The Taxation
of Municipal Bonds

The Taxation of Municipal Bonds

An Economic Appraisal

Michael L. Mussa
and
Roger C. Kormendi

with a foreword by Yale Brozen

054938

Michael L. Mussa and Roger C. Kormendi are associate professors of economics at the Graduate School of Business of the University of Chicago.

Over the course of preparing this manuscript for publication, we received advice and encouragement from a number of our colleagues at the University of Chicago. We would like now to take the opportunity to thank in particular Yale Brozen, Eugene Fama, Lawrence Fisher, Roger Ibbotson, Merton Miller, Jeffrey Skelton, and Roman Weil for their help and to acknowledge able research assistance from Chris Kudrna, Thomas Kutzen, and Mustafa Mohatarem. We are also grateful to the St. Paul Companies, Inc., for their financial support of this project. The contents of this study, however, represent our views alone and not those of any other individual or institution.

Library of Congress Cataloging in Publication Data
Mussa, Michael.
    The taxation of municipal bonds.
    (AEI studies ; 229)
    Includes bibliographical references.
    1. Municipal bonds—Taxation—United States.
I. Kormendi, Roger C., joint author.   II. Title.
III. Series: American Enterprise Institute for
Public Policy Research.   AEI studies ; 229.
HJ5905.M8   336.2'78'3326323   79-13230
ISBN 0-8447-3331-8
AEI Studies 229

HJ
5905
.M8
1979

Printed in the United States of America

CONTENTS

LIST OF TABLES

LIST OF FIGURES

FOREWORD

In this study, Michael L. Mussa and Roger C. Kormendi analyze the arguments put forward in support of the taxable bond option—a proposal under which a federal subsidy would be provided to pay a portion of the interest that would be required if state and local governments were to issue taxable bonds. They compare this with the present situation in which all interest paid on municipal bonds is tax exempt. They conclude that little, if anything, would be gained and that, in at least one important aspect, much would be lost.

At present, the interest paid on bonds issued by state and local governments is exempt from the federal personal income tax and the federal corporate earnings tax. As a result, buyers of these tax-exempt municipal bonds are willing to purchase them at yields lower than those of taxable bonds. Currently, tax-exempt bond yields range from 3.50 percent for short-term issues to 6.25 percent for long-term issues, despite the availability of yields ranging from 6.65 to 7.52 percent on short-term Treasury bills and bank certificates of deposit and from 8.44 to 9.26 percent on long-term Treasury and corporate utility bonds.

These facts show that local governments enjoy a substantial benefit from the exemption and that a substantial implicit tax is paid by holders of municipal bonds.[1] Indeed, when we consider the effects of inflation, it becomes apparent that many municipal governments actually borrow at negative real borrowing costs.

In the past year, the rate of inflation in the United States has been 6.6 percent. If inflation continues at this rate, the 6.25 percent interest

---

[1] The implicit tax is the amount by which the interest rate on municipal bonds falls short of the interest rate paid on taxable bonds of similar maturity and quality.

rate currently paid on long-term, high-grade municipals will not be sufficient to offset the loss in value of the principal invested in these bonds. In that case, the real interest rate to state and local governments and the real yield to investors will be less than zero.

Since the holder of municipal bonds is paying an inflation tax of more than 100 percent in the current inflationary climate, it is difficult to understand the claim that the tax exemption creates an inequity. Yet, that is the premise on which the case for the taxable bond option rests. As Professors Mussa and Kormendi point out, if we believe a maximum incremental personal tax rate of 70 percent and corporate tax rate of 48 percent are equitable, then the present 100 percent tax on tax-exempt interest can hardly be called inequitably low.

The authors go on to show that most of what little tax saving results from the tax exemption of interest redounds to the benefit of customers of banks and insurance companies. These firms purchase two-thirds of all tax-exempt bonds, and the majority of their customers—depositors in banks and purchasers of insurance policies—are subject to lower tax rates than the implicit tax on the holders of tax-exempt securities. It can hardly be said, then, that all the benefits of the exemption go into an inequitable avoidance of taxes by high-bracket taxpayers. The Mussa-Kormendi analysis reduces the estimate of tax inequity from the standard figure of $4–5 billion to less than $200 million, even under noninflationary circumstances.

The most enduring criticism of tax exemption for interest on municipal securities concerns the inefficient allocation of capital caused by the artificially low interest rate. Because state and local governments can borrow at rates near 6 percent, their engineers design features into their projects that yield little more than 6 percent in cost savings or service value. For example, a fleet of highway maintenance equipment may be purchased with fuel-saving features that add a million dollars to the cost of the equipment, on the basis that the fuel saved will yield a 7 percent return on the incremental investment. The cost saving, then, will pay for the borrowing cost. Capital is absorbed, however, that could instead have gone into heavier electric transmission lines, which would have reduced power losses by enough to yield 15 percent. But since the interest on utility bonds is taxable and the utility is subject to property taxes on its power lines and to corporate earnings taxes on its income, it has to earn a pretax return of 16 percent to attract capital in competition with tax-exempt uses. The utility does not invest the extra capital required to finance the extra cost of heavier transmission lines because it is not tax exempt, and the capital goes into the less productive municipal use.

While this is a significant debility of tax exemption for municipally financed projects, the taxable bond option only worsens the situation. It would reduce even further the interest cost to state and local governments, if the federal subsidy were set at levels exceeding the implicit tax on interest from municipals, and would lead to the undertaking of still more socially uneconomic projects. The taxable bond option would increase the misallocation of resources and would not meet the longest-standing criticism of tax exemption for interest from municipals.

To anyone interested in preserving our freedoms and the flexibility and adaptability allowed by the federal system of government, the most alarming feature of the taxable bond option is that it is another step down the road leading to the destruction of the federal system. As educators have learned, with the power of the purse comes the power to control. Schools that once begged for federal financial aid are now occasionally refusing it because of the increasingly onerous conditions attached.[2] Municipalities that become dependent on direct federal subsidies for paying interest on taxable bonds will, as so many other local government programs have found, find themselves increasingly subjected to Washington directives and controls.

YALE BROZEN
Graduate School of Business
University of Chicago

---

[2] Yale Brozen, "The Ethical Consequences of Alternative Incentive Systems," in *D. R. Sharpe Lectures on Social Ethics*, ed. L. Greenfield (Chicago: University of Chicago Divinity School, 1978).

1
Overview

The exemption from federal taxation of the interest paid on municipal bonds has been an enduring feature of the U.S. tax system since the income tax was established in 1913. It has also been an enduring source of controversy. Virtually from the start, economists and other tax experts have criticized the exemption as wasteful, inefficient, and inequitable. These criticisms have motivated repeated attempts to eliminate or modify the exemption. Largely because of the opposition of municipal governments, however, all attempts at reform have been defeated in Congress. For this reason, interest has grown in proposals that modify the exemption while preserving or expanding the benefits presently enjoyed by municipal governments. The most prominent such proposal is the taxable bond option. Under such a scheme, state and local governments could choose to issue either tax-exempt bonds, as at present, or taxable bonds with a direct interest subsidy paid by the U.S. Treasury.

Numerous studies have been made of the effects of the exemption and the projected consequences of the taxable bond option.[1] In general, the conclusions reached by these studies have been critical of the exemption and favorable to the option. The exemption has been criticized as being fiscally inefficient, inequitable, and the cause of an inadequate and unstable flow of credit to municipal governments. The alleged fiscal inefficiency of the exemption is measured by the amount by which the tax loss to the U.S. Treasury from the

---

[1] The most comprehensive study of the exemption is Ott and Meltzer (1963). There have been a number of recent studies of the consequences of the taxable bond option; see, especially, Ackerman and Ott (1970), Fortune (1973a and 1973b), Galper and Peterson (1971), Hufner (1970 and 1973), and Forbes and Peterson (1976).

1

exemption exceeds the implicit subsidy enjoyed by state and local governments that issue tax-exempt bonds. Because this net loss allegedly accrues as a windfall gain to high-tax-bracket investors who escape from paying their fair share of taxes by holding tax-exempt municipal bonds, the fiscal inefficiency of the exemption also corresponds to the tax inequity purported to be generated by the exemption. Moreover, it is argued that the exemption is responsible for an inadequate and unstable flow of credit to municipal governments because it limits the demand for municipal bonds to high-tax-bracket investors (including financial institutions subject to the corporate tax rate) who benefit from the exemption. Municipal governments, therefore, are supposedly isolated from the general credit market, making them especially sensitive to disturbances (such as restrictive monetary policy) that reduce the demand for tax-exempt bonds.

Proponents of the taxable bond option contend that it would deter municipal governments from issuing tax-exempt bonds unless the implicit subsidy on such bonds were at least as high as the direct subsidy paid by the U.S. Treasury on taxable municipal bonds. By inducing municipal governments to reduce the supply of tax-exempt bonds, it is argued, the option would reduce the fiscal inefficiency and tax inequity presently associated with tax-exempt municipal bonds.[2] Further, the option would allegedly reduce the instability and increase the magnitude of the flow of funds to municipal governments by enabling them to tap new sources of funds by issuing subsidized taxable bonds. This purportedly would make municipal governments less sensitive to fluctuations in the demand for tax-exempt bonds and better able to expand their borrowing in accord with their financial needs.

If these conclusions concerning the defects of the exemption and the advantages of the option are correct, there would be a strong case that the option should be adopted. In this study, however, we shall establish that many of the conclusions of previous studies are either inaccurate or irrelevant. Based on a careful appraisal of the economic effects of the exemption, our conclusion is that no significant tax inequity results from the exemption under the economic conditions

[2] There has been some disagreement among proponents of the option about the optimum rate of the direct interest subsidy on taxable municipal bonds. A subsidy rate of at least 30 percent would probably be required to induce any significant issue of taxable municipal bonds and derive any benefits from the option. Among proponents of the option, it is generally agreed that a low rate of subsidy (about 35 percent) would help to stabilize and expand the market for municipal bonds but would not have much effect in improving tax equity and increasing fiscal efficiency. A higher rate of subsidy (40 to 45 percent) would, it is argued, generate significant gains in tax equity and fiscal efficiency. For a discussion of the effects of alternative subsidy rates, see Fortune (1973a).

that have prevailed during the past decade and are likely to continue to prevail. We show that the fiscal inefficiency of the exemption has been exaggerated and is of limited significance in the absence of a convincing demonstration that it is associated with a tax inequity. We demonstrate that during the past decade the real subsidy enjoyed by municipal borrowers has increased dramatically, and it is likely to remain high for the foreseeable future. We question whether the increase in this subsidy that would be provided by the taxable bond option is necessary to meet the borrowing needs of municipal governments or is desirable from the standpoint of efficiently allocating the economy's scarce capital resources.

On the issue of stability, we show that if the taxable bond option had been in effect during the past twenty-five years the real borrowing costs of municipal governments would probably have been more unstable than they were under the exemption. Further, we question whether the redistribution of the effects of economic disturbances that would be achieved by the option would be socially desirable. Finally, we argue that the taxable bond option suffers from a number of potentially important defects: (1) its benefits would be distributed in a regressive manner; (2) speculation over changes in the subsidy provided by the option would be a possible source of increased instability in the market for municipal bonds; (3) the option might stimulate additional and undesirable borrowing by municipal governments that would divert needed capital from private investment; (4) it might complicate our international financial relations; (5) it would pose a long-range threat to the financial independence of municipal governments; and (6) it would be an open-ended subsidy that might eventually involve the federal government more deeply in the allocation of credit and capital.

It should be emphasized that some of these conclusions rely on value judgments concerning the goals of economic policy, as well as on an objective assessment of the effects of various policies. In particular, any discussion of tax equity necessarily involves value judgments concerning the tax that people should pay, as well as objective analysis of what they do pay. Throughout this study, we are careful to state explicitly the value judgments that underlie our conclusions. We believe that these value judgments are consistent with generally held beliefs concerning the principles that should guide the conduct of public policy. Others may disagree. There should be no disagreement, however, that any conclusion concerning the desirability of the exemption or the taxable bond option should be based on an objective assessment of the effects of the exemption and the probable consequences of the taxable bond option. This study is directed primarily toward providing such an assessment.

The Organization of This Study

This study is organized around the four major issues that have characterized the debate over the exemption and the taxable bond option: fiscal efficiency, tax equity, effectiveness, and stability. Chapter 2 reviews, in an uncritical fashion, the position of proponents of the option on each of these issues. This statement of the arguments that have been advanced against the exemption and in favor of the taxable bond option sets the stage for the critical examination of these arguments in chapters 3 through 10. To provide an overview of these chapters, it is useful at this stage to summarize briefly the "standard analysis" reviewed in chapter 2 and then to state the major points that are raised in criticism of this standard analysis. This brief overview is followed by a statement of some basic principles that underlie the major conclusions of this study.

In the standard analysis of the effects of the exemption, it is recognized that municipal governments (both state and local) enjoy an implicit subsidy as a result of their right to issue bonds on which the interest is exempt from federal taxes. The implicit subsidy rate on municipal bonds (s) is the amount by which the interest rate on municipal bonds is reduced below the rate that would have to be paid by municipal governments if the interest on their bonds were taxable. The implicit subsidy rate enjoyed by issuers of municipal bonds corresponds to the implicit tax rate (t^m) paid by the holders of such bonds. This implicit tax rate is the reduction in interest yield that the holder of a municipal bond must accept if he is to enjoy the privilege of receiving interest income that is exempt from federal taxation.

The standard procedure for measuring s and t^m is to calculate the proportionate differential between the nominal interest yield on taxable corporate bonds (i^c) and the nominal interest yield on tax-exempt municipal bonds of comparable quality (i^m); that is, $s = t^m = (i^c - i^m)/i^c$. If we compare long-term corporate bonds and long-term municipal bonds during the past decade, it appears that s and t^m have averaged about 30 percent. Opponents of the exemption and proponents of the taxable bond option argue that this implicit tax rate is far less than the rate that holders of municipal bonds would have had to pay if their income had been taxable. Most estimates of the average marginal tax rate for holders of municipal bonds on their taxable income ($\bar{t}$) suggest that $\bar{t}$ is somewhere between 24 and 50 percent. Because $\hat{t}$ is significantly greater than s, the loss of tax revenue to the U.S. Treasury because of the exemption is greater than the total subsidy received by municipal governments that issue tax-exempt bonds. The difference between the tax revenue lost to the Treasury and the subsidy to municipal governments is a measure of the purported fiscal inefficiency of the exemption. For 1976, the standard estimate of this fiscal inefficiency was between $4 billion and $5 billion. Further, since the difference between $\hat{t}$ and s is also the difference between $\hat{t}$ and t^m, the fiscal inefficiency of the exemption also indicates the extent to which holders of municipal bonds escape from paying their fair share of taxes—that is, it corresponds to the tax inequity resulting from the exemption.

By setting the subsidy paid by the Treasury on taxable municipal bonds (s^*) at some reasonably high level, for instance, 40 percent, municipal governments would be induced to contract the volume of tax-exempt borrowing until the implicit subsidy rate on tax-exempt bonds was also driven up to 40 percent available on subsidized taxable bonds. Because s and t^m would rise as a result of the option, the fiscal inefficiency and tax inequity associated with the exemption would be reduced. Moreover, it is argued that since municipal governments would enjoy a higher subsidy on their tax-exempt bonds, as well as on taxable municipal bonds, the financial benefit of the option to municipal governments would be significantly greater than its cost to the Treasury.

The exemption is also criticized for providing an inadequate and unstable flow of funds to municipal borrowers. It is argued that, in order to expand municipal borrowing, tax-exempt bonds must be made attractive to investors with ever-lower marginal tax rates. This requires a fall in the implicit tax rate on municipal bonds as the volume of municipal borrowing expands, the implication being that the implicit subsidy rate enjoyed by municipal borrowers must decline precisely at the moment when municipal governments are the most hard pressed for funds to finance essential public investments. Moreover, it is argued that the demand for tax-exempt bonds is not stable; it declines, for example, in response to a restrictive monetary policy that limits the willingness of commercial banks to accumulate municipal bonds. Such fluctuations in demand lead to fluctuations in the implicit subsidy rate that, in turn, cause instability in the cost and amount of credit available to municipal governments.

Proponents of the taxable bond option argue that the option would remove this instability by stabilizing the subsidy rate on all municipal bonds at the level of the direct subsidy paid by the Treasury

5

on taxable municipal bonds. Further, it is claimed that the option would increase the general level of the subsidy enjoyed by municipal borrowers and would allow municipal governments to meet any extraordinary financing requirements by selling taxable bonds to individuals and institutions that find tax-exempt bonds unattractive.

Our appraisal of these arguments against the exemption and in favor of the taxable bond option begins in chapter 3 with an examination of the effects of inflation. During the past decade, the annual rate of price inflation averaged 4 percentage points higher than during the preceding decade. This increase in the inflation rate led to a similar increase in the expected rate of inflation. The increase in the expected rate of inflation explains, almost completely, the increase in the average level of the (before-tax) *nominal* yield on taxable corporate bonds. The *real* yield on such bonds has remained approximately constant at about 3 percent. However, since investors are taxed on their nominal interest income rather than on their real interest income, the after-tax real yield on taxable corporate bonds, for investors with positive marginal tax rates, has decreased dramatically during the past decade. Indeed, for an investor in the 40 percent marginal tax bracket, the after-tax real yield on taxable bonds has been essentially zero. This means that the effective rate of tax on this investor's real interest income has been 100 percent.

These very high real effective tax rates on taxable corporate bonds have driven investors away from such bonds and toward tax-exempt municipal bonds. For this reason, during the past decade the real yield on municipal bonds has been driven down relative to its level during the preceding decade and relative to the before-tax real yield on taxable corporate bonds. Because of the combined effects of price inflation and the operation of the tax system, the real yield on municipal bonds during the past decade has averaged only about 30 percent of the before-tax real yield on corporate bonds. This means that holders of municipal bonds have paid an implicit real effective rate of tax of about 70 percent during the past decade. Moreover, as long as inflationary conditions continue, we may expect that holders of municipal bonds will continue to pay similar rates of tax. With such high real tax rates, no credible argument can be made that the availability of "tax-exempt" municipal bonds creates tax inequity by permitting holders of such bonds to escape from paying their fair share of tax. Indeed, "tax-exempt" municipal bonds may improve tax equity by permitting some escape from tax rates far in excess of 100 percent.

Chapter 4 deals with the way the yield differential between

taxable corporate bonds and tax-exempt municipal bonds varies as a function of the maturity of the bonds. The facts cited in chapter 4 indicate that the proportionate yield differential for bonds of the shortest maturity is close to 50 percent. This differential gradually declines as the maturity of the bonds is increased, reaching a differential of about 30 percent for maturities of twenty years and longer. The average differential for municipal bonds of all maturities is estimated to be at least 35 percent, which implies that the benefit of the exemption to municipal borrowers (and the implicit tax on lenders) is significantly greater than the amount suggested by standard estimates that rely on the 30 percent yield differential for long-term municipal bonds. Correspondingly, the standard estimates of the fiscal inefficiency and tax inequity resulting from the exemption are exaggerated by using an implicit tax rate that is too low.

The theoretical analysis in chapter 4 is directed toward explaining why the yield differential varies with term to maturity. The theory of equalizing differences is used to justify the following general proposition: For any investor who holds a multiplicity of assets, the benefit derived from the last dollar invested in any one of these assets must be the same as the benefit derived from the last dollar invested in any other asset. Otherwise, the investor would shift wealth from assets with low benefits to assets with high benefits until, at the margin, benefits were equalized for all assets actually held. The benefits derived from any asset depend on yield, tax status, risk, and any other properties thought relevant by the investor. In the asset markets, the yields on various assets adjust so as to compensate the holders of these assets for the differences in tax status, risk, and so on. In particular, commercial banks are the dominant holders of short-term municipal bonds and also hold short-term taxable instruments with essentially the same risk and other characteristics. The yield differential between short-term municipal bonds and comparable short-term taxable instruments is close to the corporate tax rate of 48 percent, since this is the yield differential that offsets the tax advantage of short-term municipal bonds for the dominant holder of such bonds. For long-term municipal bonds, the yield differential is not set by the tax rate for commercial banks. Banks hold long-term municipal bonds, but they do not hold any significant amount of long-term corporate bonds. Hence, the investor who is just balancing between long-term municipal bonds and long-term corporate bonds cannot be a bank but must be some other investor. For this investor, the equalizing yield differential is not 48 percent but only about 30 percent. Nevertheless, it would be incorrect to conclude that a commercial bank or any other investor who holds long-term municipal bonds gains a large advantage from doing so. For any investor who holds long-term municipal bonds, the benefit from the last dollar invested in them should be the same as the benefit derived from the last dollar invested in any other asset held. Special benefit is derived only on inframarginal holdings of municipal bonds. The magnitude of this special benefit is significantly overstated by the standard estimates of fiscal inefficiency and tax inequity that implicitly assume that the benefit derived on the last dollar of municipal bonds is the same as the benefit derived on the first dollar.

Chapter 5 focuses on the issue of tax equity as it applies to municipal bonds held directly by individual households. The basic point is that the magnitude of the inequity resulting from the exemption has been seriously exaggerated in the analysis developed by proponents of the option. This exaggeration results from three basic sources: First, as established in chapter 3, during periods of inflation the real effective rate of tax implicitly paid by holders of municipal bonds significantly exceeds the standard estimate of the implicit nominal tax rate. Second, the average marginal tax rate of present holders of municipal bonds is usually overestimated by proponents of the option. Evidence from individual tax returns and projections based on an analysis of the likely portfolio readjustment of municipal bondholders in the event of elimination of the exemption suggest that the average effective marginal tax rate for present holders of municipal bonds is probably no greater than 36 percent, rather than 42 or 50 percent. Third, the appropriate tax base to use in calculating the inequity resulting from the exemption is not the nominal interest income that holders of municipal bonds would have received if they had held taxable bonds. This tax base includes interest paid just to maintain the real value of an investor's assets, and this is not appropriately regarded as income. In 1976 the use of this exaggerated tax base resulted in an exaggeration of the true estimate of tax inequity by a factor of almost three. When account is taken of these three sources of exaggeration of the tax inequity resulting from the exemption, the corrected estimate shows that if 1976 had been a year of zero inflation, the true measure of inequity would have been only about $300 million. This sets an upper bound on the true measure of inequity at any positive rate of inflation. As the rate of inflation rises, inequity declines. At the 6 percent inflation rate that actually prevailed in 1976, the tax inequity resulting from individual holdings of municipal bonds was *minus* $500 million.

Chapter 6 deals with the issue of tax equity as it applies to municipal bonds held by institutions, predominantly commercial banks and fire and casualty insurance companies. Institutional holders of municipal bonds are dealt with separately from individual holders, because institutions cannot be regarded as the ultimate beneficiaries of any special advantage conferred by holding tax-exempt bonds. The ultimate beneficiaries must be people—either shareholders, customers, or suppliers of factor services.

Commercial banking and fire and casualty insurance are both essentially competitive industries that produce their outputs under conditions of constant returns to scale. Equity capital invested in these industries is not highly specific to a particular use, even in the short run, and earns approximately the normal rate of return for its risk. These economic characteristics indicate that the ultimate beneficiaries of any special advantage associated with institutional holdings of municipal bonds are not the owners of equity capital in these institutions. If the exemption were eliminated, or if the taxable bond option significantly reduced the tax advantage associated with tax-exempt municipal bonds, equity capital in these industries would continue to earn its normal rate of return. The burden of increased taxes resulting from eliminating the exemption or from adopting the option would be borne by the customers of banks and insurance companies, not the owners of equity capital. The customers who would bear the greatest share of this burden would probably be small savers and small businesses. There would be no gain in tax equity from imposing such a tax burden. Therefore, no one can reasonably argue that there is any tax inequity associated with the two-thirds of the outstanding stock of municipal bonds that is presently held by institutions.

Chapter 7 considers the fiscal inefficiency of the exemption and the probable fiscal effects of the taxable bond option. An estimate of the overall fiscal inefficiency of the exemption is obtained by combining the estimates of fiscal inefficiency for individual and institutional holdings of municipal bonds obtained in chapters 5 and 6. The estimated fiscal inefficiency of the exemption amounts to less than $400 million (for inflation rates of more than 2 percent), rather than the $4 billion to $5 billion suggested by standard estimates. Comparing the benefits of the exemption to municipal governments from reduced borrowing costs with its cost to the federal government from lost tax revenue, we find that for inflation rates of greater than 2 percent the "efficiency ratio" of the exemption is more than 90 percent. In other words, municipal governments enjoy more than ninety cents of benefit for each dollar of tax revenue lost by the federal government. Moreover, at inflation rates of 5 to 6 percent, the efficiency ratio of the exemption rises to 97 percent. In comparison with other federal subsidy programs, this is a very high efficiency ratio, particularly for a program that provides assistance in such a desirable form, without strings and constraints on municipal governments.

The proponents of the taxable bond option claim that its cost to the Treasury would be small relative to the benefit it would provide to municipal governments. It is argued that this high benefit-cost ratio would be achieved because the option would allow municipal governments to recapture some of the windfall gain currently accruing to nonmarginal holders of tax-exempt municipal bonds. Municipal governments purportedly would benefit from an increased implicit subsidy on tax-exempt bonds issued under the option, as well as from the explicit subsidy paid by the Treasury on taxable municipal bonds. Our analysis suggests a less optimistic view of the financial consequences of the option. Because individual holders of municipal bonds would shift to other tax shelters, the amount of additional tax revenue collected from them would be small. Although institutional holders of municipal bonds lack the extensive tax avoidance opportunities available to individuals, the net fiscal benefit from heavier taxation of such institutions is reduced by the amount of taxes that would not be paid by the individuals presently benefiting from the windfall gain on institutional holdings of municipal bonds. Moreover, the potential gain in revenue from increased effective taxation of municipal bonds is more than offset by a resulting rise in the general level of yields, which would increase the cost of servicing all outstanding government debt. When account is taken of this effect, the net fiscal benefit of the option is negative; its probable cost to the federal government exceeds its likely benefits to municipal governments.

Chapter 8 is concerned with the issue of the effectiveness of the exemption as a means of subsidizing the borrowing costs of municipal governments. Contrary to what is suggested by proponents of the option, a careful examination of the facts shows that the real effective rate of subsidy enjoyed by municipal borrowers has been very high. During the past decade, this real rate of subsidy averaged about 70 percent, in contrast with the 35 percent average of the preceding decade. Further, the fact that interest on taxable bonds is taxed on a nominal basis insures that the real rate of subsidy enjoyed by municipal borrowers will continue to be at least 70 percent, as long as the inflation rate continues in the range experienced during the past decade.

Although proponents of the option suggest otherwise, past experience with the market for tax-exempt bonds indicates that state

10

and local governments will be able to undertake the increased borrowing that is likely to occur in the next decade without any significant increase in the real borrowing costs. Moreover, while it is true that a taxable bond option with a 40 percent direct interest subsidy would increase the real subsidy enjoyed by municipal borrowers, economic analysis indicates that such an increase in the subsidy rate would not be socially desirable. Any subsidy to municipal borrowing reduces economic efficiency by encouraging municipal governments to undertake public investment projects with a lower social return than would be generated by private investment projects that could be financed with the same funds. By increasing the subsidy above its already high level, the option worsens economic efficiency.

Chapter 9 examines the issue of stability. The taxable bond option would not necessarily stabilize the real borrowing costs of municipal governments. The experience of the past twenty-five years indicates that if the taxable bond option with a 40 percent direct subsidy rate had been operating during this period, the real borrowing costs of municipal governments would have been less stable than they were under the exemption. Moreover, while it is possible that the taxable bond option would reduce the sensitivity of the municipal bond market to some types of disturbances (such as contractionary monetary policy), it is questionable whether this reduction in sensitivity would be socially desirable. This is because the option would not reduce the magnitude of most disturbances but would merely transfer their effect from the municipal bond market to some other market. In the case of contractionary monetary policy, this would probably mean an increase in the sensitivity of the mortgage market to monetary policy.

Finally, chapter 10 summarizes the basic conclusions of this study and discusses a number of potential disadvantages of the taxable bond option. One disadvantage is that the benefits of the option would be regressively distributed because the municipalities that would benefit the most are those that borrow the most, and these are, on average, wealthier municipalities. A second disadvantage is that since the level of the direct interest subsidy under the option would not be immutably fixed, both municipal governments and private investors would speculate on the possibility of changes in the subsidy rate. This would be an additional, wholly artificial source of instability in the market for municipal bonds. Third, the option would increase the danger of abuse of the subsidy to municipal borrowing by encouraging municipal governments to borrow beyond the level that is financially prudent and socially desirable. Fourth, the option might complicate our international financial relations by creating a situation in which foreigners and foreign official agencies would become substantial holders of taxable municipal bonds. Direct borrowing by municipal governments in world credit markets could exacerbate an already difficult balance of payments situation. Concern either with the balance of payments or with the implications of a default on municipal bonds held by a foreign government could provide the motivation for greater federal involvement in the management and control of municipal government finances. A fifth disadvantage is that, apart from any international complications, the option might ultimately lead to greater federal control over municipal finances. This may not be an immediate danger of the option, but the history of other federal subsidy programs suggests that it is a long-run danger. Moreover, the option would blur the constitutional principle of reciprocal immunity that has provided the primary bastion of defense for the exemption, and this would weaken the case for the exemption. Sixth, the taxable bond option would firmly establish the principle of federal subsidies for specially favored classes of borrowers. Unlike the principle of reciprocal immunity, there is nothing that naturally limits a direct interest subsidy to municipal governments. In the end, the principle embodied in the option might involve the federal government more deeply than it already is in granting specific subsidies to particular borrowers and thus controlling the allocation of credit and capital.

The Relationship between Fiscal Efficiency and Tax Equity

Criticisms of the present exemption usually cite fiscal inefficiency and tax inequity as separate defects of the exemption. The exemption is defective because the loss of tax revenue to the Treasury is greater than the subsidy to municipal governments in terms of reduced borrowing costs; this is the fiscal inefficiency of the exemption. The exemption is also defective because it permits high-tax-bracket investors to enjoy an unintended gain by reducing their federal income taxes by more than the implicit taxes they pay to municipal governments; this is the tax inequity of the exemption. Although it is recognized that fiscal inefficiency and tax inequity are opposite sides of the same coin, in the sense that the magnitude of the fiscal inefficiency corresponds to the magnitude of the tax inequity, proponents of the option argue that these two defects are really separate evils and that both must be counted to measure the total evil.

Careful reflection reveals that this double counting is not appropriate. Indeed, the argument that the fiscal inefficiency of the tax exemption measures part of the social cost of the exemption is based on a fallacy. The fallacy comes from viewing lost tax revenue as a "cost" of the tax exemption in the same sense that expenditures on military hardware are a cost of national defense. Loss of tax revenue implies a budgetary cost to the government but does not imply any real resource cost to society; what is lost by the government is gained by the private sector. In contrast, purchases of military hardware do have a real resource cost to society, as well as a budgetary cost to the government.

This does not imply that the fiscal inefficiency of the exemption is without significance. The loss of tax revenue indicated by this inefficiency must be made up by tax revenues from other sources. In general, the people who pay these other taxes will not be the people who benefit from the lower taxes resulting from the exemption. This links the fiscal inefficiency of the exemption to the question of tax equity. If the principal beneficiaries of the gain from the exemption were poor widows and orphans, the fiscal inefficiency of the exemption would not be regarded as a significant defect and might even be regarded as an advantage. The evil associated with fiscal inefficiency is that the purported beneficiaries of this inefficiency are high-tax-bracket investors who escape from paying their fair share of taxes. The fiscal attractiveness of the taxable bond option derives largely from the assertion that it would be financed primarily at the expense of these investors. In the absence of these arguments based on tax equity, however, the argument of fiscal inefficiency loses its force. Therefore, the fiscal inefficiency of the exemption is not appropriately regarded as a separate defect. It is a defect only to the extent that it is linked to a tax inequity. For this reason, we will focus primarily on the issue of tax equity and treat fiscal inefficiency as an important but subsidiary issue.

Elimination versus the Option

Until recently, the most commonly advanced proposal to remedy the alleged evils deriving from the tax-exempt status of municipal bonds was outright elimination of the exemption, or possibly substitution of a direct interest subsidy for the exemption. The taxable bond option is a relatively new proposal designed to placate municipal government officials who understandably oppose elimination of the exemption. With respect to the issues of fiscal efficiency and tax equity, the arguments in favor of the option are based on the same analysis as the arguments for elimination of the exemption. By raising the implicit tax rate paid by holders of tax-exempt municipal bonds to the level of the direct interest subsidy on taxable municipal bonds, the option would reduce the tax inequity resulting from the exemption. The upper bound of what would be achieved by the option in terms of improved tax equity is the inequity that is presently generated by the exemption. The option, of course, would have a net financial cost to the Treasury, whereas elimination of the exemption would have a net financial benefit. However, proponents of the option argue that the benefits to municipal governments in the form of reduced borrowing costs resulting from the option would significantly exceed the financial cost of the option to the Treasury. This net financial benefit to all government units combined would be achieved by recapturing part of the fiscal inefficiency that presently results from the exemption. The magnitude of the fiscal inefficiency of the exemption, therefore, sets an upper bound for the possible net fiscal benefit of the taxable bond option.

In this study, we shall frequently consider the consequences of elimination of the exemption, even though this proposal is not politically viable. We take this approach because the extreme proposal of elimination sets a useful benchmark for analyzing the benefits of the taxable bond option in the important areas of fiscal efficiency and, especially, tax equity. By showing that the gain in fiscal efficiency and tax equity from elimination of the exemption is small, we show that the gain in fiscal efficiency and tax equity from the taxable bond option must also be small.

This close analogy between the effects of elimination of the exemption and the effects of the taxable bond option in the areas of fiscal efficiency and tax equity, however, should not be permitted to obscure the very important differences between these proposals in other areas. In particular, one of the most important objections raised by those who favor elimination of the exemption is that it generates economic inefficiency. Inefficiency results from the fact that the exemption reduces the borrowing costs of municipal governments below those of private borrowers. This distorts the allocation of the economy's scarce capital resources by encouraging municipal governments to undertake public investment projects that have a lower social return than private investment projects that could be financed with the same scarce funds. For decades, this issue has been raised as a valid criticism of the exemption and as a valid argument for its elimination. In the literature favoring the taxable bond option, however, the exemption has generally not been criticized on grounds of its economic inefficiency. This neglect may be due to the fact that proponents of the taxable bond option do not believe that economic efficiency is an important concern. It is also possible that proponents of the option neglect this issue because they recognize that the option would magnify the economic inefficiency that already results from the exemption.

The Strategy of Biased Estimates

Any analysis of the effects of the exemption and the consequences of the proposed taxable bond option inevitably involves answers to hypothetical questions. What would happen to the borrowing costs of municipalities if the exemption were eliminated? What alternative assets would individual investors choose to hold if tax-exempt bonds were not available or if their yields were significantly reduced by the taxable bond option? What volume of taxable bonds would municipalities choose to issue under a 40 percent taxable bond option? Some answer to each of these hypothetical questions—and to many others —is required in order to complete our appraisal of the economic effects of the exemption and the proposed taxable bond option. Unfortunately, the established principles of economic analysis and the available empirical evidence do not always provide a firm basis for very precise answers to these questions.

Faced with this situation, we have adopted the strategy of using estimates of critical magnitudes that are biased against the basic conclusions we seek to establish. For instance, one of our basic conclusions is that the fiscal efficiency of the exemption is far greater than has been suggested by most previous studies—specifically, that municipal governments enjoy more than ninety cents of financial benefit from the exemption for every dollar lost by the U.S. Treasury. One of the critical magnitudes used in establishing this conclusion is the average nominal subsidy rate on tax-exempt municipal bonds; that is, the proportionate reduction in nominal borrowing costs that municipal governments enjoy as a result of issuing tax-exempt bonds relative to the nominal borrowing costs they would incur if they issued taxable bonds. In chapter 4 it is established that 35 percent is a *lower-bound* estimate for this average nominal subsidy rate because the procedure used in its construction intentionally neglects a number of factors that indicate that the true average nominal subsidy rate is greater than 35 percent. Because the estimate of the average nominal subsidy rate is biased in a downward direction, the fiscal efficiency achieved by the exemption is understated. In other words, the downward bias in the estimate of the average nominal subsidy rate introduces a bias against the conclusion that the exemption is highly efficient.

Another example of this strategy of using biased estimates appears in chapter 5, where the extent of the tax inequity that results from tax-exempt municipal bonds held directly by individual households is considered. A critical magnitude in estimating the extent of this tax inequity is the effective marginal tax rate for households that presently hold municipal bonds. Evidence from a variety of sources indicates that when account is taken of the alternative tax reduction opportunities available to these households their effective marginal tax rate may be as low as 32 percent, or even 30 percent. However, to guard against the possibility that these estimates of the effective marginal tax rate are too low, we choose to use a somewhat higher figure, 36 percent, in estimating the tax inequity resulting from individual holdings of municipal bonds. Since the effect of this procedure is to overstate the true magnitude of the tax inequity, it is biased against our basic conclusion that the tax inequity is much smaller than has been suggested by previous studies of the effects of the exemption.

Throughout this study are many other examples of this strategy of using estimates that are biased against our basic conclusions. In each case, we have tried to keep the size of this bias relatively small, for otherwise our estimates would produce a highly distorted picture of the true effects of the exemption and the probable consequences of the taxable bond option. Our strategy is to avoid such gross distortions, while at the same time providing a margin of safety sufficient to insure a firm basis of support for all our basic conclusions.

Summary

The purpose of this study is to conduct an economic appraisal of the consequences of the taxable bond option in comparison with the situation that presently prevails under the exemption. Our conclusions stand in sharp contrast to the conclusions of earlier studies. Taking account of the effects of inflation, a factor ignored in previous studies, we find that there is no serious tax inequity resulting from the present exemption and no potential gain in tax equity from the option. We find that the potential fiscal benefit of the option is of limited importance and of dubious magnitude. We find that the effectiveness of the subsidy implicit in the exemption has increased in recent years and is likely to remain high in the future. We find no substantial reason to believe that the taxable bond option would improve the overall stability of the municipal bond market or enhance the stability of the economic system.

These findings do not imply that the exemption is without defect or that the taxable bond option is without potential benefit. Under noninflationary conditions, there is some tax inequity resulting from the exemption that would be reduced by the option. Under all conditions, the taxable bond option would increase the effective rate of subsidy enjoyed by municipal governments (but only at the cost of decreased economic efficiency). Nevertheless, based on an appraisal of all the probable consequences of the option, our conclusion is that under the economic conditions that seem most likely to prevail in the United States the public interest would not be served by the adoption of the taxable bond option.

Once more we emphasize that this conclusion reflects certain value judgments about the appropriate objectives of economic policy. Those who start from different premises might conceivably be led to different conclusions concerning the desirability of the taxable bond option. For instance, our analysis shows that under the inflationary conditions of the past decade holders of long-term municipal bonds paid an implicit real rate of tax on their real interest income of about 70 percent. Under a taxable bond option with a 40 percent nominal subsidy rate, this implicit real tax rate would probably have risen to about 100 percent. Our value judgments become relevant when we say that no significant tax inequity results from the exemption because present holders of municipal bonds already pay the maximum legal marginal tax rate and when we say that no gain in tax equity would result from increasing the implicit real tax rate of holders of municipal bonds to something far in excess of the maximum legal marginal tax rate. Clearly, someone who believes that wealthy investors should be compelled to pay very high real rates of tax on fixed-interest investments might not accept these statements. We do believe, however, that regardless of one's opinion concerning the tax rates wealthy investors ought to pay, the decision to adopt the taxable bond option should be based on a clear and correct assessment of its economic consequences. It is to such an assessment that this study is directed.

2

A Review of the
Standard Analysis

The case in favor of the taxable bond option is based primarily on the assertion that the option would correct four important defects of the present tax exemption.

- First, proponents of the option argue that the present exemption is fiscally inefficient because it reduces the tax revenue of the U.S. Treasury by more than it reduces the borrowing costs of state and local governments.
- Second, they argue that the exemption is the source of a significant tax inequity because it permits high-income taxpayers to escape from paying their fair share of the costs of government.
- Third, they argue that the exemption is an ineffective means of subsidizing essential capital expenditures of state and local governments.
- Fourth, they argue that the exemption increases the instability of municipal borrowing by isolating the market for municipal bonds from the market for general credit instruments.

The purpose of this chapter is to provide an uncritical summary of the standard analysis upon which the case for the taxable bond option rests. We first summarize the argument that the present exemption is both fiscally inefficient and the source of an important tax inequity and then consider the standard analysis of how the taxable bond option would reduce this fiscal inefficiency and improve tax equity. Next, we present the standard analysis of why the exemption is an ineffective means of subsidizing municipal borrowing and how the taxable bond option would increase the effectiveness of the subsidy. Finally, we consider the standard analysis of why the exemption increases the instability of municipal borrowing costs and how the option would reduce this instability.

The Fiscal Inefficiency and Tax Inequity of the Exemption

The standard analysis of the fiscal inefficiency and tax inequity resulting from the present exemption is based on a simple and appealing argument.[1] This argument is conveniently illustrated by the situation that prevailed in 1976, when long-term corporate bonds had an average yield of 9 percent, subject to the federal income tax, and long-term municipal bonds of comparable quality had an average yield of 6.6 percent, exempt from federal taxation. By holding municipal instead of corporate bonds, an investor suffered a reduction in his interest income of 27 percent, that is, $(0.090 - 0.066)/0.090 = 0.27$. An investor who held municipal bonds, however, benefited from not having to pay any federal income tax on his interest income from those bonds. Assuming that corporate bonds and municipal bonds were comparable in every way, except for the yield differential and the difference in tax treatment, an investor with a 27 percent marginal income tax rate would have been indifferent between the two types of bonds. This investor would not care whether he held corporate bonds and paid an explicit tax of 27 percent to the federal government or held municipal bonds and paid an implicit tax of 27 percent (in the form of reduced interest yield) to some municipal government. Investors with tax rates less than 27 percent would choose the corporate bond, since it would have the greater after-tax yield. Investors with tax rates greater than 27 percent would choose the municipal bond, since this would limit their effective tax rate to only 27 percent.

Herein lies the fiscal inefficiency and tax inequity of the exemption. To the extent that holders of municipal bonds have marginal federal tax rates higher than 27 percent, the loss of tax revenue to the Treasury is greater than the implicit tax revenue collected by municipal governments in the form of reduced borrowing costs. The excess of the loss to the Treasury over the gain to municipal governments measures the fiscal inefficiency of the exemption. It also measures the tax inequity that results from the exemption, because the investors who capture the benefit of this fiscal inefficiency are investors with marginal tax rates in excess of 27 percent. To cover their fair share

---

[1] This argument has been advanced by most proponents of the taxable bond option; see, for instance, Fortune (1973a) and Hufner (1973). This argument has been adopted, essentially without modification, by virtually everyone who has commented on the effects of the tax-exempt status of municipal bonds; see, for instance, Pechman (1977).

of the costs of government, these investors ought to pay tax at their appropriate marginal tax rates. The availability of tax-exempt municipal bonds, however, permits them to get away with paying an effective tax rate of only 27 percent. The difference between the taxes these investors ought to pay and the implicit taxes they do pay is an inequity.

This standard analysis of the fiscal inefficiency and tax inequity resulting from the exemption can be expressed in a general form, using the notation that will be maintained throughout this study:

i^c = the nominal yield on taxable corporate bonds

i^m = the nominal yield on tax-exempt municipal bonds

$t^m = (i^c - i^m)/i^c$ = the implicit tax rate on tax-exempt municipal bonds

t = the marginal tax rate of an investor.

An investor should be indifferent between corporate bonds and comparable municipal bonds if they yield the same after-tax rates of return, that is, if $1 - t) \cdot i^c = i^m$. This implies that the investor who is on the margin of indifference between corporate and municipal bonds is the investor whose marginal tax rate is equal to t^m. Investors with marginal tax rates less than t^m should not hold municipal bonds. Investors with marginal tax rates greater than t^m capture, by holding municipal bonds, a windfall benefit equal to the excess of their marginal tax rate (t) over the implicit tax rate on municipal bonds (t^m), multiplied by the interest income they would receive if they held taxable corporate bonds.

The total fiscal inefficiency and the total tax inequity resulting from the exemption correspond to the total windfall gain accruing to all present holders of tax-exempt municipal bonds. This total windfall gain (W) is the excess of the total tax loss to the Treasury because of the exemption (T) over the total reduction in borrowing costs enjoyed by state and local governments as a result of the exemption (S). The total loss of tax revenue to the Treasury is equal to the average marginal tax rate of holders of municipal bonds ($\bar{t}$), multiplied by the taxable interest income these investors would have received if they had held corporate bonds; that is, $T = \bar{t} \cdot i^c \cdot M$, where M is the dollar value of the outstanding stock of tax-exempt municipal bonds. The benefit enjoyed by state and local governments is equal to the implicit tax rate they collect (t^m), multiplied by the interest income which holders of municipal bonds would have received on taxable corporate bonds, that is, $S = t^m \cdot i^c \cdot M = (i^c - i^m) \cdot M$. Thus, the total windfall gain accruing to holders of tax-exempt municipal bonds is $W = T - S = (\bar{t} - t^m) \cdot i^c \cdot M$.

Calculations of the windfall gain ($W = T - S$) are sensitive to the value assumed for $\bar{t}$, the average marginal tax rate of holders of municipal bonds. An estimate of $\bar{t}$ that has been widely employed in recent studies of the tax-exempt status of municipal bonds is that $\bar{t}$ equals 42 percent.[2] Using this estimate, the loss to the Treasury in 1976 resulting from the exemption (T) is calculated to be $9.4 billion, which is equal to 42 percent of the interest that would have been earned on the $248 billion of municipal bonds at the corporate yield of 9 percent; that is, $9.4 billion is equal to $(0.42) \cdot (0.09) \cdot$ ($248 billion). The benefit of the exemption to state and local governments (S) was $6.0 billion, which is equal to 27 percent of the interest that would have been paid on the stock of municipal bonds at the corporate interest rate; that is, $6.0 billion is equal to $(0.27) \cdot (0.09) \cdot$ ($248 billion). The windfall gain accruing to holders of municipal bonds in 1976 using this calculation was $W = T - S = \$3.4$ billion, which was equal to $(\bar{t} - t^m) \cdot i^c \cdot M = [(0.42) - (0.27)] \cdot (0.09) \cdot$ ($248 billion).

Corporations held about two-thirds of the outstanding stock of municipal bonds in 1976 and were generally subject to marginal tax rates of 48 percent. Individual holders of municipal bonds are generally believed to be taxed at marginal rates that average in excess of 50 percent. For this reason, an estimate of 42 percent for the average marginal tax rate for all holders of municipals seems too low. If the average marginal tax rate for individual holders of municipal bonds was 55 percent, then a reasonable estimate for $\bar{t}$ would be 50 percent, a weighted average of the marginal tax rate for corporations and the marginal tax rate for households, with two-thirds of the weight given to corporations. Using this estimate of $\bar{t}$, the loss to the Treasury in 1976 rises from $9.4 billion to $11.2 billion. The estimated subsidy to state and local governments remains at $6.0 billion, and the estimate of the windfall gain rises from $3.4 billion to $5.2 billion.[3]

In order to put these figures into historical perspective, Table 1 reports estimates of Treasury loss (T), the subsidy to state and local

---

[2] This estimate of the average marginal tax rate of holders of municipal bonds is derived by Ott and Meltzer (1963) on the basis of the conditions prevailing in 1960, including the provisions of the tax law as of that date. Despite the changes in economic conditions and in the tax laws that have occurred since 1960, this estimate of the average marginal tax rate has continued to be used; see for instance, Fortune (1973a) and Ackerman and Ott (1970).

[3] Break and Pechman (1975) report $4.9 billion as the estimated revenue gain from taxing interest on state and local government bonds in 1976. This figure is close to $5.2 billion. However, it is not clear whether the Break and Pechman estimate refers to the gross gain of tax revenue to the U.S. Treasury or the net gain to the Treasury, less the loss to state and local governments.

governments (S), and the windfall gain to holders of municipal bonds $(W = T - S)$ for the years 1952 through 1976. The estimates of T and W are reported both for an assumed value of $\bar{t}$ of 42 percent and for an assumed value of $\bar{t}$ of 50 percent.[4] It is apparent that the higher value of $\bar{t}$ results in significantly higher estimates of T and W. It is also apparent that all of the dollar magnitudes reported in Table 1 grow significantly over time. To some extent, this is accounted for by the real growth of the U.S. economy and by the substantial increase in the price level during the past twenty-five years. In relation to the money value of gross national product, the windfall gain to holders of municipal bonds during the past decade was slightly less than double what it was during the preceding decade.

A dramatic way to illustrate the fiscal inefficiency of the exemption is to calculate its "efficiency ratio," that is, the ratio of the benefits of the exemption to municipal governments to its cost to the Treasury. Obviously, the efficiency ratio of the exemption depends on the assumed value of the average marginal tax rate of holders of municipal bonds, $\bar{t}$. The efficiency ratios for $\bar{t} = 42$ percent and $\bar{t} = 50$ percent are easily calculated from the results given in Table 1. These efficiency ratios are reported in Table 2. It is apparent that for both values of $\bar{t}$, the efficiency ratio during the last ten years was generally higher than during the 1950s and early 1960s. However, even for $\bar{t} = 42$ percent, it has been a relatively rare occurrence for the efficiency ratio to exceed 70 percent. Indeed, for the decade 1967 to 1976 the average value of the efficiency ratio was 68 percent, which indicates that, out of each dollar of tax revenue lost by the Treasury, municipal governments enjoyed a financial benefit of only 68 cents. The remaining 32 cents accrued as an inequitable windfall to investors who held tax-exempt municipal bonds.

The Effects of the Taxable Bond Option

Elimination of the exemption of municipal bond interest from federal taxation would increase Treasury revenues by more than it would increase the borrowing costs of state and local governments. This net fiscal benefit corresponds to the fiscal inefficiency of the present exemption, as measured by the windfall gain presently accruing to holders of tax-exempt municipal bonds. This standard measure of fiscal inefficiency indicates the *maximum* fiscal benefit and the *maximum* gain in tax equity that could be generated by the taxable bond

---

[4] The estimates of T and W are linear in $\bar{t}$. Therefore, the appropriate estimates of T and W for values of $\bar{t}$ other than 42 or 50 percent are easily determined by interpolation or extrapolation.

TABLE 1

Estimated Effects from Tax Exemption of Municipal Bonds:
Treasury Loss, Subsidy to State and Local Governments, and
Windfall Gain to Holders of Municipal Bonds
(billions of dollars)

Year	Treasury Loss $(\bar{t} = 42\%)^{a}$ (1)	Treasury Loss $(\bar{t} = 50\%)$ (2)	Subsidy to State and Local Governments (3)	Windfall Gain to Holders of Municipal Bonds $(\bar{t} = 42\%)$ (4)	Windfall Gain to Holders of Municipal Bonds $(\bar{t} = 50\%)$ (5)
1952	0.40	0.48	0.29	0.11	0.19
1953	0.60	0.71	0.21	0.29	0.50
1954	0.54	0.64	0.28	0.16	0.36
1955	0.63	0.75	0.31	0.32	0.44
1956	0.74	0.88	0.31	0.43	0.57
1957	0.95	1.13	0.35	0.60	0.78
1958	1.03	1.23	0.47	0.46	0.76
1959	1.28	1.52	0.60	0.68	0.92
1960	1.41	1.68	0.74	0.67	0.94
1961	1.48	1.76	0.80	0.68	0.96
1962	1.57	1.87	1.07	0.50	0.80
1963	1.64	1.95	1.06	0.58	0.89
1964	1.78	2.12	1.20	0.58	0.92
1965	1.96	2.33	1.30	0.66	1.03
1966	2.38	2.83	1.53	0.85	1.30
1967	2.78	3.31	2.08	0.70	1.23
1968	3.37	4.01	2.50	0.87	1.51
1969	4.12	4.90	2.17	1.95	2.73
1970	5.16	6.14	3.02	2.14	3.12
1971	5.40	6.43	3.76	1.64	2.17
1972	5.68	6.76	4.13	1.65	2.63
1973	6.34	7.54	4.99	1.35	2.55
1974	8.04	9.57	5.95	2.09	3.62
1975	8.89	10.58	5.39	3.50	5.19
1976	9.37	11.15	5.95	3.42	5.20

[a] The value of $\bar{t}$ is the assumed average marginal tax rate of holders of municipal bonds.

Source: The formulas for Treasury loss, subsidy to state and local governments, and windfall gain are given in the text. The values for i^{e}, the yield on long-term corporate bonds, i^{m}, the yield on long-term municipal bonds, and M, the dollar value of the outstanding stock of tax-exempt bonds, come from the *Federal Reserve Bulletin*.

TABLE 2

Efficiency Ratio of the Exemption

Year	Assumed Average Marginal Tax Rate of Holders of Municipal Bonds ($\bar{t}$)	
	42 Percent (1)	50 Percent (2)
1952	73	60
1953	35	30
1954	52	44
1955	49	41
1956	42	35
1957	37	31
1958	46	38
1959	47	39
1960	52	44
1961	54	45
1962	68	57
1963	65	54
1964	67	57
1965	66	56
1966	64	54
1967	75	63
1968	74	62
1969	53	44
1970	59	49
1971	70	58
1972	73	61
1973	79	66
1974	74	62
1975	61	51
1976	64	53
Average		
1952–76	60	50
1952–66	54	46
1967–76	68	57

Source: For $\bar{t} = 42$ percent the ratio is that of column 3 to column 1 of Table 1. For $\bar{t} = 50$ percent the ratio is that of column 3 to column 2 of Table 1.

option. To achieve these maximums, however, the direct interest subsidy offered by the Treasury under the option would have to be so high that state and local governments would willingly forgo the issue of *any* tax-exempt bonds. Proponents of the option generally do not argue for the 60 to 70 percent subsidy rates that would be required to achieve this result. Rather, it is usually argued that most of the benefits of the option could be captured with a direct interest subsidy rate (s^*) of 40 percent and that such a subsidy would involve relatively modest costs to the Treasury.[5]

Under a taxable bond option with a 40 percent direct subsidy rate, the implicit subsidy rate on tax-exempt municipal bonds would also ultimately rise to 40 percent.[6] The reason for this is that municipal governments would find it attractive to issue tax-exempt municipal bonds only if the implicit subsidy on them was as high as the direct subsidy available from the Treasury. For a while after the introduction of the option, this condition would probably not be met (at least for long-term bonds); the large outstanding stock of tax-exempt bonds would keep the implicit subsidy rate at less than 40 percent. In this situation, municipal governments would find it attractive to finance their new borrowing largely with taxable bonds and also to retire some outstanding tax-exempt issues and replace them with taxable issues. As the supply of tax-exempt bonds contracts, competition among investors to hold these bonds would drive their yields down and therefore increase the implicit subsidy rate obtainable on new issues of tax-exempt bonds. Equilibrium would result when the implicit subsidy rate on tax-exempt bonds reached the 40 percent subsidy rate on taxable bonds. This equilibrium would be automatically maintained by municipal borrowers, because they have an incentive to divide up new issues of municipal bonds between taxables and tax-exempts so that the 40 percent implicit subsidy rate on tax-exempts is sustained.

Assuming that this equilibrium condition prevailed in 1976, and assuming that the yield on taxable bonds would have been unchanged at 9.0 percent, the 40 percent option would have reduced the yield on tax-exempt bonds from 6.6 to 5.4 percent. State and local governments would have benefited from this reduction in borrowing costs on all of their outstanding bonds—both tax-exempt bonds and taxable bonds with the 40 percent direct interest subsidy. Assuming that the outstanding stock would have remained constant at $248 billion, the benefit to state and local governments from the option would have

[5] For instance, Fortune (1973b) estimates that, if a 40 percent taxable bond option had been instituted in 1968, by 1970 the net interest savings to municipal governments would have amounted to $288 million per year and the net cost to the U.S. Treasury would have been only $84 million per year.

[6] This is the assumption that is made in virtually all studies of the effects of the taxable bond option. It neglects the differences between municipal bonds and corporate bonds in terms of marketability and risk.

been $3.0 billion $= (0.012) \cdot$ ($248 billion). The general formula for the calculation of this benefit is given by the difference between the direct subsidy rate under the option (s^*) and the implicit tax rate on tax-exempt bonds without the option (t^m), multiplied by the yield on taxable bonds (i^c), multiplied by the outstanding stock of state and local government debt (M); that is, $(s^* - t^m) \cdot i^c \cdot M$.

To calculate the cost of the option to the Treasury, and the resulting reduction in the windfall to holders of tax-exempt bonds, it is necessary to know something about the demand function for tax-exempt bonds. Figure 1 shows a hypothetical demand function for tax-exempt bonds consistent with a total 1976 windfall gain of $3.4 billion and with an average marginal tax rate for holders of tax-exempt bonds of 42 percent. The horizontal axis of Figure 1 shows the quantity of tax-exempt bonds. The vertical axis shows the yield on tax-exempt bonds (i^m) and the yield on taxable bonds (i^c). The demand curve slopes upward because an increase in the yield on tax-exempt bonds (given the yield on taxable bonds) increases the number of investors who will find tax-exempt bonds attractive and also increases the attractiveness of such bonds to investors who already hold some of them. At a yield of 6.6 percent in 1976, the demand for tax-exempt bonds is shown to equal the outstanding stock for that year, $248 billion. The subsidy to state and local governments resulting from the exemption ($S = $6.0 billion) is shown by the rectangular area above the horizontal line $i^m = 6.6$ percent, below the horizontal line $i^c = 9.0$ percent, and to the left of the vertical line $M = $248 billion. The windfall gain to holders of tax-exempt bonds ($W = $3.4 billion) is the triangular-shaped area above the demand curve and below the horizontal line $i^m = 6.6$ percent.

Under the taxable bond option with a 40 percent subsidy rate, the yield on tax-exempt bonds in 1976 would have been reduced to 5.4 percent. The demand curve in Figure 1 indicates that at this value of i^m the demand for tax-exempt bonds would have been only $138 billion. The remaining $110 billion of state and local debt would have been financed by the issuance of subsidized taxable bonds. On the $138 billion of tax-exempt bonds, state and local governments would enjoy an increase in the implicit subsidy rate from 27 to 40 percent, for a total increased benefit of $1.7 billion. This $1.7 billion comes wholly at the expense of the windfall presently accruing to holders of tax-exempt bonds. On the $110 billion of subsidized taxable bonds, state and local governments would enjoy an increased subsidy of $1.3 billion (the difference between the new cash subsidy of $4.0 billion and the former implicit subsidy of $2.7 billion). Subsidy

FIGURE 1

Demand Function for Tax-Exempt Bonds

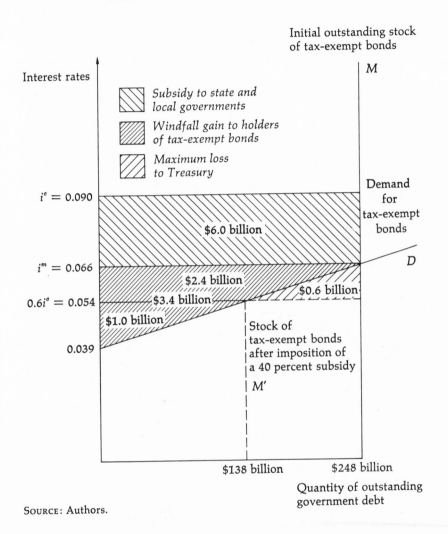

Source: Authors.

payments by the Treasury would be $4.0 billion = (0.40) · (0.09) · ($110 billion). However, the Treasury would recover the bulk of these subsidy payments in taxes collected from the holders of the subsidized taxable bonds. Indeed, an upper-bound estimate of what the Treasury would not recover is the small triangle below the demand

27

TABLE 3

Effects of Taxable Bond Option at an Average Marginal
Tax Rate of 42 Percent
(billions of dollars)

Subsidy Level (percent)	Windfall Captured (1)	Total Benefits to State and Local Governments (2)	Cost to Treasury (3)	Ratio of Benefits to Costs (2)/(3) (4)
30	0.70	0.74	0.04	18.5
40	2.32	2.98	0.66	4.5
50	3.18	5.21	2.03	2.6

Source: The calculations for columns 1–4 are summarized in the text; the relevant data come from the *Federal Reserve Bulletin*.

curve, above the horizontal line 0.6 i^c = 5.4 percent, and between the vertical lines M' = \$138 billion and M = \$248 billion.[7] The area of this triangle is \$0.6 billion. Thus, for a net cost to the Treasury of at most \$0.6 billion, state and local governments benefit to the extent of \$3.0 billion (the sum of \$1.7 billion and \$1.3 billion). The benefit cost ratio is a favorable five to one. Moreover, since the excess of the benefits to state and local governments over net Treasury cost of \$2.4 billion comes at the expense of an inequitable windfall presently accruing to high-bracket holders of tax-exempt bonds, there is a gain in tax equity to the extent of \$2.4 billion.

The effects of the taxable bond option depend on the rate of the direct interest subsidy (s^*) paid by the Treasury on taxable municipal bonds. Given the demand curve shown in Figure 1, it is possible to calculate different subsidy rates. The results of these calculations for subsidy rates of 30, 40, and 50 percent are summarized in Table 3. It is noteworthy that as s^* increases, the benefit to state and local governments and the cost to the Treasury increase. The ratio of benefit to cost, however, decreases as s^* rises. This is because the fraction of the benefit to state and local governments that comes from the windfall of present holders of tax-exempt bonds declines as s^* rises.

The estimated effects of the taxable bond option also depend on

---

[7] The linear demand curve in Figure 1 is constructed so as to be consistent with the estimate that the average marginal tax rate of holders of municipal bonds is 42 percent and the windfall gain accruing to holders of municipal bonds is \$3.4 billion.

TABLE 4

EFFECTS OF TAXABLE BOND OPTION AT AN AVERAGE MARGINAL
TAX RATE OF 50 PERCENT
(billions of dollars)

Subsidy Level (percent)	Windfall Captured (1)	Total Benefits to State and Local Governments (2)	Cost to Treasury (3)	Ratio of Benefits to Costs (2)/(3) (4)
30	0.71	0.74	0.03	24.6
40	2.54	2.98	0.44	6.8
50	3.88	5.21	1.33	3.9

SOURCE: The calculations for columns 1–4 are described in the text; the relevant data come from the *Federal Reserve Bulletin*.

what is assumed about the demand curve for tax-exempt bonds. Consider, as an alternative to the demand curve in Figure 1, a linear demand curve based on an estimated windfall gain to holders of tax-exempt bonds of $5.1 billion and an average marginal tax rate of 50 percent. This demand curve must pass through the point where $i^m =$ 6.6 percent and $D = \$248$ billion and must have a steeper slope than the demand curve in Figure 1.[8] Using this demand curve, we can derive alternative estimates of the effects of the taxable bond option. These estimates, for subsidy rates of 30, 40, and 50 percent, are summarized in Table 4. Since the effect of a given subsidy rate on the borrowing costs of state and local governments does not depend on the shape of the demand curve for tax-exempt bonds, the estimates of the benefits to state and local governments given in Table 4 are the same as those given in Table 3. The steeper demand curve, however, implies that a greater fraction of these benefits comes at the expense of the windfall gains presently accruing to holders of tax-exempt bonds and that a smaller fraction comes at a net cost to the Treasury. For this reason, the benefit-cost ratio, for any given subsidy rate, is always higher for the steeper demand curve.

These results embody the basic position of proponents of the taxable bond option on the issues of fiscal efficiency and tax equity.

[8] The assumptions that the demand curve is linear and that the windfall gain to holders of municipal bonds with average marginal tax rates of 50 percent is equal to $5.1 billion imply that the vertical intercept of the demand curve must be at $i^m = 0.025$.

The magnitude of the problem is measured by the windfall gain currently accruing to holders of tax-exempt municipal bonds. This windfall gain measures both the fiscal inefficiency and the tax inequity resulting from the exemption. A taxable bond option with a subsidy rate of 40 percent would not completely eliminate the problems created by the exemption, but it would greatly improve both fiscal efficiency and tax equity. The option would achieve these benefits because it would enable government units to recapture a substantial part of the windfall gain currently accruing to holders of tax-exempt municipal bonds, and at a low cost to the U.S. Treasury.

The Effectiveness Issue

The case in favor of the taxable bond option is not based exclusively on the purported inefficiency and inequity of the present exemption. Proponents of the option also argue for its adoption on the grounds that it would increase the effectiveness of the federal subsidy on the borrowing costs of municipal governments. At present, these governments enjoy the implicit subsidy that results from the privilege of issuing tax-exempt bonds. The implicit subsidy rate (s) is equal to the proportionate reduction in the borrowing costs of municipal governments relative to taxable corporations; that is, the implicit subsidy rate is equal to the implicit rate paid by holders of tax-exempt municipal bonds, $s = t^m = (i^c - i^m)/i^c$. It is a fact, however, that this implicit subsidy has not prevented a substantial increase in the nominal borrowing costs of municipal governments during the past fifteen years. Presumably, this increase in borrowing costs has compelled municipal governments to restrict the amount of public investment.

Concern with the effectiveness of the present exemption as a means of subsidy is not limited to problems encountered in the past. Proponents of the taxable bond option also argue that the present exemption is unlikely to meet the needs of the future. During the past decade, the outstanding dollar volume of state and local government debt increased more than twofold. Projecting this rate of increase into the next decade, proponents of the option argue that a similar increase in municipal borrowing cannot be absorbed by the tax-exempt market alone without a further substantial increase in the borrowing costs of municipalities. In other words, the effectiveness of the present exemption as a means of subsidy is likely to be further eroded as the pressure of increased municipal borrowing drives up the yields on municipal bonds and thereby reduces the effective rate of subsidy implicit in the privilege of issuing tax-exempt bonds.

Proponents of the taxable bond option argue that its adoption would have resolved the difficulties of the past and will, if adopted, provide a flexible mechanism for meeting the needs of the future. Under an option with a 40 percent direct subsidy rate on taxable municipal bonds, the effective subsidy rate on municipal bonds would be increased from an average of about 30 percent to a fixed rate of 40 percent. This is because municipalities would only issue tax-exempt municipal bonds up to the point where the implicit subsidy on these bonds is equal to the direct subsidy available on taxable bonds. In particular, if the 40 percent taxable bond option had been in effect during the past decade, municipalities would have issued far fewer tax-exempt bonds and would have taken extensive advantage of the opportunity to issue subsidized taxable bonds. This would have reduced significantly the borrowing costs of municipalities and would have enabled them to undertake additional desirable investments. Moreover, the option would operate as an escape valve for any pressures that might develop in the municipal bond market in the future. If their need for capital funds grows more rapidly than the demand for tax-exempt bonds, municipalities will be able to exercise their option to issue subsidized taxable bonds. This will permit any expansion of the total supply of municipal bonds to be absorbed without any increase in the borrowing costs of municipalities relative to the borrowing costs of taxable corporations.

The Instability of Municipal Borrowing Costs

Proponents of the taxable bond option argue that the implicit subsidy provided by the exemption is not only inadequate in terms of its average level, but also is inherently unstable and an important source of variability in the borrowing costs of municipal governments. In particular, they argue that the operation of the exemption makes the yields on municipal bonds especially sensitive to the disturbances created by contractionary monetary policy.[9] The taxable bond option would reduce the instability of municipal borrowing costs by stabilizing the effective subsidy rate on both taxable and tax-exempt municipal bonds at the direct subsidy rate paid on taxable bonds. This would also reduce the sensitivity of municipal borrowing costs to contractionary monetary policy because it would make municipalities less dependent on commercial banks during periods of tight credit.

The contentions of the proponents of the taxable bond option are

---

[9] This specific criticism of the exemption is raised by Fortune (1973a), among many others.

supported by the historical record, which shows significant fluctuations in the implicit subsidy rate. Specifically, column 3 of Table 5 shows that during the past twenty-five years s has fluctuated from a low of 15 percent in 1957 to a high of 33 percent in 1973. During this same period, the nominal yield on municipal bonds has also shown significant fluctuations, as indicated by the standard deviation of i^m reported at the bottom of column 2. The importance of fluctuations in s as a source of instability in i^m is illustrated by comparing columns 2 and 4. Column 4 reports what the yield on municipal bonds would have been if there had been a 40 percent taxable bond option since 1952. This series is referred to as i^{m*} and is constructed by taking 60 percent of the yield on taxable corporate bonds reported in column 1. The standard deviation of i^{m*} is 1.3 percent in comparison with a standard deviation of 1.4 percent for i^m. This indicates that the taxable bond option would have reduced the variability of municipal borrowing costs had it been in operation during the past twenty-five years.

The special role of commercial banks in the market for tax-exempt municipal bonds is indicated by the facts reported in Figure 2 and Table 6 concerning the distribution of municipal bonds by class of holder. For many years, commercial banks have been the single most important group of holders of municipal bonds. But the demand by banks for additions to their holdings of municipal bonds has not grown in a smooth and predictable fashion. In particular, during the credit crunch of 1966, commercial banks did not increase their share of the market, whereas in preceding years their share had grown steadily. In the credit crunch of 1969, the share held by commercial banks actually declined. It is argued that these episodes reflect the special sensitivity of the municipal bond market to contractionary monetary policy. Commercial banks regard municipal bonds as the residual component of their portfolio. When the Federal Reserve tightens credit, banks sell off municipal bonds (or cease acquiring them) in order to maintain loan commitments to their favored customers. The result is a severe restriction in the availability of bank credit to municipal borrowers during periods of monetary contraction.

Proponents of the taxable bond option argue that it would ameliorate the problem of the special sensitivity of the municipal bond market to contractionary monetary policy, because the option would make municipalities less dependent on banks as a source of credit. Taxable municipal bonds would be attractive to many investors—such as pension funds, life insurance companies, and various tax-exempt institutions—who do not find tax-exempt bonds particularly attrac-

FIGURE 2

The Share of Municipal Bonds Held by Commercial Banks and
the Nominal Subsidy to Holders of Municipal Bonds

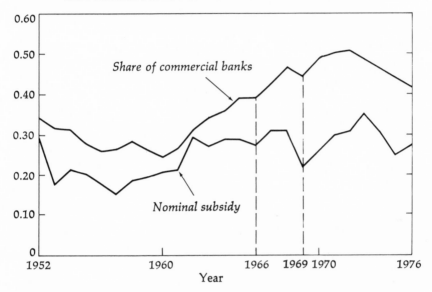

SOURCE: The nominal subsidy is from column 3, Table 5. The share of commercial banks comes from a computer printout of holdings of municipal bonds by type of holder, 1952–76, provided by the Board of Governors of the Federal Reserve System. The figures are reported in column 5, Table 6.

tive. During periods of monetary constraint, when bank demand for municipal bonds falls off, municipal governments would be able to issue more subsidized taxable bonds, and these bonds would find an active market.

Summary

In this chapter we have outlined the logical and factual analysis that is usually presented in support of the taxable bond option. We have pointed out that the case in favor of the option is based on the contention that the present exemption suffers from four major defects that would be corrected by the option. The first defect is *fiscal inefficiency*: the tax revenue lost by the U.S. Treasury as a result of the exemption exceeds the reduction in borrowing costs of municipal governments. The second defect is *tax inequity*: the fiscal loss to the government

33

TABLE 5

NOMINAL YIELDS ON CORPORATE AND MUNICIPAL BONDS, IMPLICIT
SUBSIDY RATE, AND ESTIMATED MUNICIPAL BOND RATE UNDER
TAXABLE BOND OPTION
(percent)

Year	i^c (1)	i^m (2)	s (3)	$i^{m*} = 0.6i^c$ (4)
1952	3.12	2.22	.30	1.9
1953	3.43	2.82	.18	2.1
1954	3.16	2.46	.22	1.9
1955	3.25	2.57	.21	2.0
1956	3.57	2.94	.18	2.1
1957	4.21	3.56	.15	2.5
1958	4.16	3.36	.19	2.5
1959	4.65	3.74	.20	2.8
1960	4.73	3.69	.22	2.8
1961	4.66	3.60	.23	2.8
1962	4.62	3.30	.29	2.8
1963	4.50	3.28	.27	2.7
1964	4.57	3.28	.28	2.7
1965	4.64	3.34	.28	2.8
1966	5.34	3.90	.27	3.2
1967	5.82	3.99	.31	3.5
1968	6.51	4.48	.31	3.9
1969	7.36	5.73	.22	4.4
1970	8.51	6.42	.25	5.1
1971	7.94	5.62	.29	4.8
1972	7.63	5.30	.31	4.6
1973	7.80	5.22	.33	4.7
1974	8.98	6.19	.31	5.4
1975	9.46	7.05	.25	5.7
1976	9.01	6.61	.27	5.4
1952–76 mean	5.7	4.2	.25	3.4
standard deviation	2.1	1.4	.05	1.3
1952–66 mean	4.2	3.2	.23	2.5
standard deviation	0.7	0.5	.05	0.4
1967–76 mean	7.9	5.7	.29	4.7
standard deviation	1.1	1.0	.04	0.7

NOTE: i^c = nominal yield on long-term corporate bonds; i^m = nominal yield on long-term municipal bonds; $s = (i^c - i^m)/i^c$ = implicit subsidy rate; $i^{m*} = 0.6i^c$ = nominal yield on long-term municipal bonds under hypothetical taxable bond option rate of 40 percent.

SOURCE: The data come from the *Federal Reserve Bulletin*. The calculations are described above and in the text.

TABLE 6

Distribution of Municipal Bonds by Class of Holder
(amounts in billions of dollars)

Year	Total Debt (1)	Held by Households Amount (2)	Held by Households Percent (3)	Held by Commercial Banks Amount (4)	Held by Commercial Banks Percent (5)	Held by Others Amount (6)	Held by Others Percent (7)
1952	$ 30	$12	40	$ 10	33	$ 8	27
1953	35	13	37	11	31	11	31
1954	41	16	39	13	32	12	29
1955	46	19	41	13	28	14	30
1956	49	21	43	13	27	15	31
1957	54	23	43	14	26	17	31
1958	59	24	41	17	29	18	31
1959	65	27	42	17	26	21	32
1960	71	31	44	18	25	22	31
1961	76	32	42	21	28	23	30
1962	81	31	38	26	32	24	30
1963	87	32	37	30	35	25	29
1964	93	35	38	34	37	24	26
1965	100	36	36	39	39	25	25
1966	106	40	38	41	39	25	24
1967	114	38	33	50	44	26	23
1968	123	37	31	59	48	27	22
1969	133	46	33	60	45	27	20
1970	144	45	31	70	49	29	20
1971	162	45	28	83	51	34	21
1972	177	47	27	90	51	40	23
1973	194	54	28	96	49	44	23
1974	213	66	31	101	47	46	22
1975	224	74	33	103	46	47	21
1976	248	81	33	106	43	61	25

Note: Percentages may not total 100 because of rounding.

Source: The data are from computer printouts of the holdings of municipal bonds by types of holder, 1952–76, provided by the Board of Governors of the Federal Reserve System.

accrues as a windfall gain to high-bracket taxpayers who escape from paying their fair share of tax by holding tax-exempt municipal bonds. The third defect is *ineffectiveness*: the subsidy enjoyed by municipal governments as a result of the exemption is too low and is likely to fall lower as the supply of municipal bonds expands relative to the demand for them. The fourth defect is *instability*: by isolating the market for municipal bonds from the general credit market, the exemption makes municipal borrowing especially sensitive to a variety of economic disturbances, particularly contractionary monetary policy.

Proponents of the option argue that its introduction would go a long way toward correcting the defects of the exemption, provided that the direct interest subsidy on taxable municipal bonds is set at a sufficiently high level. Under the option, the effective implicit tax rate paid by holders of municipal bonds would be raised from its present level of approximately 30 percent to the level of the direct interest subsidy on taxable municipal bonds. This increase in the implicit tax rate would enable municipal governments and the Treasury to capture a substantial portion of the windfall gain currently accruing to holders of tax-exempt municipal bonds, thereby improving fiscal efficiency and reducing tax inequity. The taxable bond option would also increase the subsidy enjoyed by municipal borrowers and stabilize the rate of subsidy on both taxable and tax-exempt bonds at the direct subsidy rate paid by the Treasury. This would solve both the problem of the ineffectiveness of the present exemption and the problem of the instability created by the exemption.

3

Inflation, Real Yields, and Effective Tax Rates

During the past decade, the United States has experienced an average rate of price inflation of 6 percent per year. It appears that people expect a similar rate of inflation to prevail into the foreseeable future. In the literature of theoretical economics, it has long been recognized that the expectation of continued inflation has important consequences for the yields on all types of securities.[1] More recently, it has become apparent that the functioning of the U.S. tax system is severely affected by inflation.[2] Yet, in the literature dealing with the effects of the tax-exempt status of municipal bonds and with the implications of a taxable bond option, no mention is made of the consequences of inflation.

In this chapter, we argue that this omission is the source of serious error. The existence of inflation has profound implications for the standard argument that the tax-exempt status of municipal bonds results in a substantial inequity in the functioning of the U.S. tax system. During the past decade of high inflation, holders of municipal bonds have paid real implicit tax rates that, on average, have exceeded both the maximum marginal rate prevailing under U.S. law and the effective tax rate on virtually every other form of income. From this

---

[1] At least since the early writings of Irving Fisher (1896), it has been recognized that the nominal rate of interest is the sum of the real rate of interest and the expected rate of price inflation. Fisher's distinction between nominal and real interest rates is now widely employed in the economic analysis of the effects of inflation; see, for instance, Fama (1975), Mundell (1963), and Sargent (1972). Some recent evidence indicates that the real rate of interest on U.S. Treasury bills has been essentially constant during the postwar period and that fluctuations in the nominal rate of interest have been due primarily to fluctuations in the expected rate of inflation; see Fama (1975).

[2] A useful survey of the effects of inflation on the operation of the U.S. tax system can be found in Aaron (1976).

fact, we conclude that as long as the inflation rate remains at or near the level of the past decade holders of municipal bonds will not escape paying their "fair share" of the costs of government.

To develop the basis for this conclusion, we first discuss why the existence of inflation makes it necessary to distinguish between the nominal yield on a security and the real yield on that same security. Next, we examine how inflation affects the operation of the U.S. tax system, with particular reference to the effective tax rate on interest income. Then, we show how the combined effects of inflation and the operation of the tax system affect the real yield on municipal bonds and the real effective rate of tax implicitly paid by holders of such bonds. Finally, we explore the implications of this analysis for the purported inequity generated by the availability of tax-exempt municipal bonds.

Real and Nominal Yields

The nominal yield on a security is the rate of return on that security measured in terms of money. The real yield on a security is the rate of return on that security measured in terms of real goods and services. Nominal and real yields differ when the price of real goods and services—measured, for example, by the consumer price index (CPI)—is changing. In fact, the real yield on a security is the nominal yield on that security minus the percentage rate of price inflation.

To see this, consider a corporate bond that sells for $1,000 at the beginning of the year, pays coupons of $80 during the year, and is resold at the end of the year for $1,000. An investor who purchased this bond at the beginning of the year would have earned a nominal yield of 8 percent. He could have spent 8 percent of the initial *dollar* value of his investment ($80) and still had the same *dollar* value of his investment remaining at the end of the year. If there had been no inflation during the year, the investor would also have earned a real yield of 8 percent. He could have spent 8 percent of the initial *real* value of his investment and still had the same *real* value of his investment at the end of the year. Suppose, however, that the rate of price inflation during the year had been 5 percent. The investor's nominal yield would still be 8 percent, but his real yield would only be 3 percent. Inflation of 5 percent means that the investor's principal at the end of the year is worth only $950 in terms of dollars of constant real purchasing power. Therefore, to keep the real value of his investment intact, the investor must "save" $50 to add to the dollar value of his principal. This means that the investor can spend only $30, or 3 percent of the real value of his initial investment.

In discussing yields on securities, it is also important to distinguish between realized yields and anticipated yields. The realized yield is the rate of return (real or nominal) an investor actually earns, viewed in retrospect, taking account of actual interest and dividends, actual capital gains and losses, and actual inflation. The anticipated yield is the rate of return an investor expects to earn, viewed in prospect, taking account of expected interest and dividends, expected capital gains and losses, and expected inflation. This distinction between realized and anticipated yields is particularly important during periods in which anticipated yields are changing rapidly. If the anticipated nominal yield on long-term bonds rises in the current year, the price of previously issued long-term bonds will decline. Investors who purchased long-term bonds in the preceding year may actually earn negative *realized* rates of return, taking account of the change in the market value of their investments. These negative realized rates of return, however, are not representative of the rates of return that these investors expected to earn when they purchased the bonds.

The distinction between nominal and real yields and the distinction between realized and anticipated yields imply four possible measures of the yield on any security. Table 7 reports the values of three of these measures of yield for long-term corporate bonds, for the last twenty-five years, from 1952 through 1976. Column 1 reproduces the series on realized nominal yields calculated by Ibbotson and Sinquefield (1977). This measure of yield includes both interest payments and realized capital gains, calculated on the assumption that an investor purchased a representative long-term corporate bond and resold it one year later. Column 2 reproduces the Ibbotson-Sinquefield series on realized real yields. This measure adjusts the realized nominal rate to take account of the effects of inflation over the holding period. Column 3 reproduces the series on the anticipated nominal yield on long-term corporate bonds reported in the *Federal Reserve Bulletin*. This yield is calculated by finding the average annual rate of return an investor would earn if he held a representative long-term corporate bond from the time of purchase to maturity.[3] For comparative purposes, column 4 reports a series on the actual rate of inflation each year, calculated as the percentage change in the consumer price index

---

[3] The Ibbotson and Sinquefield study examines the realized yields on high-grade corporate bonds, whereas the Federal Reserve interest rate series in column 3 of Table 7 refers to an average of bonds of different grades. This difference, however, is not of major importance for the issues presently under discussion.

TABLE 7

NOMINAL AND REAL YIELDS ON LONG-TERM CORPORATE BONDS
(percent)

Year	Realized Nominal Rates (1)	Realized Real Rates (2)	Anticipated Nominal Rates (3)	Inflation (4)
1952	3.5	2.6	3.2	2.2
1953	3.4	2.8	3.4	0.8
1954	5.4	5.9	3.2	0.5
1955	0.5	0.1	3.3	− 0.4
1956	− 6.8	− 9.4	3.6	1.5
1957	8.7	5.5	4.2	3.5
1958	− 2.2	− 3.9	4.2	2.7
1959	− 1.0	− 2.4	4.7	0.8
1960	9.1	7.5	4.7	1.6
1961	4.8	4.1	4.7	1.0
1962	7.9	6.7	4.6	1.1
1963	2.2	0.5	4.5	1.2
1964	4.8	3.5	4.6	1.3
1965	− 0.5	− 2.4	4.6	1.7
1966	0.2	− 3.1	5.3	2.8
1967	− 5.0	− 7.8	5.8	2.8
1968	2.6	− 2.1	6.5	4.1
1969	− 8.1	−13.5	7.4	5.2
1970	18.4	12.3	8.5	5.8
1971	11.0	7.4	7.9	4.2
1972	7.3	3.7	7.6	3.2
1973	1.1	− 7.1	7.8	6.0
1974	− 3.1	−13.7	9.0	10.4
1975	14.6	7.2	9.5	8.7
1976	18.6	13.2	9.0	5.6
Average				
1952–76	3.9	0.7	5.7	3.1
1952–66	2.7	1.2	4.2	1.5
1967–76	5.7	−0.04	7.9	5.6

SOURCE: Data in columns 1–2 from Ibbotson and Sinquefield (1977). Data for column 3 are taken from Table 5, column 1. Data for column 4 are the consumer price index (CPI) from the *Federal Reserve Bulletin*. Inflation is calculated as $lnCPI_t - lnCPI_{t-1}$, when $lnCPI_t$ is the natural logarithm of the consumer price index in year t.

between one year and the next. The entries at the bottom of each column report the average values of the corresponding series for the whole period 1952 to 1976, for the subperiod 1952 to 1966, and for the subperiod 1967 to 1976.

Two general facts are apparent from the data in Table 7. First, the series on realized nominal yields show much more erratic behavior than the series on anticipated nominal yields. In particular, in years that were followed by increases in the anticipated nominal yield, realized yields tended to be low or negative. This is due to the capital losses caused by the rising nominal rates. In contrast, anticipated nominal yields were always positive. Second, the general upward trend of anticipated nominal yields during the past twenty-five years is associated with a general upward trend in the inflation rate. In particular, the anticipated nominal yield frequently showed significant increases in years in which the inflation rate increased significantly.

These facts are consistent with what economic theory suggests about the effects of inflation on interest rates. The observation of higher rates of inflation ought to lead people to expect higher rates of inflation in the future. The immediate increase in the expected rate of inflation is usually less than the observed increase in the actual rate of inflation because people know that some increases in inflation rates are transitory rather than permanent. Persistence of high rates of inflation, however, eventually persuades people that they should expect similar rates of inflation in the future. When the expected rate of inflation increases, the nominal yield ought to rise by an approximately equal amount; the anticipated real yield ought to remain approximately unchanged. This is because anticipated real yields, not nominal yields, regulate the desire of borrowers to borrow and the willingness of lenders to lend. If greater inflation is anticipated, borrowers and lenders simply adjust nominal interest rates so as to achieve the same bargain in terms of anticipated real interest rates.

This explains why nominal yields rose as people experienced and then came to anticipate higher rates of inflation in the late 1960s and in the 1970s. Furthermore, the increases in nominal yields occasioned by increases in the expected rate of inflation caused capital losses for holders of previously issued long-term bonds. This capital loss effect explains why the average realized real yield on long-term corporate bonds for the decade 1967 to 1976 was minus 0.04 percent. In addition to capital losses due to increases in nominal yields, investors suffered unanticipated losses of real purchasing power due to underprediction of the rate of inflation.

Anticipated Inflation and Anticipated Real Yields

The amount of income a bondholder actually earns is determined by his realized yield rather than by the yield he expected to earn when he purchased the bond. For this reason, it might be thought appropriate to base the analysis of the issues concerning the tax-exempt status of municipal bonds on realized yields rather than on anticipated yields. There are, however, two important reasons why it is better to rely on anticipated yields rather than realized yields. First, an investor's decisions about which assets he will hold depend on the yields that he anticipates earning on these assets. Hence, for the analysis of any issue concerning choices among alternative assets, it is essential to focus on anticipated yields rather than realized yields. Second, the analysis of the effects of the exemption is fundamentally concerned with its long-run effects rather than its effects in any particular year. In the long run, realized yields ought to correspond to anticipated yields. In any particular year, realized yields deviate from anticipated yields because of unforeseen circumstances which are not characteristic of the situation that will prevail on average in the long run.

The measurement of anticipated nominal yields presents little difficulty. For the purposes of the present discussion, we may safely assume that the anticipated nominal yield on a bond is equal to the ordinary measure of yield to maturity on that bond. The measurement of anticipated real yields presents much greater difficulties. The basic problem is that there is no direct measure of the expected rate of inflation or of the anticipated real yield on any security. There are, however, procedures for estimating the expected rate of inflation and for imputing a value for anticipated real yields.

One procedure is to assume that the average anticipated real yield on taxable bonds is constant, independent of changes in the expected rate of inflation. Given this assumption, it remains to determine the correct, average value of the real yield on long-term bonds. For this purpose, it seems appropriate to take the difference between the average nominal yield on long-term bonds and the average rate of inflation over some period of time. The period should be long enough and stable enough so that it is plausible to assume that the average actual inflation rate corresponds to the average expected inflation rate. Except for the years 1957 and 1958, the period from 1953 to 1965 seems to have been a fairly stable period with low inflation. Thus, there is some presumption that this procedure will be relevant for that period. Using the anticipated nominal yields and the rates of inflation reported in Table 7 for the period 1953 to 1965 (excluding 1957 and 1958), the implied estimate of the average real yield on long-term corporate bonds of average grade is 3.2 percent (4.2 percent average nominal yield minus 1.0 percent inflation rate).

Applying this same procedure to the inflationary period in the late 1960s and 1970s, it is appropriate to focus on the years 1969 through 1976, excluding 1974 and 1975. By 1969, inflation was already well under way, and experience with inflation had probably already had a significant impact on expectations of future inflation. The years 1974 and 1975 should be excluded because, like 1957 and 1958, they were years of high inflation (relative to previous and subsequent years) followed by deep recession. The average of anticipated nominal yields for the years 1969 through 1976 (excluding 1974 and 1975) was 8.0 percent. The average of inflation rates for these years was 5.0 percent. The difference between 8.0 percent and 5.0 percent indicates a real yield of 3.0 percent, slightly less than the estimated real yield of 3.2 percent for the years 1953 through 1965 (excluding 1957 and 1958).

Another piece of evidence on the anticipated real rate comes from a study of realized yields over the fifty-year period from 1926 to 1976 by Ibbotson and Sinquefield (1977). On the basis of the evidence on realized real yields, they find the anticipated real yield on high-grade long-term corporate bonds to be about 2.0 percent. A portfolio of corporate bonds of all qualities is riskier than a collection made up solely of high-grade bonds, so the investor must be compensated with a real yield higher than that of high-grade bonds. The compensation or risk premium is less than a full percentage point and probably only about half a percentage point. Thus, the average anticipated real yield for long-term corporate bonds of average quality that is suggested by the long-run evidence on realized real yields is about 2.5 to 3.0 percent.

An alternative procedure for estimating the expected rate of inflation and the anticipated real yield on corporate bonds is to assume that expectations of inflation are based on some mechanism for predicting future inflation rates using past inflation rates. One such mechanism that has been widely employed in studies of inflation and has been found to be a reasonable mechanism for predicting inflation in the United States (in the postwar period) is the mechanism of adaptive expectations.[4] Under adaptive expectations, people are assumed to

---

[4] Several empirical studies have shown that the adaptive expectations perform well in predicting the rate of inflation in the United States during the postwar period. Adaptive expectations are close to being the optimal statistical predictor of the future inflation rate based on past observed inflation rates.

form some initial expectation of the future rate of inflation (π). If the actual rate of inflation in the initial year exceeds this initial value of π, then people are assumed to adjust their expectation of the future rate of inflation upward by some fraction, B, of the excess of the actual inflation rate over the expected inflation rate. This procedure is continued in subsequent years; specifically, in each year the expected future rate of inflation is adjusted (upward or downward) by a fraction B of the difference between the observed inflation rate and the previously expected inflation rate.

Using the mechanism of adaptive expectations, together with the actual inflation rates in Table 7, it is possible to construct series for the expected rate of inflation and for the anticipated real yield on corporate bonds. In particular, values of B of one-third, one-fourth, and one-fifth produce the series for the expected rate of inflation reported in Table 8. (These series are constructed on the assumption that the expected rate of inflation was zero in 1952.) Table 8 also reports three series on the anticipated real yield on corporate bonds. These series are obtained by subtracting each of the three series on the anticipated rate of inflation from the series on the anticipated nominal yield on long-term corporate bonds reported in column 3 of Table 7. The figures at the bottom of the columns in Table 8 indicate the averages of the corresponding series for the whole period 1952 to 1976, for the subperiod 1952 to 1966, and for the subperiod 1967 to 1976.

The data in column 3 of Table 7 indicate that the anticipated nominal yield on long-term corporate bonds increased from an average of 4.2 percent during the noninflationary subperiod 1952 to 1966 to an average of 7.9 percent in the inflationary subperiod 1967 to 1976. For all three of the series on the expected rate of inflation in Table 8, it is apparent that the bulk of this increase in the anticipated nominal yield is accounted for by the increase in the expected rate of inflation between the two subperiods. Anticipated real yields, in contrast to anticipated nominal yields, have remained essentially constant between the two subperiods. Indeed, the maximum estimate for the anticipated real yield on corporate bonds for the decade 1967 to 1976 is 4.0 percent. This is the anticipated real yield for the case where the speed of adjustment of expectations (the fraction B) is equal to one-fifth. Since the series on the expected inflation rate that is derived under the assumption that B is equal to one-fifth shows a consistent tendency to underpredict the inflation rate, it is likely that the estimate of a 4.0 percent anticipated real yield is too high. Moreover, the price and wage controls that were imposed from August of 1971 through the summer of 1973 tended to depress the measured inflation rate relative to the true underlying inflation rate in the economy. For this reason, it is likely that estimates of the expected rate of inflation that are based on the mechanical use of measured inflation rates probably understate to some extent the true value of the expected rate of inflation during this period. All things considered, the evidence in Table 8 indicates that the bulk of the increase in the anticipated nominal yield on corporate bonds that occurred during the past decade was due to the increase in the expected rate of price inflation. The evidence in this table is also broadly consistent with the notion that the anticipated real yield on long-term corporate bonds is in the range of 3 percent and is essentially constant in the face of significant changes in the expected rate of price inflation.

In recent years, a controversy has arisen over an assertion by Eugene F. Fama that the anticipated real yield on U.S. Treasury bills is constant and that variations in the nominal yield on Treasury bills reflect variations in the market's expectation of the future rate of inflation.[5] After extensive debate and data analysis, the consensus on these issues is that the anticipated real yield on Treasury bills is not constant but that major movements in the nominal yield on Treasury bills do primarily reflect changes in expectations concerning future inflation rates.[6] For present purposes, however, the critical issue is not the absolute constancy of the real yield on taxable bonds but rather whether there is any pronounced tendency for the average anticipated real yield on taxable corporate bonds to be significantly affected by changes in the anticipated rate of inflation. Theoretical analyses of this issue have produced ambiguous conclusions.[7] No empirical study of which we are aware shows a pronounced positive or negative effect or is inconsistent with the hypothesis that there is no

[5] See Fama (1975 and 1977), Carlson (1977), Joines (1977), and Nelson and Schwert (1977).

[6] In Fama (1975), it was claimed that the data were consistent with the hypothesis that the anticipated real yield on Treasury bills is constant. Subsequent work, particularly that of Nelson and Schwert (1977), disconfirms this strong hypothesis. However, the results of Nelson and Schwert are consistent with the hypothesis that "expectations of inflation have accounted for most of the variation in short-term interest rates during the postwar period."

[7] Mundell (1963) has argued that an increase in the expected rate of inflation should depress the real interest rate. Darby (1975) and Gandolfi (1976) have questioned whether this result is applicable to before-tax yields or after-tax yields. Sargent (1973) and Mussa (1976) have presented theoretical models in which changes in the expected rate of inflation have no effect on real yields.

TABLE 8

ANTICIPATED INFLATION RATES AND ANTICIPATED NOMINAL AND REAL YIELDS

(percent)

Year	Anticipated Nominal Yields (1)	Anticipated Inflation (B = 1/3)ᵃ (2)	Anticipated Real Yields (B = 1/3) (3)	Anticipated Inflation (B = 1/4) (4)	Anticipated Real Yields (B = 1/4) (5)	Anticipated Inflation (B = 1/5) (6)	Anticipated Real Yields (B = 1/5) (7)
1952	3.2	0.0	3.2	0.0	3.2	0.0	3.2
1953	3.4	0.3	3.2	0.2	3.2	0.2	3.2
1954	3.2	0.3	2.9	0.3	2.9	0.2	3.0
1955	3.3	0.1	3.2	0.1	3.2	0.1	3.2
1956	3.6	0.6	3.0	0.6	3.0	0.4	3.2
1957	4.2	1.5	2.7	1.3	2.9	1.0	3.2
1958	4.2	1.9	2.3	1.7	2.5	1.3	3.2
1959	4.7	1.5	3.2	1.4	3.3	1.2	3.5
1960	4.7	1.6	3.1	1.5	3.2	1.3	3.4
1961	4.7	1.4	3.3	1.4	3.3	1.2	3.5
1962	4.6	1.3	3.3	1.3	3.3	1.2	3.4
1963	4.5	1.3	3.2	1.3	3.2	1.2	3.3
1964	4.6	1.3	3.3	1.3	3.3	1.2	3.4
1965	4.6	1.4	3.2	1.4	3.2	1.3	3.3
1966	5.3	1.9	3.4	1.7	3.6	1.6	3.7
1967	5.8	2.2	3.6	2.0	3.8	2.3	4.2

1968	6.5	2.8	3.7	2.5	4.0	1.9	3.9
1969	7.4	3.6	3.8	3.2	4.2	2.9	4.5
1970	8.5	4.3	4.2	3.9	4.6	3.5	5.0
1971	7.9	4.3	3.6	3.9	4.0	3.6	4.3
1972	7.6	3.9	3.7	3.8	3.8	3.5	4.1
1973	7.8	4.6	3.2	4.3	3.5	4.0	3.8
1974	9.0	6.5	2.5	5.9	3.1	5.3	3.7
1975	9.5	7.3	2.2	6.6	2.9	6.0	3.5
1976	9.0	6.7	2.3	6.3	2.7	5.9	3.1
Average							
1952–76	5.7	2.5	3.2	2.3	3.4	2.1	3.6
1952–66	4.2	1.1	3.1	1.0	3.2	0.9	3.3
1967–76	7.9	4.6	3.3	4.2	3.7	3.9	4.0

NOTE: The figures reported in this table are rounded off at a single decimal place. When used in subsequent calculations, however, two decimal places are used before rounding. This procedure yields more accurate results, but also the appearance of minor numerical inconsistencies.

[a] The value of B indicates the degree to which anticipations of inflation are assumed to change in response to past errors in prediction. A larger value implies a faster response.

SOURCE: Column 1 comes from column 3, Table 7. See text for method of calculating columns 2–7. For example, column 2 is calculated as $\pi_t = B(\Delta_t) + (1 - B)\pi_{t-1}$, where π_t is the anticipated inflation in year t, and Δ_t is the actual inflation in year t. Note that $\pi_{1952} = 0$ by assumption. Column 3 is then $i_t^e - \pi_t$.

effect of changes in the expected rate of inflation on the (before-tax) real yield on long-term corporate bonds.[8]

Given the best available evidence on the behavior of yields on taxable bonds, the following conclusions are justified. First, the increase in the general level of yields that has occurred during the past decade is due primarily to the increase that has occurred in the expected rate of price inflation. Second, on average, in the long run the anticipated real yield on long-term corporate bonds is about 3 percent and is almost certainly below 3.3 percent. Third, although the anticipated real yield on taxable bonds is not absolutely constant, the average anticipated real yield on corporate bonds is not significantly affected by changes in the expected rate of inflation. Given these conclusions, we shall assume throughout the remainder of this study that 3.3 percent is a reasonable upper-bound estimate of the anticipated real yield on taxable corporate bonds of average quality. Further, for purposes of assessing the effects of the exemption and the consequences of the taxable bond option, we shall assume that, for any given value of the expected rate of inflation, the long-run average level of the anticipated nominal yield on taxable corporate bonds is equal to an anticipated real yield of 3.3 percent plus the expected rate of price inflation.

Inflation and Taxation

There is general agreement that the appropriate base for an income tax is an individual's real income, that is, the amount an individual could spend on current consumption and still hold his real wealth intact. At present, however, the base of the U.S. income tax is measured in dollars which correspond to real income only when the rate of price inflation is zero. When the rate of price inflation is low, as during the period 1952 to 1966, this definition of the tax base creates only minor problems. However, during periods of high inflation, the present definition of the tax base results in serious distortions in the operation of the tax system.

---

[8] In one test, Nelson and Schwert (1977) find that an increase in the anticipated rate of inflation has a slight positive effect on the anticipated real yield on Treasury bills. In another test, they find a somewhat stronger negative effect. In tests of the effect of changes in the anticipated inflation rate on the nominal yield on long-term government bonds, Fama and Schwert (1978) find that the coefficient is sometimes greater than one and sometimes less than one and in no test significantly different from one. This indicates that the anticipated real yield on long-term government bonds is not affected by changes in the anticipated rate of inflation.

The most serious distortion arises with respect to the taxation of interest income on taxable bonds. This is because all of the interest paid on such a bond is treated as income subject to tax, including that part of interest income that is required simply to maintain the real value of the bond during a period of price inflation. To illustrate the problem, consider an investor with a 40 percent marginal tax rate who holds a taxable bond with 3.3 percent before-tax real yield. If the inflation rate is zero, this investor will also earn a nominal yield of 3.3 percent and pay 40 percent of this nominal yield as tax. After tax, he will be left with a nominal yield and a real yield of 2.0 percent. Under noninflationary conditions, the investor will have paid 40 percent of his before-tax real yield as tax. Now, consider what happens if the rate of inflation (actual and expected) is 6 percent. A before-tax real yield of 3.3 percent corresponds to a before-tax nominal yield of 9.3 percent. On his nominal yield of 9.3 percent, the investor must pay 40 percent tax, reducing his after-tax nominal yield to 5.6 percent. Subtracting the 6 percent inflation rate, he receives an after-tax real yield of minus 0.4 percent. Thus, the 40 percent tax applied to the investor's nominal yield takes away more than 100 percent of his before-tax real yield. In fact, on his before-tax real yield of 3.3 percent, the investor is forced to pay tax at the real effective rate of 113 percent.

This distortion becomes more severe as the investor's marginal tax rate increases, as it inevitably does when inflation pushes everyone into higher nominal tax brackets. When the inflation rate is 6 percent, an investor in the 60 percent bracket will have to pay 60 percent tax on a nominal yield of 9.3 percent, leaving him with an after-tax nominal yield of only 3.7 percent. This after-tax nominal yield corresponds to an after-tax real yield of minus 2.3 percent (3.7 percent minus the inflation rate of 6 percent). Clearly, this investor pays far more than his before-tax real yield of 3.3 percent to the government. His real effective tax rate is actually 169 percent.

From these examples, it is apparent that during periods of inflation holders of taxable bonds pay tax on their real interest income at rates substantially in excess of their nominal marginal tax rates. To take account of the effect of inflation on taxes paid on real interest income, it is useful to introduce the concept of the "real effective rate of tax" on taxable interest income, t^{ec}, defined as the proportion of real yield which must be paid as tax; that is,

$$t^{ec} = t \cdot i^c / (i^c - \pi) = t \cdot (r^c + \pi)/r^c,$$

where t is the investor's nominal marginal rate, i^c is the nominal yield on taxable corporate bonds, π is the expected rate of inflation, and

r^o is the before-tax real yield on corporate bonds. From this formula, it follows that the real effective rate of tax will exceed the nominal tax rate whenever the expected rate of inflation is positive, and that the difference between t^{eo} and t will grow as π grows and also as t rises.

The effect of higher expected rates of inflation on the real effective tax rate paid by holders of taxable bonds is indicated in Table 9. The columns of this table indicate the nominal marginal tax rate of the investor (t), and the rows indicate the expected rate of inflation (π). The entries in the body of the table indicate the real effective tax rate (t^{eo}) corresponding to each combination of t and π. The values of t^{eo} are calculated on the assumption that the real yield on long-term corporate bonds remains at 3.3 percent in the face of variations in the expected rate of inflation.

It is apparent that the real effective rate of tax reaches very high levels, even at moderate rates of inflation, for investors with modest nominal tax rates. Since inflation rates of at least 4 to 6 percent seem likely to prevail for some time to come, the entries in Table 9 for this range of inflation rates have particular relevance. In this range of inflation rates, investors with nominal tax rates of 50 percent or more

TABLE 9

REAL EFFECTIVE TAX RATES FOR HOLDERS OF TAXABLE BONDS
(percent)

Expected Inflation Rate	Marginal Tax Rate of the Investor			
	30	40	50	60
0	30	40	50	60
1	39	52	65	78
2	48	64	80	96
3	57	76	95	115
4	66	88	111	133
5	75	101	126	151
6	85	113	141	169
7	94	125	156	187
8	103	137	171	205
9	112	149	186	224
10	121	161	202	242

NOTE: The real effective tax rate, t^{eo}, is calculated from the formula, $t^{eo} = t \cdot (.033 + \pi)/.033$, where t is the marginal tax rate of the investor, π is the percentage rate of anticipated price inflation, and 3.3 percent is the before-tax real yield on a taxable bond.

will face real effective tax rates consistently in excess of 100 percent. This means that such investors would earn negative after-tax real income from taxable bonds. Moreover, even investors in the 30 percent nominal tax bracket will face real effective tax rates in the range of 66 to 85 percent when the inflation rate is in the range of 4 to 6 percent.

As indicated in Table 9, the distortionary effect of inflation is larger, the higher the nominal tax brackets. This is so because inflation has a multiplicative rather than an additive effect on an investor's real effective tax rate. This effect is most dramatically illustrated when we consider investors with a zero nominal tax rate. For them, the real effective tax rate is always zero, regardless of the inflation rate. This fact is of some importance, because substantial amounts of taxable bonds are held in pension funds, retirement accounts, and life insurance reserves. The nominal tax rate on these bonds is zero or very close to zero. Hence, the ultimate beneficiaries of these pension funds, retirement accounts, and life insurance reserves enjoy very low real effective tax rates, relative to taxable investors who hold bonds directly in their own portfolios. Since the law imposes quantitative limits on the amount that may be sheltered from taxation in pension funds and retirement accounts, wealthy investors are far more likely to be exposed to very high real effective tax rates on taxable bonds than are poorer investors.

Inflation affects the taxation of real income earned on assets other than taxable bonds. For equity assets such as common stocks and real estate, any increase in money value is regarded as a capital gain that is taxable upon realization (that is, when the asset is sold). During periods of inflation, however, only the excess of the rate of nominal capital gains over the rate of price inflation constitutes real income for the investor. Since all nominal capital gains are taxable, the effective rate of tax on real income earned on equity assets rises as the inflation rate rises. This increase in the real effective tax rate on equity assets, however, is much smaller than the increase in the real effective tax rate on taxable bonds. The basic reason for this is that the effective nominal tax rate on equity assets is lower than that applicable to taxable bonds. Equity assets benefit from two significant tax advantages relative to taxable bonds: realized long-term capital gains are taxed at a lower nominal tax rate than interest income; and, more important, holders of equity assets can delay the taxation of capital gains by continuing to hold the asset rather than selling it. The magnitude and significance of the lower real effective tax rate on equity assets will be further explored in chapter 5.

Inflation also affects the taxation of wage income but in a fundamentally different way than it affects the taxation of income from capital. As the price level rises, wage rates also rise, maintaining real wages at the level dictated by real labor productivity. Higher price inflation does push wage earners into higher tax brackets. For example, the doubling of prices and wages that has occurred in the last decade has pushed a married wage earner with an income of $12,000 in 1967 from the 25 percent marginal tax bracket to the 36 percent marginal tax bracket. However, the wage earner's nominal tax rate still measures his real tax rate. Unlike taxable bonds, wages are never taxed at a real rate above the wage earner's nominal tax rate. The reason for this fundamental difference is well explained in the study, "Inflation and the Definition of Personal Disposable Income," prepared by Roger Brinner for the Brookings Institution Conference on Inflation and the Income Tax:

> It is important to recognize that taxes levied on wages are distorted by inflation only because the system of progressive tax rates and nonindexed exemptions, deductions, and rate brackets is progressive. In contrast, the measurement of capital income is currently distorted in two respects during inflation. First, capital income shares with wages the arbitrary inflation-induced increases associated with a progressive tax structure. Second, the contribution of capital income to taxable capacity is overstated if a deduction is not allowed for that component of the return that merely maintains the purchasing power of initial net worth.

Thus, the distortion of the tax system that is induced by inflation is greater for income from capital than it is for wage income. Among capital assets, the greatest distortionary effect of inflation falls on taxable bonds, where real effective tax rates can easily exceed 100 percent. Among investors in taxable bonds, those most severely affected by this distortion are those in the highest tax brackets.

Inflation and the Implicit Tax on Municipals

The interest on municipal bonds is exempt from federal income tax. However, it is widely recognized that while holders of municipal bonds do not pay any direct income tax to the federal government they do pay an implicit tax to the municipal governments that issue tax-exempt bonds. The magnitude of this implicit tax is the reduction in (before-tax) interest income that holders of municipal bonds suffer as a result of holding such bonds rather than comparable corporate bonds. This implicit tax is collected by state and local governments in the form of a lower interest obligation on their tax-exempt bonds.

The nominal implicit tax rate for holders of municipal bonds (t^m) is defined as the proportionate reduction in nominal yield on municipal bonds relative to corporate bonds; that is,

$$t^m = (i^c - i^m)/i^c,$$

where i^c is the nominal yield on taxable corporate bonds and i^m is the nominal yield on tax-exempt municipal bonds. This definition is based on the assumption that corporate bonds and municipal bonds are strictly comparable in every way, except for tax status and yield, and that in the absence of the exemption municipal bonds would have the same yield as corporate bonds.[9]

During periods of inflation, as we have shown, nominal interest income does not correspond to real interest income. Therefore, the nominal implicit tax rate (t^m) paid by municipal bondholders does not accurately measure the real implicit tax rate paid by these bondholders during periods of inflation. To obtain a measure of the tax rate paid by municipal bondholders on their prospective real interest income, it is necessary to define the real implicit tax rate on municipal bonds (t^{em}) as the proportionate reduction in real yield suffered by holders of municipal bonds relative to the (before-tax) real yield on corporate bonds; that is,

$$t^{em} = (r^c - r^m)/r^c = (i^c - i^m)/(i^c - \pi),$$

where $r^c = i^c - \pi$, $r^m = i^c - \pi$, and π is the expected rate of price inflation. If we compare the formulas for t^m and t^{em}, it is apparent that the real implicit tax rate on municipal bonds (t^{em}) will be greater than

---

[9] Municipal bonds are not exactly comparable to corporate bonds for at least two important reasons. First, municipal bonds are usually issued in serial form, with many different maturities included in a single issue. For this reason, the number of bonds of any given maturity in any given issue is likely to be small. This limits the breadth of the resale market for municipal bonds and presumably makes them less attractive than "comparable" corporate bonds. For a discussion of this point, see West (1964). Second, the tax advantage of municipal bonds due to the exemption of interest payments from federal income taxation does not extend to capital gains and losses associated with fluctuations in the market value of such bonds. In fact, it can be shown that the risk associated with a tax-exempt municipal bond (due to fluctuations in market value) is greater than the risk associated with a "comparable" corporate bond. For a discussion of this point, see Skelton (1978). Ignoring the issue of risk and the issue of marketability tends to exaggerate the measured gain accruing to holders of municipal bonds.

the nominal implicit tax rate (t^m) whenever the expected rate of price inflation is positive.[10]

The importance of the distinction between the nominal implicit tax rate on municipal bonds (t^m) and the real implicit tax rate (t^{em}) is dramatically illustrated in Table 10. Column 1 reproduces the series on the nominal yields on long-term corporate bonds of average quality reported in the *Federal Reserve Bulletin*. Column 2 reproduces a similar series for long-term municipal bonds. Column 3 reports the value of t^m calculated from the yields reported in columns 1 and 2. These are the nominal implicit tax rates referred to in the standard analysis of the effects of the tax-exempt status of municipal bonds. Column 4 reports a series for the real implicit tax rate on municipal bonds. These tax rates are calculated on the assumption that the real yield on taxable corporate bonds is 3.3 percent; that is, for each year, the real implicit tax rate on municipal bonds is calculated by dividing the difference between column 1 and column 2 by a fixed real yield of 3.3 percent.

It is apparent from Table 10 that while the nominal implicit tax rate for holders of long-term municipal bonds (t^m) has fluctuated during the past twenty-five years its average level has not been much affected by the increase in the inflation rate. For the fifteen years from 1952 to 1966, when inflation rates were relatively low, t^m aver-

---

[10] In private communications, Harvey Galper of the Office of Tax Analysis and Richard Kopcke of the Federal Reserve Bank of Boston have raised a theoretical objection to our use of the real implicit tax rate on municipal bonds in discussing tax equity. They agree that, because interest income is taxed on a nominal basis rather than a real basis, inflation decreases the after-tax real yield on taxable bonds *relative* to the before-tax real yield on such bonds. This spills over into the municipal bond market; the real yield on municipal bonds falls *relative* to the before-tax real yield on corporate bonds, or, as we have put it, the real implicit tax rate on municipal bonds rises. But, they argue, the decrease in the real yield on municipal bonds *relative* to the before-tax real yield on corporate bonds could be achieved exclusively by an increase in the before-tax real yield on corporate bonds, without any change in the real yield on municipal bonds. This point is related to an argument made in Darby (1975). In this situation, it would still be true that the real implicit tax rate on municipal bonds (as we have defined it) would rise due to an increase in the anticipated inflation rate. However, this increase in the real implicit tax rate would not indicate that municipal bond-holders were any worse off than before the increase in the anticipated inflation rate. They would still be earning the same real yield. We believe that this argument is theoretically correct but empirically irrelevant. The results presented in this study and the results of many other studies indicate that before-tax real yield on corporate bonds has remained approximately constant in the face of a substantial increase in the anticipated inflation rate. The increase in the real implicit tax rate on municipal bonds has been achieved by a decline in the real yield on municipal bonds against an essentially constant before-tax real yield on corporate bonds.

TABLE 10

Effective Tax Rates on Municipal Bonds
(percent)

Year	i^o	i^m	t^m	t^{em}
1952	3.2	2.2	30	30
1953	3.4	2.8	18	18
1954	3.2	2.5	22	21
1955	3.3	2.6	21	21
1956	3.6	2.9	18	21
1957	4.2	3.6	15	18
1958	4.2	3.4	19	24
1959	4.7	3.7	20	30
1960	4.7	3.7	22	30
1961	4.7	3.6	23	33
1962	4.6	3.3	29	39
1963	4.5	3.3	27	36
1964	4.6	3.3	28	39
1965	4.6	3.3	28	39
1966	5.3	3.4	27	58
1967	5.8	4.0	31	55
1968	6.5	4.5	31	61
1969	7.4	5.7	22	52
1970	8.5	6.4	25	64
1971	7.9	5.6	29	70
1972	7.6	5.3	31	70
1973	7.8	5.2	33	79
1974	9.0	6.2	31	85
1975	9.5	7.0	25	76
1976	9.0	6.6	27	73
Average				
1952–76	5.7	4.2	25	46
1952–66	4.2	3.2	23	31
1967–76	7.9	5.7	29	68

Note: i^o = nominal yields, long-term corporate bonds; i^m = nominal yields, long-term municipal bonds; t^m = implicit nominal tax rate paid by holders of municipal bonds; t^{em} = implicit real tax rate paid by holders of municipal bonds. Source: The data for i^o and i^m are from Table 5. The formulas for calculating t^m and t^{em} are given in the text. Calculations are based on unrounded data.

aged 23 percent, whereas during the past decade of high inflation it edged up to only 29 percent. In contrast, the real implicit tax rate paid by holders of long-term bonds (t^{em}) increased dramatically during the period of high inflation rates, from an average of 31 percent for the fifteen years 1952 to 1966 to an average of 68 percent for the decade 1967 to 1976.

Further, the real effective tax rates reported in Table 10 significantly understate the real effective tax rates that will be paid on average by municipal bondholders during a period of sustained and correctly anticipated inflation. There are three reasons why this is so. First, the real yield of 3.3 percent on long-term taxable bonds that is assumed in calculating the series for t^{em} in Table 10 is an upper-bound estimate. The effect of using too high a value of r^o is to understate the true value of t^{em}. Second, the inflation that occurred during the decade 1967 to 1976 was not fully anticipated. Hence, the anticipated nominal yields on taxable and tax-exempt bonds that prevailed during this decade did not fully reflect the actual inflation rate; they reflect only the generally lower value of the expected inflation rate. This, too, tends to understate the value of t^{em} relative to a period with the same actual rate of inflation but with inflation correctly anticipated. Third, the difference between the nominal yield on taxable bonds (i^o) and the nominal yield on tax-exempt bonds (i^m) is smaller for long-term bonds than for short- or medium-term bonds. This implies that both the series for the nominal implicit tax rate (t^m) and the series for the real implicit tax rate (t^{em}) reported in Table 10 understate the true values of these tax rates for municipal bonds of average maturity.

Evidence that will be presented in chapter 4 indicates that for bonds of average maturity, the proportionate nominal yield differential between taxable and tax-exempt bonds ($(i^o - i^m)/i^o$) has been at least 35 percent during the past decade, and probably very close to this figure during the previous, noninflationary period. This implies that the nominal implicit tax rate paid by municipal bondholders on bonds of average maturity is close to 35 percent rather than the 25 to 29 percent figure suggested by looking exclusively at long-term bonds. This significantly higher value of the nominal implicit tax rate implies much higher values for the real implicit tax rate. This is apparent from the formal relationship between t^{em} and t^m; specifically,

$$t^{em} = (i^o/r^o) \cdot t^m = (r^o + \pi)/r^o \cdot t^m.$$

This formula says that the real implicit tax rate (t^{em}) is proportional to the nominal implicit tax rate (t^m), with a factor of proportionality equal to the ratio of the nominal yield on taxable bonds ($i^o = r^o + \pi$) to the real yield on taxable bonds (r^o). It is apparent that this factor of proportionality is greater than unity whenever the expected rate of inflation (π) is positive. Hence, any increase in t^m has a magnified effect on the value of t^{em} when inflation is anticipated.

Using the formula for t^{em} that is given above, we may construct Table 11, which presents the real implicit tax rates that would be paid under conditions of correctly anticipated inflation for different levels of the expected inflation rate. Consistent with the evidence presented in chapter 4, it is assumed that the nominal implicit tax rate ($t^m = (i^c - i^m)/i^c$) is equal to 35 percent for municipal bonds of average maturity. To insure that the estimates of t^{em} have a downward rather than an upward bias, it is assumed that the real yield on taxable bonds (r^c) is 3.3 percent (an upper-bound estimate of r^c). For each expected inflation rate, the estimated value of t^{em} for municipal bonds of average maturity is determined by multiplying $t^m = 35$ percent by the ratio $(0.033 + \pi)/0.033$. To obtain estimates of t^{em} for bonds of longer maturities (15 to 30 years), it is assumed that t^m is 30 percent rather than 35 percent.

It is useful to focus attention on inflation rates in the range of 4 to 6 percent. This range of inflation rates indicates the lower end of the range of expected inflation rates that seems likely to prevail in the U.S. economy for the foreseeable future. For an expected inflation

TABLE 11

REAL IMPLICIT TAX RATES ON MUNICIPAL BONDS AT
DIFFERENT EXPECTED INFLATION RATES
(percent)

Expected Inflation Rate	Real Implicit Tax Rate	
	Bonds of average maturity	Long-term bonds
0	35	30
1	46	39
2	56	48
3	67	57
4	77	66
5	88	75
6	99	85
7	109	94
8	120	103
9	130	112
10	141	121

NOTE: The formula for calculating the real implicit tax rate is $[(3.3 + \pi)/3.3] \cdot t^m$, where $t^m = 35$ for bonds of average maturity, $t^m = 30$ for long-term bonds, and π is the expected inflation rate.

rate of 4 percent, Table 11 indicates that the real implicit tax rate paid by holders of longer-term municipal bonds will be 66 percent. Holders of municipal bonds of average maturity will pay an even higher real implicit tax rate, 77 percent. And for higher inflation rates, the real implicit tax rate rises markedly higher. With a continuation of recent (early 1977) inflation rates in excess of 6 percent, the real implicit tax rates paid by municipal bondholders will exceed 100 percent.

The question that remains to be answered is, Why are municipal bondholders willing to pay such high real implicit tax rates? It is because, for these individuals, municipal bonds are the best available security. The next best alternative earns an even lower (even more negative) after-tax real return. Given a 4 percent inflation rate, the investor in the 30 percent bracket faces a real effective tax rate of 66 percent on earnings from corporate bonds (see Table 9). This investor is willing to bear the equally high real implicit tax rate (66 percent) that prevails on longer-term municipal bonds. Investors in higher nominal tax brackets have an even stronger incentive to hold municipal bonds. For instance, for an inflation rate of 4 percent, an investor in the 50 percent tax bracket faces a real effective tax rate on corporate bonds of 111 percent. To escape this very high real effective tax rate, this investor is willing to pay a real implicit tax rate of 77 percent on municipal bonds of average maturity, and even more for higher-quality or shorter-term municipal bonds.

Not only does the effect of inflation explain why real implicit tax rates on municipal bonds have been so high during the past decade, it also indicates why these rates are likely to remain high. At present, it appears likely that inflation rates of at least 4 to 6 percent will prevail for the foreseeable future. As long as expected inflation rates remain in or above this range, the figures in Table 9 indicate that many middle- and upper-tax-bracket investors will face real effective tax rates on taxable bonds of at least 90 percent and sometimes much more. Therefore, these investors will continue to prefer municipal bonds on which the real implicit tax rate is in the range of 70 to 100 percent. The demand for municipal bonds that is generated by this strong incentive will maintain the real implicit tax rate on municipal bonds in the range of at least 70 to 100 percent.

Equity and Inflation

The allegation that the tax exemption results in a significant tax inequity is based on the assertion that holders of municipal bonds escape from paying their fair share of the costs of government. This assertion is supported by an indisputable fact: The taxes that holders of municipals implicitly pay by accepting lower yields are less than the taxes they would pay if they held taxable corporate bonds. This fact, however, does not prove that there is any inequity. To prove that there is an inequity, it is necessary to establish that the taxes implicitly paid by holders of municipals are less than these taxpayers ought to pay.

In the standard analysis, this part of the argument is glossed over by implicitly assuming that the taxes that holders of municipals ought to pay are the taxes that they would pay if they held corporate bonds. This would be a reasonable assumption if nominal tax rates on interest income corresponded to real effective tax rates. However, as we have seen, price inflation forces an extreme divergence between nominal tax rates and real effective tax rates for holders of taxable bonds. Indeed, if the typical holder of municipal bonds during the past decade had held taxable corporate bonds, he would have paid a real effective rate of tax substantially in excess of 100 percent. It is difficult to argue that considerations of tax equity require that anyone pay a marginal rate of tax in excess of 100 percent on his real income.

Thus, a strong case can be made that the present method of taxing interest income is inequitable during periods of price inflation. The U.S. tax system was designed with a noninflationary economy in mind. Under conditions of price stability, real interest income would be taxed on the same basis and at the same rates as other types of income. There is no good reason why the fact of inflation should lead to much higher real rates of tax on interest income than on other forms of income. This is an unintended and undesirable consequence of price inflation operating on a tax system that was designed for a noninflationary economy.

Unquestionably, the excessively high real effective tax rates on corporate bonds have increased the relative attractiveness of tax-exempt municipal bonds. By holding municipal bonds, investors have been able to escape paying real effective tax rates substantially in excess of 100 percent. The fact that municipal bonds have provided this avenue of escape, however, does not imply that the availability of such bonds creates inequity in the tax system. During the past decade, holders of municipal bonds have paid real tax rates close to and exceeding the maximum nominal marginal tax rates currently applicable under U.S. law. If the nominal tax rate schedule is accepted as the measure of what individuals in different income classes ought to pay as tax on their real incomes, municipal bondholders have paid at least their fair share of the costs of government. Indeed, it can be argued that the availability of tax-exempt municipal bonds has actually improved the equity of the tax system during the past decade of inflation. Municipal bonds have provided an avenue of escape from real tax rates that, because of inflation, substantially exceed equitable tax rates, but they have not permitted anyone to escape from paying his fair share of taxes.

Further, the real implicit tax rate paid by holders of municipal bonds during periods of substantial inflation exceeds the real tax rates paid on virtually any other form of income by any taxpayer. Real implicit tax rates on municipal bonds are far in excess of the maximum tax rate of 50 percent on wage income and other forms of "earned income." Real implicit tax rates on municipal bonds also exceed the real effective tax rate on common stocks and other equity assets. The only real tax rate that exceeds that on municipal bonds is the real effective tax rate on taxable bonds for high-bracket investors. However, since high-bracket investors can and do avoid the very high real tax rate on taxable bonds (induced by the distortionary effect of inflation) by holding municipal bonds and equity assets, the highest real tax rate actually paid is the real implicit tax rate on municipal bonds. It is difficult to see why a further increase in this highest real tax rate contributes to greater tax equity.

As long as the taxation of interest income continues on its present basis, and as long as the inflation rate remains as high as 4 to 6 percent, high real effective tax rates on taxable bonds will continue to induce investors to pay real implicit tax rates on municipal bonds of 70 to 100 percent and more. Since inflation rates of at least 4 to 6 percent seem likely for the foreseeable future, it follows that holders of municipal bonds will continue to pay real implicit tax rates that exceed both the maximum legal tax rate and the highest real tax rate actually paid on any other form of income. In this situation, it is reasonable to conclude that tax-exempt municipal bonds provide a socially desirable avenue of escape from the inequitably high tax rates that are the unintended consequence of a tax system severely distorted by inflation and do not, in any meaningful sense, permit the holders of such bonds to get away with paying tax rates that are too low.

This conclusion stands in sharp contrast to the conclusions reached by opponents of the exemption and proponents of the taxable bond option. This difference in conclusions is due to the failure of previous analyses to account adequately for the effects of inflation and, particularly, to distinguish between nominal tax rates and real tax rates. Opponents of the exemption argue that it is inequitable because it permits people who hold municipal bonds to pay tax at a rate of 30 percent when they should pay tax at rates of 50 to 70 percent. In an inflationary environment, however, this argument is deceptive. It relies on nominal tax rates as a proxy for real rates in a situation where the real rates are much higher. Phrased correctly to take account of the effects of inflation, the argument that the exemption creates inequity must be put as follows: The exemption is inequitable because it permits people to pay real implicit tax rates of only 70 to 100 percent, when they ought to pay tax rates substantially in excess of 100 percent. This argument for the inequity created by the exemption is logically consistent, provided one is willing to argue that real tax rates of 150 to 200 percent on real interest income are the tax rates that high-bracket investors ought to pay. However, truth in advertising requires that if this argument is to be made it should be clearly stated. Opponents of the exemption and proponents of the taxable bond option should not rely on the deceptive use of nominal tax rates but should argue clearly and convincingly why real effective tax rates of 150 to 200 percent are both equitable and socially desirable. We believe that there are few who would make this argument and few who would accept it.

Summary

In this chapter we have examined the effects of inflation on the yields on securities and on the taxes paid by the holders of securities. We discussed why, during an inflationary period, it is important to distinguish between the nominal yield on a bond and the real yield on that bond. Specifically, the anticipated real yield on a bond is equal to the anticipated nominal yield on that bond *minus* the expected rate of inflation. The expected rate of inflation is subtracted from the anticipated nominal yield because the investor needs to earn a yield equal to the inflation rate in order to maintain the value of his asset in terms of real purchasing power. The real yield earned by the investor is only the excess of his nominal yield over the rate of price inflation.

Under the U.S. tax system, the holder of a taxable bond is taxed on his nominal interest income, including both his real interest income and the part of his nominal interest income that is required merely to keep pace with inflation. For this reason, during periods of inflation real effective tax rates on taxable bonds will significantly exceed nominal tax rates for all taxable investors. In particular, for inflation rates in the range of 4 to 6 percent, investors in the 50 percent nominal tax bracket will face real effective tax rates on taxable bonds of 111 to 141 percent. The magnitude of this distortion is proportional to the investor's nominal tax rate and, therefore, is greatest for those in the highest tax brackets. Moreover, the distortionary effect of inflation on the taxation of interest income is far greater than on income from equity assets or from wages and salaries.

Because of the very high real effective tax rates on taxable bonds during periods of inflation, middle- and high-tax-bracket investors have a strong incentive to hold municipal bonds. Competition among these investors for the limited stock of municipal bonds drives down the real yield on such bonds relative to the before-tax real yield on taxable bonds (which remains approximately constant). This means that the real implicit tax rate paid by holders of municipal bonds increases as a result of inflation. This real implicit tax rate is the proportionate differential between the real yield on taxable bonds and the real yield on municipal bonds of comparable quality. This sacrifice of real yield by investors in municipal bonds accrues as a direct financial benefit to the state and local governments issuing the bonds. At inflation rates of 4 to 6 percent, the real implicit tax rate paid by holders of municipal bonds (and received by the governments issuing the bonds) ranges between 70 percent and 100 percent. This is much higher than the implicit nominal tax rates derived by looking at nominal rather than real yields.

The high real implicit tax rate paid by municipal bondholders during periods of inflation casts doubt on the purported inequity of the municipal bond tax exemption. In the standard analysis of the inequity of the exemption, it is argued that investors in the higher tax brackets (say, 50 percent and above) avoid paying their fair share of tax by holding tax-exempt municipal bonds. Specifically, it is argued that higher-bracket investors get away with paying nominal implicit tax rates of only about 30 percent on municipal bond income rather than their legal tax rates of 50 to 70 percent. When we examine real yields and real implicit tax rates on municipal bonds, however, we find that during the past decade of inflation the real implicit tax rate paid by holders of long-term municipal bonds has been in the range of 52 to 85 percent and the real implicit tax rate on municipal bonds of average maturity has been significantly higher. Moreover, given the expectation that inflation rates of at least 4 to 6 percent will prevail for the foreseeable future, it follows that the real implicit tax rate that will be paid by municipal bondholders will be at least 70 to 100 percent.

This real implicit tax rate exceeds the maximum legal tax rate and also the highest real tax rate actually paid on virtually any other component of income. Therefore, we conclude that no tax inequity presently results from the exemption, nor is any likely to result for the foreseeable future.

4

The Nominal Subsidy Provided
by the Exemption

Municipal governments derive financial benefit from the right to issue tax-exempt bonds. The magnitude of this benefit is the reduction in borrowing costs that municipal governments enjoy on tax-exempt bonds relative to what their borrowing costs would be if they issued taxable bonds. The standard procedure for calculating the magnitude of this benefit is to multiply the difference between the nominal yield on long-term taxable bonds and the nominal yield on long-term tax-exempt bonds by the volume of outstanding municipal debt. In this chapter we argue that this procedure yields an underestimate of the benefit of the exemption to municipal governments. Specifically, the standard analysis suggests that the subsidy provided by the exemption is less than 30 percent of the nominal borrowing costs municipal governments would incur if they issued taxable bonds. The analysis in this chapter establishes that the true subsidy is at least 35 percent of nominal borrowing costs.

To establish this conclusion, we first examine the level of the subsidy that municipal governments enjoy when they issue long-term tax-exempt bonds. Consideration of the yield differential between newly issued bonds and seasoned bonds indicates that the subsidy provided by the exemption on long-term bonds is about 32 percent of the nominal borrowing costs municipal governments would incur on long-term taxable bonds. The higher level of yields on privately placed corporate bonds and the special characteristics of municipal borrowing suggest that the subsidy rate on long-term borrowing is even greater than 32 percent.

The next issue to be considered is how the subsidy rate varies with the length of the borrowing period. This requires an examination of the "term structure of interest rates" for both taxable and tax-exempt bonds. The term structure of interest rates is the relationship between the yield on a bond and the term to maturity of that bond. For taxable bonds, the evidence indicates that yield increases with term to maturity. This effect is even more pronounced for tax-exempt bonds. Hence, the nominal subsidy rate enjoyed by municipal governments on short-term bonds is greater than the nominal subsidy rate for long-term bonds. Specifically, the evidence indicates that the nominal subsidy rate for bonds of one-year maturity is about 45 percent, significantly greater than the 32 percent nominal subsidy rate for long-term bonds. Based on analysis of the distribution of outstanding municipal bonds by their term to maturity at the date of original issue, the average nominal subsidy rate is estimated to be at least 35 percent.

The Subsidy Rate for Long-Term Bonds

The implicit subsidy rate to municipal borrowers (s) corresponds to the implicit tax rate (t^m) paid by municipal bondholders and is measured by the proportionate differential between the nominal yield on long-term corporate bonds (i^c) and the nominal yield on long-term municipal bonds (i^m); that is, $s = (i^c - i^m)/i^c$. The nominal yields used in measuring $s = t^m$ in chapter 3 were for bonds of average quality, both corporates and municipals, as reported in the *Federal Reserve Bulletin*. For the twenty-five-year period from 1952 to 1976, the average subsidy rate implied by the proportionate differential between the yield on corporate bonds and the yield on municipal bonds is 25 percent. For the fifteen-year period from 1952 to 1966, this subsidy rate is only 22 percent. For the ten-year period from 1967 to 1976, the subsidy rate is 29 percent.[1] For reasons that will now be examined, however, it is doubtful that these figures provide a wholly adequate measure of the subsidy provided by the exemption to long-term borrowing by municipalities.

One problem is the comparability of rating classes from corporate and municipal bonds. Does "average quality" mean the same thing for municipal bonds as it does for corporate bonds? Is the relationship

---

[1] These average subsidy rates are reported at the bottom of Table 8. Approximately 120 bonds were used in constructing the series for the nominal yield on long-term corporate bonds, divided about equally between the four rating classes, Aaa, Aa, A, and Baa, and the three industrial classifications, industrial, utility, and railroad. In 1970 these bonds had an average term of maturity of twenty-five years. The yield series for municipal bonds is based on twenty general obligation bonds with an average maturity of about twenty years.

TABLE 12

THE NOMINAL SUBSIDY RATE ON AAA-RATED BONDS

(percent)

Year	Nominal Yield, Moody's Aaa-Rated Seasoned Corporate Bonds (1)	Nominal Yield, Moody's Aaa-Rated Municipal Bonds (2)	Nominal Subsidy Rate (3)
1952	2.96	1.80	39
1953	3.20	2.31	28
1954	2.90	2.04	30
1955	3.06	2.18	29
1956	3.36	2.51	25
1957	3.89	3.10	20
1958	3.79	2.92	23
1959	4.38	3.35	23
1960	4.41	3.26	26
1961	4.35	3.27	25
1962	4.33	3.03	30
1963	4.26	3.06	28
1964	4.40	3.09	30
1965	4.49	3.16	30
1966	5.13	3.67	28
1967	5.51	3.74	32
1968	6.18	4.20	32
1969	7.03	5.45	22
1970	8.04	6.12	24
1971	7.39	5.22	29
1972	7.21	5.04	30
1973	7.44	4.99	33
1974	8.57	5.89	31
1975	8.83	6.42	27
1976	8.43	5.66	33
Average			
1952–76	5.34	3.82	28.2
1952–66	3.93	2.85	27.6
1967–76	7.46	5.27	29.3

SOURCE: Columns 1 and 2 are from the *Federal Reserve Bulletin*, various issues. Column 3 is calculated by taking the difference between column 1 and column 2 and dividing by column 1.

between the quality of an "average quality" corporate bond and an "average quality" municipal bond unchanging over time? Since the criteria used in rating corporate and municipal bonds are not the same and are not constant over time, the answer to both of these questions is probably no. In this situation, a better procedure would be to compare the highest rated corporate bonds with the highest rated municipal bonds—specifically, to compare Aaa-rated corporates with Aaa municipals. Since both sets of bonds are the least risky of their type, the variability in quality between them over time is the smallest among all bonds of their type. The nominal yields for Aaa-rated corporate bonds and Aaa-rated municipal bonds are reported in columns 1 and 2 of Table 12. From these nominal yields, it is possible to calculate the proportionate yield differential between Aaa-rated corporates and Aaa-rated municipals. This differential is reported in column 3 of Table 12.

The proportionate yield differential in column 3 of Table 12 is a measure of the percentage subsidy that municipal governments enjoy on long-term bonds of all qualities. This is so because the proportionate yield differential for the highest quality bonds captures the pure effect of the exemption, least clouded by differences in the meanings of different rating classifications for corporate and municipal bonds. The distinctive feature of the subsidy rate measured in Table 12, in comparison with the subsidy rate derived from the comparison of "average quality" bonds in Table 5, is its relative constancy. In particular, the average subsidy rate for the fifteen years from 1952 to 1966 is 27.6 percent, only 1 percent less than the average subsidy rate for the ten years from 1967 to 1976. This result strengthens our confidence in the assertion that the average nominal subsidy rate provided by the exemption has remained essentially constant in the face of the economic changes of the past twenty-five years.

The average nominal subsidy rate measured in Table 12 is only about 28 percent. There are, however, good reasons to believe that this is too low an estimate of the subsidy rate. One important reason involves the distinction between newly issued bonds and "seasoned" bonds (those that have been in the market for some time). The subsidy rates reported in column 3 of Table 12 are based on an index of yields on seasoned corporate bonds (column 1) and an index of yields on a mixture of new and seasoned municipals (column 2).[2] Thus, the

---

[2] The construction of the yield series for long-term municipal bonds is described in Moody's *Municipal and Government Manual*: "The averages have been constructed from a small sampling of general market issues. Under the relatively stable market conditions that system performed satisfactorily. However, under

data are not strictly comparable, and a bias is introduced into the calculation of the subsidy rate.

The appropriate yields to compare in measuring the subsidy rate are the yields on *new* issues of corporate and municipal bonds. New issues are relevant because the fundamental question is how much a municipal government gains when it issues a tax-exempt bond rather than a taxable bond. The use of yields on seasoned corporate bonds to measure the subsidy rate tends to underestimate the true subsidy rate because the yields on seasoned corporate bonds are typically less than the yields on newly issued corporate bonds. Corporate bonds are usually issued at prices that are very close to the par value of the bond. This requires that the coupon on the bond be very close to the nominal yield on the bond at the date of issue. During periods of rising interest rates, however, the yield on a seasoned bond must increase in order for the bond to compete with new, higher-coupon bonds. Since the coupon dollar amount is fixed, the only way for the yield to rise is for the bond to decline in price to below par; that is, the bond becomes a discount bond. The purchaser of such a bond earns a lower coupon yield than the purchaser of a newly issued bond, but he also expects to enjoy a capital gain when the bond is redeemed at par. Because capital gains receive more favorable tax treatment than interest income, the before-tax yield to maturity on a discount bond will actually be less than the before-tax yield to maturity on newly issued par bond.

The effect of using yields on seasoned bonds on the calculation of the subsidy rate is indicated by the data in Table 13. Column 1 reproduces the series on nominal yield on Aaa-rated corporate bonds reported in column 1 of Table 12. Column 2 reports a series on the nominal yield on newly issued Aaa-rated corporate bonds, calculated from monthly data reported in Moody's *Industrial Manual* (1977). The difference between new-issue yields and seasoned-issue yields (measured in percentage points) is reported in column 3. In every year, except for 1976, the new-issue yield is higher than the seasoned-issue yield; the average difference for the twenty-five-year period is 24 basis points (one basis point equals one-hundredth percentage point). Since new issues have higher nominal yields, the subsidy rates

---

depressed market conditions, an average geared to specific issues quickly becomes an average based upon discount bonds. Consequently, for some time Moody's averages have been in a transitory stage, as weight has been given not only to quality and maturity but also to factors of prevailing interest rates to determine what present yields would be if bonds of the same quality bore current coupons. Thus, it was progressively, by degrees, that Moody's averages have become colored by the new-issue market."

calculated using these yields are higher than the subsidy rates calculated using the seasoned-issue yields. Specifically, column 4 of Table 13 reports the estimates of the subsidy rate implied by proportionate differential between the nominal yield on newly issued corporate bonds (column 2 of Table 13) and the nominal yield on municipal bonds (column 2 of Table 12). For comparative purposes, column 5 of Table 13 reproduces the estimates of the subsidy rate based on the nominal yields on seasoned corporate bonds (column 3 of Table 12).

A comparison of columns 4 and 5 of Table 13 shows that the use of yields on newly issued corporate bonds results in a higher estimate of the subsidy rate provided by the exemption. The estimated subsidy rate is higher for every year except 1976. The estimate of the average subsidy rate increases from 28.2 percent to 31.7 percent.

Further, the estimate of 31.7 percent is still too low because it fails to take account of the effect of seasoning on the yields on municipal bonds. For municipal bonds, seasoning has the opposite effect that it has for corporate bonds. For corporate bonds, there is a tax advantage from receiving part of the yield in the form of a capital gain because capital gains are taxed at a lower rate than taxable interest income. For municipal bonds, there is a tax disadvantage from receiving part of the yield in the form of a capital gain because capital gains are taxed and the interest income is not. This implies that during periods of rising interest rates seasoned municipal bonds, which (like corporate bonds) will sell at a discount, will typically have higher yields than newly issued municipal bonds. For this reason, an estimate of the subsidy rate that is based on yields on seasoned municipal bonds is likely to be biased downward during a period of generally rising interest rates.

An indication of the possible size of this bias is provided by Table 14. Column 1 of this table reproduces the series on the nominal yield on Aaa-rated municipal bonds given in column 2 of Table 12 for the years 1957–61 and 1970–76. Column 2 reports a series on the nominal yield on newly issued Aaa-rated municipal bonds. For the years 1957 through 1961, this series comes from table A-3 in Ott and Meltzer (1963); for the years 1970 through 1976, it comes from an average of reoffering yields on newly issued Aaa-rated municipal bonds (20-year maturity) compiled by the *Bond Buyer*.[3] Column 3 of Table 14 reports the difference (in basis points) between the yield

---

[3] These reoffering yields are for general obligation bonds and are reported on a weekly basis for every week in which new issues were reoffered by the underwriting syndicates. The figures reported in Table 14 are the averages of all weekly observations.

TABLE 13

The Nominal Subsidy Rate Based on New-Issue Yields
(percent)

Year	Nominal Yield, Moody's Aaa-Rated Seasoned Corporate Bonds (1)	Nominal Yield, Moody's Aaa-Rated New-Issue Corporate Bonds (2)	Seasoned Issue Premium (percentage points) (3)	Nominal Subsidy Rate Based on Aaa-Rated New-Issue Corporate Bonds (4)	Nominal Subsidy Rate Based on Aaa-Rated Seasoned Corporate Bonds (5)
1952	2.96	3.12	0.16	42	39
1953	3.20	3.46	0.26	33	28
1954	2.90	3.00	0.10	32	30
1955	3.06	3.16	0.10	31	29
1956	3.36	3.56	0.20	29	25
1957	3.89	4.42	0.53	30	20
1958	3.79	4.05	0.26	28	23
1959	4.38	4.76	0.38	30	23
1960	4.41	4.77	0.36	32	26
1961	4.35	4.53	0.18	28	25
1962	4.33	4.36	0.03	31	30
1963	4.26	4.30	0.04	29	28
1964	4.40	4.46	0.06	31	30
1965	4.49	4.57	0.08	31	30
1966	5.13	5.44	0.31	33	28
1967	5.51	5.83	0.32	36	32

1968	6.18	6.55	0.38	36	32
1969	7.03	7.74	0.71	30	22
1970	8.04	8.53	0.49	27	24
1971	7.39	7.52	0.13	31	29
1972	7.21	7.32	0.11	31	30
1973	7.44	7.76	0.32	36	33
1974	8.57	9.00	0.43	35	31
1975	8.83	9.01	0.18	29	27
1976	8.43	8.33	−0.10	32	33
Average					
1952–76	5.34	5.58	0.24	31.7	28.2
1952–66	3.93	4.13	0.20	31.3	27.6
1967–76	7.46	7.76	0.30	32.3	29.3

SOURCE: Column 1 is from the *Federal Reserve Bulletin*, various issues. Column 2 is from Moody's *Industrial Manual* (1977) average of monthly figures. Column 3 = column 2 minus column 1. Column 4 = the difference between column 13 and column 2 of Table 13, divided by column 2 of Table 13.

TABLE 14

The Seasoning Effect for Municipal Bonds

Year	Yield on Seasoned Aaa-Rated Municipals (percent) (1)	Yield on Newly Issued Aaa-Rated Municipals (percent) (2)	Seasoned Issue Premium for Municipal Bonds (basis points) (3)	Seasoned Issue Premium for Corporate Bonds (basis points) (4)
1957	3.10	2.96	−14	53
1958	2.92	2.82	−10	26
1959	3.35	3.26	− 9	38
1960	3.26	3.20	− 6	36
1961	3.27	3.23	− 4	18
1970	6.12	5.80	−32	49
1971	5.22	5.12	−10	13
1972	5.04	5.08	4	11
1973	4.99	5.02	− 3	32
1974	5.89	5.76	−13	43
1975	6.42	6.34	− 8	18
1976	5.66	5.77	11	−10

Source: Column 1 is from column 2 of Table 12. Column 2: 1957–61, is from Ott and Meltzer (1963), table A-3; 1970–76, is from the *Bond Buyer* compilation of reoffering yields on Aaa-rated, twenty-year municipal bonds, average of weekly figures. Column 3 = column 2 minus column 1. Column 4 is from column 3 of Table 13.

on new issues and the Moody series in column 1. For comparative purposes, column 4 of Table 14 reproduces the series on the difference between nominal yields on new and seasoned issues of Aaa-rated corporate bonds from column 3 of Table 13 (converted to basis points).

As expected, the entries in column 3 of Table 14 show the reverse pattern of the entries in column 4. When the difference between the nominal yields on new and seasoned corporate bonds is substantial and positive, the difference between nominal yields on new and seasoned municipals tends to be substantial and negative; and conversely. The average excess of the yield on seasoned municipals over that on new issues is 8 basis points. When account is taken of this 8 basis point difference, the estimate of the average subsidy rate provided by the exemption rises from 31.5 percent to 32.9 percent.[4]

The evidence on the effect of seasoning on the yields on municipal bonds is too disjointed to justify a firm revision of the subsidy rate estimate. It is sufficiently strong, however, to suggest that the estimate of 31.5 percent derived in Table 13 is too low and that, as a lower-bound estimate, 32 percent is justified by the available evidence.

Support for this conclusion is provided by another consideration raised by Ott and Meltzer. Citing interviews with capital market experts concerning the appropriate measure of the yield that municipal governments would have to pay on taxable bonds, Ott and Meltzer concluded, "The yield series should be a new issue series, but it should account for the new issue yields on the much more important private placements in addition to the present yield series on public offerings." The data analyzed by Ott and Meltzer indicated that the yields on privately placed corporate bonds were generally more than 50 basis points higher than the yields on new issues of publicly offered corporate bonds of supposedly comparable quality.[5] Since these data are not completely reliable, and since it is difficult to estimate the extent of private placement of municipal bonds that would occur if the bonds were taxable, we cannot estimate precisely the increase in municipal borrowing costs that would result from the need for private placements of taxable bonds. However, if the effect of private placement were to increase the relevant measure of the nominal yield on newly issued taxable bonds by only 10 basis points, it may be calculated that this would mean a 1.5 percentage point increase in the true measure of the subsidy rate provided by the exemption; that is, an increase from 32 percent to 33.5 percent.[6] Thus, the higher level of yields on privately placed issues of taxable bonds strengthens the conclusions that 32 percent is a lower-bound estimate of the subsidy provided by the exemption on long-term municipal bonds.

---

[4] The effect of an 8 basis point reduction in the yield on municipal bonds on the average nominal subsidy rate is obtained by dividing 8 basis points by the average nominal yield on newly issued, Aaa-rated, long-term corporate bonds, 5.54 percent. This implies that the increase in the subsidy rate would be 1.4 percent, equal to 8/554.

[5] The ratings on directly placed corporate bonds are those reported by the life insurance companies purchasing such bonds. It is difficult to know whether the criteria used in establishing these ratings correspond to those used by Moody's Investors Services in rating publicly traded corporate bonds.

[6] The effect of a 10 basis point increase in the yield on corporate bonds on the average nominal subsidy rate is obtained by recalculating what nominal subsidy rates would have been if nominal yields on corporate bonds had been 10 basis points higher than those reported in column 2 of Table 13.

Two additional characteristics of municipal borrowing also contribute support to this conclusion. First, municipal bonds are generally issued in "serial form" with a different maturity date for each series. This means that the volume of bonds in any particular series is likely to be small relative to the volume of bonds in a corporate issue with a single maturity date. For this reason, the resale market for municipal bonds is likely to be thinner than for the typical corporate bond, and this thinness of the resale market requires a higher initial yield in order to sell the bond to the initial purchaser. (This additional yield is a "liquidity premium.") Second, many municipalities borrow very small amounts relative to the size of most corporate borrowings. It is argued that in order to market such small issues in the taxable market, municipalities would have to pay a substantial premium over the yields paid by large-scale corporate borrowers.

The available evidence on the effect of serial issues and small issues does not indicate that these factors are of dominant importance in measuring the subsidy rate provided by the exemption.[7] There is little doubt, however, of the direction of the effect. It is clear that serial issues do tend to thin out the resale market, and hence they have some marginal effect in increasing the borrowing costs of municipalities relative to the corporate borrower. Small-scale municipal borrowers might well find themselves limited to the private placement market, in which yields are generally higher than in the public offering market. Therefore, taking account of the higher yield on private placements and of the other special characteristics of municipal borrowing, it is reasonable to conclude that 32 percent is a lower-bound estimate of the subsidy rate enjoyed by municipalities on their long-term borrowings.

The Term Structure of the Subsidy Rate

It has long been recognized that the yield to maturity on a bond usually varies with its term to maturity. Indeed, the term structure of interest rates has been one of the most extensively studied subjects in finance and economics.[8] This subject is relevant to the measurement of the subsidy provided to municipal governments by the exemption because the term structure of interest rates for tax-exempt bonds

---

[7] In assessing the available evidence, Ott and Meltzer (1963) conclude that the effect of serial issues and of small-size issues is not very great. There is some evidence, however, that transactions costs in the resale market for municipal bonds are somewhat greater than those in the market for corporate bonds.

[8] A useful review of the literature on the term structure of interest rates is provided by Van Horne (1978), chapter 4.

differs markedly from the term structure of interest rates for taxable bonds. This implies that the subsidy rate enjoyed by municipal borrowers cannot be summarized by a single rate for long-term bonds but must instead be described by a term structure of subsidy rates for bonds of different maturities.

Recent studies of the term structure of interest rates have focused primarily on U.S. government obligations. This is because there is no question of default risk for these obligations and because there are a large number of obligations of different maturities, all issued by the same agency, that are outstanding at any moment of time. In general, studies of the term structure of interest rates have found that interest rates on longer maturities are influenced by the market's expectations of the future course of short-term interest rates.[9] For example, if short-term interest rates are expected to be significantly lower five years from now than they are today, bonds with maturities of more than five years will have generally lower yields than bonds with maturities of less than five years.

Expectations aside, there also appears to be a "liquidity effect" for short-term issues. Except for periods of very high short-term interest rates (that are not expected to be permanent), the yield on three-month Treasury bills is almost always significantly less than the yield on medium-term notes and long-term bonds. There is also some indication that long-term bonds carry a term premium relative to medium-term notes: Given expectations of constant short-term interest rates for the foreseeable future, twenty-year government bonds will have slightly higher yields than five-year Treasury notes.

For the purpose of determining the term structure of the subsidy rate provided by the exemption, however, the term structure of interest rates for U.S. government obligations is not the most useful standard of comparison. There is general agreement among all who have studied the issue that the relevant standard for comparison for judging the yields that municipal governments would have to pay on taxable bonds is the yield prevailing on taxable corporate bonds. Unfortunately, there is less reliable information on the term structure of interest rates for corporate bonds than for U.S. government bonds.

One source of information is the series on "basic yields" on corporate bonds by term to maturity, originally constructed by Durand (1958) and subsequently updated by others. The series for the years

---

[9] Empirical studies of the term structure of interest rates have generally found that expectations of future short-term interest rates have an important influence on the observed term structure. For a summary of the studies of this expectations effect, see Van Horne (1978).

1952 through 1970 is reproduced here in Table 15. In using and interpreting this series, it is useful to keep in mind the method of its construction, as described by the Federal Reserve:

> The series on basic yields . . . represents the yields estimated to have prevailed in the first part of each year on the highest grade corporate issues, classified by term to maturity. Each estimate is based on quotations for practically all high-grade, seasoned, nonconvertible, corporate bonds for which valid quotations were available during the period covered and which were not subject to special influences, with occasional reference to municipal and Government yield quotations for interpolation of maturities. For each year the yields to maturity of outstanding bonds were plotted by term to maturity on a scatter diagram. The basic yield curve for each year is a freehand curve so fitted that it passes below most of the yields on the chart but usually above a few isolated low ones. Basic yields for each maturity are read from the curve.[10]

From this description of the construction of the basic yield series, it follows that the basic yield understates the yield that an Aaa-rated corporate borrower had to provide on a new issue of any maturity. There are two downward biases. First, the basic yields are derived from data on seasoned (rather than new-issue) corporate bonds; and second, the basic yield curve was drawn below the observed yields on virtually all Aaa-rated seasoned bonds. An indication of the size of the downward bias in the basic yield series is provided by the last column in Table 15, which reports average yield on newly issued, Aaa-rated corporate bonds for the first three months of each year. This new issue series should be compared with the basic yield series for twenty-year maturity. Without exception, the basic yield series is less than the new-issue series. On average, for the nineteen years covered in the table, the basic yield for twenty-year maturity is 29 basis points lower than the yield on newly issued bonds.

For corporate bonds, the data on basic yields indicate a relatively flat term structure of interest rates similar to the term structure for U.S. government obligations. Comparable data for the term structure of U.S. government obligations are reported in Table 16. For both the basic yields and for the yields on government bonds, the years 1966 through 1970 are somewhat peculiar. During these years, the yield on short-term bonds equaled or exceeded the yield on long-term bonds. There is reason to believe, however, that this unusual term

---

[10] For further discussion of the characteristics and possible defects of this series of basic yields, see Durand (1958).

TABLE 15

BASIC YIELDS ON CORPORATE BONDS BY TERM TO MATURITY
(percent per year)

	Years to Maturity							Moody's Corporate Aaa New-Issue Yield
Year	1	5	10	15	20	25	30	
1952	2.73[a]	2.73[a]	2.73	2.81	2.88	2.94	3.00	3.12
1953	2.62[a]	2.75[a]	2.88	2.97	3.05	3.11	3.15	3.46
1954	2.40	2.52	2.66	2.78	2.88	2.95	3.00	3.00
1955	2.60	2.70	2.80	2.88	2.95	3.00	3.04	3.16
1956	2.70	2.78	2.86	2.93	2.99	3.04	3.09	3.56
1957	3.50[a]	3.50[a]	3.50	3.50	3.50[a]	3.60	3.68	4.42
1958	3.21[a]	3.25[a]	3.33	3.40	3.47	3.54	3.61	4.05
1959	3.67	3.80	4.03	4.10	4.10	4.10	4.10	4.76
1960	4.95	4.73	4.60	4.55	4.55	4.55	4.55	4.77
1961	3.10	3.75	4.00	4.06	4.12	4.16	4.22	4.53
1962	3.50	3.97	4.28	4.37	4.40	4.41	4.42	4.36
1963	3.25	3.77	3.98	4.05	4.10	4.14	4.16	4.30
1964	4.00	4.15	4.25	4.29	4.33	4.33	4.33	4.46
1965	4.15	4.29	4.33	4.35	4.35	4.35	4.35	4.57
1966	5.00	4.97	4.91	4.85	4.80	4.78	4.75	5.44
1967	5.29	5.28	5.23	5.08	5.00	4.95	4.95	5.83
1968	6.24	6.24	6.20	6.08	6.00	5.99	5.93	6.55
1969	7.05	7.05	7.05	6.95	6.77	6.60	6.54	7.74
1970	8.15	8.10	8.00	7.75	7.60	7.60	7.60	8.53

[a] More than usually subject to error.

SOURCE: *Banking and Monetary Statistics, 1941–1970* (Washington, D.C.: Board of Governors, Federal Reserve System, 1976), Table 12.14, p. 761; and Moody's *Industrial Manual* (1977).

structure was due to the expectation that short-term interest rates during this period were higher than they would be later on (an expectation that was reasonable at the time, though it turned out to be inaccurate). In any case, it may be argued that the quiescent period of the early 1960s provides a more appropriate benchmark for judging the effect of term to maturity on the yield on corporate bonds. During this period, interest rates on both seasoned and newly issued corporate bonds were quite stable, and the difference between these yields was small. There was little reason for the market to form expectations of

TABLE 16

Yields on U.S. Government Securities by Term to Maturity
(percent per year)

Year	\multicolumn{5}{c}{Years to Maturity}
	1	5	10	20	30
1952	1.87	2.03	2.47	2.68	N.A.
1953	2.13	2.57	2.78	2.92	N.A.
1954	1.03	1.89	2.43	2.57	2.76
1955	1.97	2.58	2.72	2.83	2.95
1956	2.89	3.13	3.08	3.07	3.10
1957	3.48	3.63	3.54	3.45	3.44
1958	2.17	2.98	3.27	3.45	3.48
1959	3.90	4.26	4.18	4.12	4.08
1960	2.93	4.13	4.23	4.13	4.12
1961	2.34	3.69	3.84	3.90	3.94
1962	3.05	3.71	3.96	4.02	4.06
1963	3.29	3.80	3.98	4.04	4.07
1964	3.80	4.08	4.17	4.18	4.19
1965	4.07	4.20	4.25	4.23	4.22
1966	5.12	5.14	4.86	4.72	4.69
1967	4.77	5.00	4.97	4.93	4.90
1968	5.54	5.56	5.48	5.40	5.35
1969	6.95	6.73	6.46	6.25	6.17
1970	7.05	7.43	7.21	6.79	6.73

N.A.: Not available.

Source: Salomon Brothers, *Analytical Record of Yields and Yield Spreads*, pt. 1, table 1.

changes in interest rates and for these expectations to influence the observed term structure.

These considerations suggest that the five years from 1961 through 1965 provide the best basis for judging the effect of term to maturity on the yield on corporate bonds and for measuring the term structure of the subsidy provided by the exemption. To measure the term structure of the subsidy rate, it is necessary to compare these yields on corporate bonds with yields on municipal bonds of the same maturities. Data on yields for prime-grade municipals of maturities of one, two, five, ten, twenty, and thirty years are provided in Salomon Brothers' *Analytical Record of Yields and Yield Spreads*. Even a cursory examination of this data indicates that the term structure of interest rates for municipal bonds exhibits a much steeper gradient than that for either corporate or U.S. government bonds. Relative to longer-term bonds of the same type, yields on shorter-term municipals are much lower than are yields on shorter-term corporates and governments. This pattern is apparent in the data reported in Table 17. These data are the averages for the first three months of each year of the yields on prime municipals of various maturities. The first three months of the year were selected to insure comparability with the basic yield series that refers to "the first part of each year."

From the data in Tables 15 and 17, it is possible to estimate the term structure of the subsidy rate provided by the exemption for the representative years, 1961 through 1965. Specifically, for each year and for each maturity of one, five, ten, twenty, and thirty years, we may calculate the implicit subsidy rate provided by the exemption by taking the proportionate differential between the basic yield in Table 15 and the corresponding municipal yield in Table 17. The results of these calculations are reported in Table 18.

From Table 18, it is apparent that the subsidy rate is greatest for municipal bonds of the shortest maturity. Specifically, for municipal bonds of one-year maturity, the average subsidy rate for the five years covered in this table is 50 percent. As maturity is lengthened, the subsidy rate declines, reaching an average of 43 percent at five-year maturity, 35 percent at ten-year maturity, 29 percent at twenty-year

TABLE 17

Yields on Prime Municipal Bonds by Term to Maturity
(percent per year)

| Year | Years to Maturity | | | | | |
	1	2	5	10	20	30
1961	1.50	1.70	2.15	2.65	3.09	3.32
1962	1.70	1.84	2.25	2.68	3.08	3.28
1963	1.60	1.75	2.05	2.45	2.90	3.14
1964	2.01	2.11	2.45	2.71	3.05	3.21
1965	2.23	2.35	2.57	2.75	3.00	3.20

Source: Salomon Brothers, *Analytical Record of Yields and Yield Spreads*, average of January, February, and March.

TABLE 18

NOMINAL SUBSIDY RATE FOR MUNICIPAL BONDS BY TERM TO MATURITY,
USING BASIC YIELDS

(percent per year)

Year	Years to Maturity				
	1	5	10	20	30
1961	52	43	34	25	21
1962	51	43	33	30	26
1963	51	46	38	29	25
1964	50	41	36	30	25
1965	46	40	36	31	26
1961–65 avg.	50	43	35	29	25
Adjusted average	50	44	37	32	28

SOURCE: Subsidy rates for each year and maturity are calculated from data in Tables 15 and 17. The adjusted average subsidy rates reflect a correction of the lower yield on seasoned corporate bonds.

maturity, and 25 percent at thirty-year maturity. Moreover, this term structure of subsidy rates is not a special phenomenon of the five years covered in Table 18. Examination of the nineteen years from 1952 through 1970 reveals a similar pattern of subsidy rates for every year. In fact, the average subsidy rate for each maturity, based on the entire nineteen years, is in every case close to the average subsidy rate for that maturity reported in Table 18.[11] The details for some individual years, however, diverge from the average due to the peculiarities of the term structure of interest rates in some individual years.

The average subsidy rate for twenty-year bonds in Table 18 is only 29 percent, somewhat less than the 32 percent that was suggested in the preceding section as a lower-bound estimate of the subsidy rate for long-term bonds. One reason for this has already been pointed out. The basic yield series underestimates the borrowing costs of corporations on newly issued, Aaa-rated bonds. Specifically, a comparison of the basic yield for twenty-year bonds with Moody's index of yields for newly issued Aaa corporate bonds (see Table 15) indi-

[11] In every one of the nineteen years, the nominal subsidy rate declines with term to maturity. While the extent of this decline varies from year to year, the fact that the general pattern is always the same is persuasive evidence that the nominal subsidy rate on shorter-term municipal bonds is significantly greater than the nominal subsidy rate on longer-term municipal bonds.

cates that the magnitude of this underestimate for the years 1961 through 1965 is an average of 13 basis points. When the basic yield for twenty-year bonds is adjusted by this amount, the estimate of the subsidy rate for this maturity rises from 29 percent to 31 percent. The other considerations mentioned in the discussion of the subsidy rate (pp. 65–74) easily justify a further upward adjustment from 31 percent to 32 percent. This figure is what is reported as the adjusted average subsidy rate for twenty-year municipal bonds at the bottom of Table 18. The same upward adjustment of the subsidy rate (three percentage points) is also applied to the subsidy rate for thirty-year municipal bonds, producing an adjusted subsidy rate of 28 percent. For bonds of less than twenty-year maturity, however, it is doubtful that the appropriate adjustment factor is as great as for twenty- and thirty-year bonds. The effect of seasoning declines with term to maturity. Taking account of this fact, it is assumed that no correction is required for the subsidy rate on one-year bonds, one percentage point correction is required for five-year bonds, and two percentage points correction is required for ten-year bonds. These correction factors are incorporated into the adjusted subsidy rates reported in Table 18.

To strengthen our confidence in these adjusted estimates of the term structure of the subsidy rate, and also to assess the possible

TABLE 19

Yields on GMAC Bonds by Term to Maturity
(percent per year)

	Years to Maturity			
Year	1–2	4–6	9–11	19–21
1965	...	4.60	4.69	4.67
1966	5.69	6.07	5.88	5.65
1967	5.75	6.02	5.87	5.89
1968	5.33	6.48	6.71	6.53
1969	7.76	7.80	7.87	7.39
1970	8.15	8.24	8.35	8.02
1971	6.42	6.96	7.39	7.32
1972	6.24	6.28	7.02	7.38
1973	7.68	7.48	7.65	7.63
1974	8.67	8.73	8.87	8.97
1975	7.18	8.20	8.60	9.04

Source: Calculated from market quotations on General Motors Acceptance Corporation (GMAC) bonds of different terms to maturity.

TABLE 20

Yields on Prime Municipal Bonds by Term to Maturity
(percent per year)

Year	Years to Maturity					
	1	2	5	10	25	30
1965	2.35	2.50	2.75	2.90	3.10	3.30
1966	3.40	3.45	3.50	3.55	3.65	3.75
1967	3.00	3.15	3.40	3.55	3.75	3.90
1968	3.30	3.45	3.75	3.95	4.20	4.35
1969	4.55	4.70	4.85	5.10	5.45	5.65
1970	4.35	4.50	4.85	5.35	6.10	6.35
1971	2.90	3.10	3.65	4.35	5.25	5.55
1972	2.75	3.00	3.60	4.15	4.95	5.20
1973	3.95	4.05	4.25	4.75	5.00	5.20
1974	4.75	4.80	4.90	5.15	5.70	5.90
1975	3.91	4.21	4.83	5.44	6.29	6.59

Source: Salomon Brothers, *Analytical Record of Yields and Yield Spreads*, pt. 3, table 1.

changes that have occurred in this structure due to the events of the past few years, it is useful to examine an alternative estimate of the term structure of interest rates for corporate bonds. Since 1965, General Motors Acceptance Corporation (GMAC) has had a sufficient number of bonds of diverse maturities outstanding (on which publicly quoted yields are available) to permit the estimation of a term structure of interest rates for this single borrower. The relevant data on yields to maturity on bonds of different maturities are reported in Table 19.[12] For comparative purposes, Table 20 reports data on yields for municipal bonds of different maturities.[13] For each year and each maturity, the implicit subsidy rate provided by the exemption may be calculated by computing the proportionate yield differential between

---

[12] These data were obtained by securing quarterly quotations on the market price of GMAC bonds with different maturities and coupons. The yield to maturity for each bond was calculated from this data. The yield for each year and each maturity class is the average of the four quarterly observations of all bonds within (or close to) that maturity class.

[13] The yields chosen are those for prime municipals. Yields for good-grade municipals are generally higher than for prime municipals but have the same term structure. Thus, the use of good-grade municipals would lower the estimated nominal subsidy rate at each maturity but would not materially effect the term structure of the subsidy rate.

the yield on that maturity of GMAC bond and the yield on that maturity of municipal bonds. The results of these computations are reported in Table 21.

It is immediately apparent that the term structure of subsidy rates in Table 21 is very nearly the same as that in Table 18. Short-maturity municipal bonds enjoy the greatest subsidy rate, and the subsidy rate declines as term to maturity increases. Moreover, the average subsidy rates for bonds with maturities of five, ten, and twenty years are very close to the adjusted subsidy rates reported in Table 18. The average subsidy rate for bonds of one to two-year maturity, however, is distinctly lower than the adjusted subsidy rate for similar bonds in Table 18. As will be discussed later in this chapter, the reason for this decline in the subsidy rate for short-term municipal bonds between 1961–65 and 1965–75 is the decline in the corporate tax rate from 52 percent to 48 percent.

The average subsidy rate for bonds of twenty-year maturity in Table 21 is 32 percent. Thus, it is not necessary to make any adjustment to this subsidy rate in order to make it consistent with the 32 percent subsidy rate for long-term municipal bonds indicated by the

TABLE 21

NOMINAL SUBSIDY RATE FOR MUNICIPAL BONDS BY TERM TO MATURITY,
USING GMAC YIELDS
(percent per year)

| Year | Years to Maturity | | | |
	1–2	4–6	9–11	19–21
1965	N.A.	40	38	34
1966	40	42	40	35
1967	47	44	40	36
1968	37	42	41	36
1969	40	38	35	26
1970	46	41	36	24
1971	53	48	41	28
1972	54	43	41	33
1973	48	43	42	34
1974	45	44	42	36
1975	43	41	37	30
1965–75 average	45	42	39	32

N.A.: Not available.
SOURCE: Calculated from data in Tables 19 and 20.

analysis of the previous section. No adjustment is required, because the seasoning effect on GMAC bonds of twenty-year maturity (a factor tending to reduce yields) was almost exactly balanced by the fact that GMAC bonds were only Aa-rated rather than Aaa-rated (a factor tending to increase yields).[14] This suggests that no adjustment is required for the average subsidy rates reported in Table 21 for maturities of less than twenty years.

The procedure for estimating the term structure of the subsidy rate using the term structure of interest rates for taxable bonds issued by GMAC may be replicated for taxable bonds issued by other corporations. For this purpose, a sample of yield structures for other corporations with diverse maturities of outstanding bonds (on which publicly quoted yields are available) was examined.[15] For particular years and particular corporations, the results differed in minor respects from the results reported in Table 21. However, correcting for differences in the average yield on long-term bonds of different corporations, the average term structure of subsidy rates implied by the yields on bonds issued by these other corporations is fully consistent with the results reported in the last row of Table 21.

To produce a final estimate of the term structure of the subsidy rate, it is useful to combine the results in the last row of Table 21 with those in the last row of Table 18. To insure that the subsidy rate for any maturity is not too high, we specify that the subsidy rate for any maturity is the lower of the two subsidy rates for that maturity reported in the two tables. This specification implies the term structure of subsidy rates that is reported in Table 22. In this table, the subsidy rates for maturities between those listed in Tables 18 and 21 are determined by linear interpolation between the two nearest (listed) maturities, rounded off to the nearest percentage point. The previous discussion of the 32 percent estimate of the subsidy rate

---

[14] For the eleven years from 1965 to 1975, the average nominal yield on GMAC bonds of nineteen to twenty-one-year maturity was 7.14 percent. The average nominal yield for newly issued, Aaa-rated, corporate bonds (column 2 of Table 13) for the same years was 7.21 percent. If a correction were made for this difference, it would require an *increase* in the estimated average subsidy rate for the nineteen to twenty-one-year maturity class of about one percentage point.

[15] Examined were Pacific Gas and Electric, Philadelphia Edison, and Southern California Edison, the companies that provided the widest diversity of different maturities of outstanding bonds. If an average of the yields on the bonds of these companies (together with GMAC) were used to calculate the nominal subsidy rate on municipal bonds of different maturities, the result would be a higher nominal subsidy rate for most maturities in most years and a higher average nominal subsidy rate for all maturities based on the years 1965 through 1975.

TABLE 22

Estimated Term Structure of the Nominal Subsidy Rate

Years to Maturity	Subsidy Rate (percent)	Years to Maturity	Subsidy Rate (percent)
1	45	21	32
2	45	22	31
3	44	23	31
4	43	24	30
5	42	25	30
6	41	26	30
7	40	27	29
8	39	28	29
9	38	29	28
10	37	30	28
11	37	31	28
12	36	32	28
13	36	33	28
14	35	34	28
15	35	35	28
16	34	36	28
17	34	37	28
18	33	38	28
19	33	39	28
20	32	40	28

SOURCE: From interpolation of the results given in Tables 18 and 21.

for long-term (20-year) municipal bonds, together with the method of constructing the estimate of the term structure of the subsidy rate, suggest that these subsidy rates are probably underestimates of the true subsidy rate enjoyed by municipalities issuing tax-exempt bonds of various maturities.

The Average Subsidy Rate

To determine the total benefit that municipal governments enjoy as a result of the exemption, it is necessary to calculate the average subsidy rate provided by the exemption. Obviously, if the subsidy rate were the same for all maturities, the calculation of this average would present no difficulty. However, since the subsidy rate varies significantly with term to maturity, it is essential to know the correct weight to apply to each maturity in calculating the average subsidy rate.

In general, the previous literature on the effects of the exemption and the consequences of the taxable bond option has neglected the issue of the average subsidy rate and has simply assumed that the average subsidy rate is the subsidy rate for long-term bonds.[16] The one exception to this general rule is the estimate of the average subsidy rate suggested by Peter Fortune.[17] To construct his estimate, Fortune assumes that the subsidy rate for municipal bonds of one to ten-year maturity is 45 percent, the subsidy rate for municipal bonds of ten to twenty-year maturity is 35 percent, and the subsidy rate for municipal bonds of more than twenty-year maturity is 30 percent. He also assumes that 40 percent of outstanding municipal bonds have terms to maturity of less than ten years, 30 percent have terms to maturity of ten to twenty years, and 30 percent have terms to maturity of over twenty years. Multiplying the assumed subsidy rate for each maturity class by the fraction of municipal bonds assumed to be in that class yields an estimate of the average subsidy rate of 38 percent; that is, $0.38 = (0.40) \cdot 0.45 + (0.30) \cdot 3.35 + (0.30) \cdot 0.30$.

The fact that this estimated average is so much higher than the subsidy rate on long-term bonds indicates the importance of considering both long- and short-term bonds in an estimate of the average subsidy rate. The procedure used in constructing this estimate is suggestive of the correct procedure. However, there is reason to believe that the estimate of 38 percent for the average subsidy rate may be too high a figure, and it is certainly not a downward-biased estimate of the average subsidy rate. It is too high a figure because a subsidy rate of 45 percent is probably too high for all bonds in the one to ten-year maturity class, and a subsidy rate of 35 percent may be too high for bonds in the ten to twenty-year maturity class,[18] and because the weights assigned to the short maturity classes may be too large.

---

[16] Ott and Meltzer (1963) recognize that the yield advantage enjoyed by municipal borrowers is greater on short-term bonds than on long-term bonds. They do not, however, attempt to construct an estimate of the average nominal subsidy rate; instead, they satisfy themselves with a rather broad range of estimates for the yield advantage enjoyed by municipal borrowers. In general, proponents of the taxable bond option have focused on the nominal subsidy rate for long-term bonds (pointing out that it is low) and have neglected the fact that the nominal subsidy rate for short-term bonds is significantly higher than for long-term bonds.

[17] See Fortune (1976). Fortune makes no pretense that his estimate is very precise. He merely suggests that it is appropriate to take account of the fact that the subsidy rate varies with term to maturiy and that his estimate is approximately the right figure.

[18] Since our estimates of the nominal subsidy rate are biased in a downward direction, it is possible that Fortune's estimates are correct. Based on the available evidence, however, it appears that 45 percent is too high an estimate for the average subsidy rate for all bonds in the one to ten-year maturity class.

We turn now to the question of the appropriate weight to assign to municipal bonds in different maturity classes. The relevant weight to attach to each maturity is not the fraction of outstanding municipal bonds of that many years remaining to maturity but, rather, the fraction of outstanding municipal bonds that were originally of a given maturity. This is because the subsidy that a municipal government enjoys on a tax-exempt bond throughout its life is the difference between the nominal yield to maturity on that bond at its date of issue and the nominal yield on a newly issued taxable bond of the same quality and maturity, issued at the same date.

Unfortunately, no one has compiled figures on the distribution of outstanding municipal bonds by their original term to maturity. However, it is possible to infer what this distribution must look like from information on the maturity structure of new issues. Table 23 uses data from a summary of reoffering yields for newly issued municipal bonds compiled by the *Bond Buyer* for the calendar year 1976. For each rating class, the numbers in the table report the number of weeks in which the reoffering yield on the longest-quoted maturity was five, ten, fifteen, twenty, twenty-five, or thirty years, and also the number of weeks when there were no reoffering yields for that rating class. Clearly, if more than one issue of any rating class was reoffered in any given week, the longest maturity among all of these issues is what is registered in Table 23. For this reason, the summary figures in the last column of this table on the percentage distribution of new issues by the length of longest maturity clearly overstate the relative importance of issues with long maturities, at the expense of those with short maturities.[19]

To complete the picture of the maturity structure of outstanding municipal bonds (by maturity at original issue), it is essential to know something about the pattern of principal repayment. A survey of a

Moreover, from the results developed later in this section, it is apparent that the weight given to this maturity class in calculating the average subsidy rate is too high.

[19] Some indication of the presence of this bias may be obtained by comparing the distribution of maximum maturities for different rating classes. For the Aaa rating class, there were ten weeks in which no reoffering yields were quoted, in comparison with only one week for the Aa rating class, no weeks for the A rating class, and six weeks for the Baa rating class. Presumably, this is because there are fewer issues of Aaa-rated and Baa-rated bonds than of either Aa-rated or A-rated bonds. It is noteworthy, therefore, that the distribution of maximum maturities for the Aaa rating class has a much lower density of long maturities than either the Aa or the A rating class and is similar to the distribution for the Baa rating class. This is an indication of the extent of the bias that results from the simultaneous reoffering of series of municipal bonds with different maximum maturities within the same week.

TABLE 23

DISTRIBUTION OF NEW ISSUES OF MUNICIPAL BONDS, IN CALENDAR
YEAR 1976, BY MAXIMUM MATURITY OF ISSUE

Maximum Maturity (years)	Number of Weeks the Reoffering Yield Was in Each Maximum Maturity Class, by Rating				Total Number of Weeks	Percent of Total Weeks
	Aaa	Aa	A	Baa		
5	1	0	0	0	1	0.5
10	1	2	0	1	4	2.1
15	11	7	1	7	26	13.3
20	18	21	14	21	79	40.5
25	4	16	17	17	54	27.7
30	8	6	16	1	31	15.9
No issue	10	1	0	6	—	—
Total					195	100.0

SOURCE: From the *Bond Buyer's* annual compilation of reoffering yields on general obligation municipal bonds.

sample of municipal bond issues reveals the following facts. In a large fraction of municipal bond issues there is a flat repayment schedule, with a constant amount of principal retired each year. In another large fraction of issues, principal repayments rise gradually as the final maturity date is approached.[20] A common pattern among these issues is for the principal sum of the loan to be amortized in the same fashion as a home mortgage; that is, annual payments of interest and principal combined are constant over the maturity of the loan, with an increasing share of these payments going to principal retirement as the final maturity date is approached. In some cases, retirement of principal does not begin until a few years after the bonds are issued. Furthermore, bonds are sometimes called for retirement before their final maturity date (or ahead of the schedule of mandatory sinking fund retirements). These considerations suggest that the average pattern of principal repayment for a new issue of municipal bonds with a maximum maturity of, say, twenty-five years is one in which the rate of principal repayment rises moderately as the final maturity date is approached but not as rapidly as in the standard home mortgage.

---

[20] These general impressions were obtained by analyzing the principal repayment schedules for a number of outstanding series of municipal bonds, as reported in Moody's *Municipal and Government Manual* (1977).

To estimate the maturity structure of outstanding municipal bonds, by maturity at original issue, two further factors must be taken into account. First, the bonds with an original maturity of twenty-five years that are currently outstanding include not only newly issued twenty-five-year bonds, but also twenty-five-year bonds issued during the preceding twenty-four years. In contrast, bonds with an original maturity of ten years that are currently outstanding include only ten-year bonds issued during the present year and the preceding nine years. Second, since the volume of municipal borrowing has been growing (at an annual average rate of 9 percent for the past twenty-five years), the average volume of twenty-five-year bonds issued each year during the past twenty-four years is considerably less than the volume of twenty-five-year bonds issued this year. This is also true, but to a much lesser extent, for ten-year bonds. This factor counter-balances the fact that principal retirement for a municipal bond issue with a maximum maturity of twenty-five years is more heavily concentrated in the years immediately before the final maturity date.

When all factors are taken into account, the following procedure emerges as a reasonable one for estimating the distribution of the outstanding stock of municipal bonds by original term to maturity. This procedure is applied separately to municipal bond issues with specific maximum maturities. Consider, for example, municipal bonds that were originally issued as parts of series in which the maximum maturity was twenty years. Such series will include bonds with maturities of one, two, three, and so on up to twenty years. Bonds with one-year original maturities will be outstanding only from the present year; bonds with two-year original maturities will be outstanding from this year and last year; bonds with three-year original maturities will be outstanding from this year, last year, and the preceding year; and so on up to bonds with twenty-year original maturities that will be outstanding from this year and the preceding nineteen years. Given the normal pattern of principal repayments, the volume of twenty-year bonds issued this year will exceed the volume of one-year bonds issued this year (within series with a maximum maturity of twenty years). However, because of the growth of municipal borrowing, the average volume of twenty-year bonds issued in the preceding nineteen years will be less than the volume of twenty-year bonds issued this year. Assuming that these two factors just balance, a weight of twenty should be assigned to a maturity of twenty years, a weight of nineteen should be assigned to a maturity of nineteen years, and so on down to a weight of one, which should be assigned to a maturity of one year. These weights indicate the relative importance of the respective maturities in that part of the total outstanding stock of municipal bonds generated by issues with a twenty-year maximum maturity.

Using the weights described above, together with the term structure of subsidy rates given in Table 22, we may calculate an average subsidy rate for the outstanding municipal bonds issued as parts of series in which the maximum maturity was twenty years. This calculation yields an average subsidy rate of 35.7 percent. This is reported in Table 24 as the average subsidy rate for series with twenty-year maximum maturities. Similar calculations of the average subsidy rate for outstanding municipal bonds from series with maximum maturities of five, ten, fifteen, twenty-five, thirty, and forty years are also reported in Table 23.[21] The average subsidy rate for bonds originating in series with a maximum maturity of twenty-five years is 34 percent. Since Table 23 indicates that more than 80 percent of new issues of municipal bonds come in series with maximum maturities of twenty-five years or less, this 34 percent average subsidy rate is surely a lower bound for the average subsidy rate on all outstanding municipal bonds.

To obtain a more precise (but still a lower-bound) estimate of the average subsidy rate for all outstanding municipal bonds, it is necessary to take a weighted average of the subsidy rates in Table 24. The appropriate weights to use are the fractions of the total outstanding that are accounted for by series with maximum maturities of five, ten, fifteen, twenty, twenty-five, thirty, and forty years. These weights may be inferred from the distribution of new issues given in the last column of Table 23 (assuming that one-half of the thirty-year issues are actually forty-year issues) and from the growth rate of municipal borrowing (9 percent per year).[22] The relevant weights are reported in Table 24. The application of these weights to the subsidy rates yields the average subsidy rate for all outstanding municipal bonds that is reported at the bottom of the table, namely, 34.9 percent.

Two facts about this estimate of the average subsidy rate deserve

---

[21] It has been assumed that the nominal subsidy rate for municipal bonds in the thirty to forty-year maturity range is the same 28 percent as the nominal subsidy rate for thirty-year municipal bonds. Since there are very few corporate bonds with maturities of forty years, it is difficult to test the accuracy of this assumption. To the extent that there is evidence available, however, this assumption is consistent with that evidence.

[22] Assuming a growth rate of 9 percent per year, it is possible to calculate the volume of outstanding issues of any maximum maturity relative to the new issues of that maximum maturity. This information—together with the assumed distribution of new issues by maximum maturity—implies the weights given in Table 24.

TABLE 24

THE AVERAGE NOMINAL SUBSIDY RATE BY MAXIMUM MATURITY CLASS

Maximum Maturity Class (years)	Relative Weight of Maximum Maturity Class[a]	Average Subsidy Rate for Bonds from the Class (percent)
5	0.002	43.3
10	0.015	40.0
15	0.116	38.7
20	0.397	35.7
25	0.291	34.0
30	0.088	32.4
40	0.091	30.5
Weighted average		34.9

[a] Weights are inferred from the distribution of new issues (Table 23) and from an annual growth rate of 9 percent for municipal borrowing.
NOTE: Calculations are described in the text.

further emphasis. First, 34.9 percent is clearly a lower-bound estimate of the average subsidy rate for outstanding municipal bonds. This is true because the term structure of subsidy rates reported in Table 22 understates the true subsidy rates and because the weight given to longer-maturity municipal bonds in calculating the average subsidy rate is probably excessive. Second, the estimated average subsidy rate of 34.9 percent refers only to municipal obligations that are classified as bonds and neglects short-term municipal borrowing in the form of tax warrants, bills, and bond anticipation notes. Over the past decade, such short-term municipal borrowing has averaged about 8 percent of total outstanding municipal debt. The subsidy rate on such short-term borrowing has been at least as great as the 45 percent subsidy rate for one-year bonds indicated in Table 22. When account is taken of short-term municipal borrowing, the estimate of the average subsidy rate rises to 35.7 percent. (This is computed by taking a weighted average of subsidy rates of 34.9 percent for long-term borrowing and 45 percent for short-term, with weights of 0.92 and 0.08, respectively.) Therefore, all things considered, we may be quite confident that the average nominal subsidy rate that municipal governments enjoy as a result of the tax-exempt status of their bonds is at least 35 percent of the nominal borrowing costs they would incur if they issued taxable bonds.

Equalizing Differences and the Theory of the Subsidy Rate

It is clear from the preceding analysis that municipal borrowers enjoy much higher subsidy rates on their short-term bonds than on their long-term bonds—as high as 45 percent for bonds of one-year maturity and as low as 28 percent for thirty-year bonds. What remains to be explained is the economic reason why the subsidy rate on short-term bonds is greater than the subsidy rate on long-term bonds. This requires an analysis of the incentives that different investors have for holding municipal bonds of various maturities.

Suppose that municipal bonds and corporate bonds of the same rating class and the same term to maturity were identical (in the eyes of the investor) in terms of risk, liquidity, and every other relevant factor, except yield and tax status. (This may not be a completely accurate assumption, but it serves to illustrate the basic principles determining the subsidy rate.)[23] If this assumption is valid, then common sense suggests that an investor will hold both municipal bonds and corporate bonds (of the same rating class and term to maturity) only if the advantage of the tax-exempt status of the municipal bond exactly compensates for the yield advantage of the corporate bond. To avoid the problem of the differential taxation of interest and capital gains, suppose that both the municipal bond and the corporate bond are selling at par. Then the investor will be indifferent between corporate and municipal bonds when the proportionate yield differential (in nominal terms) between the bonds is equal to his nominal marginal tax rate. The investor will hold both the municipal bond and the corporate bond (of the same rating class and term to maturity) only if he is indifferent between them. If the proportionate nominal yield differential is greater than the investor's nominal marginal tax rate, he should hold only the corporate bond. Conversely, if the proportionate nominal yield differential is less than the investor's nominal marginal tax rate, he should hold only the municipal bond. These simple, common-sense principles are implied by "the theory of equalizing differences." All other things being equal, an investor will hold both a taxable bond and a tax-exempt bond only if the yield differential compensates for the difference in tax status; otherwise, he will hold only the asset that yields the highest after-tax return.[24]

---

[23] There is reason to believe that long-term municipal bonds are of somewhat higher risk than long-term corporate bonds and that this difference in risk explains at least part of the observed term structure of the nominal subsidy rate. This issue has been explored in a paper by Skelton (1978).

[24] In analyzing empirical data on security holdings of different investors, it is unreasonable to expect that this principle will always hold exactly. There are

This theory may be applied to various investors who hold municipal bonds. Consider commercial banks. The *Federal Reserve Bulletin* reports that, on 30 June 1976, all commercial banks held a total of $103 billion of municipal government debt. This amounted to about 42 percent of total outstanding municipal debt and to about 11 percent of total bank assets. In general, the nominal tax rate applied to bank profits is the corporate tax rate of 48 percent. Hence, for commercial banks, the equalizing proportionate yield differential between taxable bonds and tax-exempt bonds that are identical in all relevant respects, except tax status and yield, is 48 percent.

Detailed evidence on the asset holdings of commercial banks indicates that they hold substantial amounts of *both* short-term taxable debt and short-term tax-exempt debt. The principal business of commercial banks (other than providing services to depositors) is making loans to businesses and individuals. Predominantly, bank loans are short-term loans. The only significant exceptions are loans secured by real estate mortgages. However, out of the $350 billion of bank loans not secured by real estate in June of 1976, the vast bulk must have been loans with less than two or three years' duration. Moreover, commercial banks also show a strong preference for shorter-term securities in their holdings of U.S. Treasury obligations, as indicated by the following breakdown for large, weekly reporting banks in June of 1976: Treasury bills, 31 percent; Treasury notes and bonds due within one year, 15 percent; Treasury notes and bonds due in two to five years, 49 percent; Treasury notes and bonds due after five years, 6 percent.

In the tax-exempt market, commercial banks are the preponderant holders of short-term municipal debt that is officially classified as "tax warrants, short-term notes, and bills." The detailed breakdown of assets held by large, weekly reporting banks indicates that, in June of 1976, 13 percent of these banks' holdings of municipal government obligations were in this official short-term category. Assuming that

---

always special circumstances that account for small-scale holdings of securities that economic theory suggests an investor should not be holding. People make mistakes in their investment decisions. Assessments of risk and expected return by individual investors differ from the average of all investors. In some cases, securities may have been acquired in the past, when either general economic conditions or the specific circumstances of the investor were different from what they are today. In some cases, securities may have special properties (such as convertible bonds) that are not reported in the data. All things considered, therefore, the theory of equalizing differences suggests that investors in high tax brackets should not be holding substantial amounts of taxable long-term bonds. Small-scale holdings of such bonds by high-tax-bracket investors, however, should not be regarded as contradicting the theory.

TABLE 25

The Nominal Subsidy Rate on Short-Term Municipal Bonds
(percent)

Year	Yield on One-Year Prime Municipal Bonds (1)	Yield on Four–Six Month Prime Commercial Paper (2)	Nominal Subsidy Rate on Short-Term Municipal Bonds (3)
1952	1.00	2.33	57
1953	1.30	2.52	48
1954	0.75	1.58	53
1955	1.15	2.18	47
1956	1.70	3.31	49
1957	2.15	3.18	32
1958	1.30	2.46	47
1959	2.20	3.97	45
1960	2.05	3.85	47
1961	1.50	2.97	49
1962	1.60	3.26	51
1963	1.75	3.55	51
1964	2.10	3.97	47
1965	2.35	4.38	46
1966	3.40	5.55	39
1967	3.00	5.10	41
1968	3.30	5.90	44
1969	4.55	7.33	38
1970	4.35	7.72	44
1971	2.90	5.11	43
1972	2.75	4.69	41
1973	3.95	8.15	48
1974	4.75	9.78	51
1975	3.91	6.33	38
Average			
1952–75	2.49	4.55	45.7
1952–65	1.64	3.11	47.8
1966–75	3.69	6.57	42.7

Source: Column 1 is from Salomon Brothers, *Analytical Record of Yields and Yield Spreads.* Column 2 is from the *Federal Reserve Bulletin.* Column 3 is the difference between columns 2 and 1, divided by column 2.

the same percentage applies to all banks, it follows that total bank holdings of tax warrants, short-term notes, and bills issued by municipal governments were approximately $13 billion, out of a total outstanding stock of such obligations of $15 billion. Thus, virtually all of the officially classified short-term municipal debt was held by commercial banks.

Since commercial banks hold both short-term taxable obligations and short-term tax-exempt obligations, the theory of equalizing differences implies that the yield differential between two such obligations of the same risk and quality should be 48 percent. The evidence is consistent with the theory. Specifically, the evidence presented in Tables 18 and 21 indicates that the proportionate yield differential between taxable and tax-exempt bonds at the short end of the maturity spectrum is close to the corporate tax rate, close enough that any minor divergences can easily be explained by deficiencies of the data and lack of exact comparability between taxable and tax-exempt bonds.

This evidence is supplemented by the results reported in Table 25. Column 1 reports the series on the nominal yield on one-year municipal bonds from Salomon Brothers' *Analytical Record of Yields and Yield Spreads*. Column 2 reports the series on nominal yield on four to six-month prime commercial paper taken from various issues of the *Federal Reserve Bulletin*. These yields are probably representative of the yields that banks earn on short-term corporate loans of highest quality and security. Column 3 reports the nominal subsidy rate provided on short-term municipal bonds, calculated by taking the proportionate differential between the taxable yield in column 2 and the tax-exempt yield in column 1. The average of these subsidy rates, reported at the bottom of column 3, is 45.7 percent. This average subsidy rate is slightly less than the average corporate tax rate for the period covered in the table, 50.5 percent. Part of this difference is explained by the fact that nominal yields on four to six-month taxable instruments are somewhat lower than one-year taxable instruments.[25]

---

[25] For the years since 1959, Salomon Brothers' *Analytical Record of Yields and Yield Spreads* provides yields for three-month and six-month Treasury obligations, as well as one-year Treasury obligations. For the seventeen years from 1959 through 1975, the average yield on Treasury obligations of three-month maturity was 4.67 percent, that on Treasury obligations of six-month maturity was 4.79 percent, and that on Treasury obligations of one-year maturity was 5.05 percent. The average yield differential between one-year Treasury obligations and the average of three-month and six-month obligations was 26 basis points. If the effect of longer maturity on corporate obligations is the same as on Treasury obligations, this suggests that 26 basis points should be added to the yield on four to six-month commercial paper in order to compare that yield with the yield on one-year municipal bonds. The result of this correction would be to increase the estimated nominal subsidy rate on short-term municipal bonds by about 5 percentage points.

Any remaining difference is easily accounted for by the fact that prime commercial paper and prime municipal bonds are not exactly comparable instruments with respect to risk, liquidity, and other relevant characteristics. Thus, all things considered, the evidence is consistent with the conclusion that the proportionate yield differential between short-term taxable instruments and short-term tax-exempt instruments is the equalizing difference that compensates for the difference in tax status for the dominant holder of short-term tax-exempt obligations. At the short end of the maturity spectrum, the nominal subsidy rate provided by the exemption is the nominal corporate tax rate facing commercial banks.[26]

Commercial banks also hold substantial amounts of longer-term municipal bonds. Some evidence on the distribution of banks' holdings of municipal bonds by term to maturity is available from surveys compiled by the Federal Reserve Bank of Cleveland during the 1960s, which are summarized in Table 26. These results confirm that banks' holdings of municipal bonds are concentrated in short-range and intermediate-range maturities. Nevertheless, it is apparent from Tables 18 and 21 that for some of the maturities held by banks the nominal subsidy rate is significantly below the corporate tax rate. This implies no inconsistency with the theory of equalizing differences, however, because banks do not hold significant amounts of *both* longer-term municipal bonds and longer-term corporate bonds. During the past twenty years, municipal bonds have frequently exceeded 10 percent of bank assets, but corporate bonds have never exceeded 1 percent of bank assets.[27]

The explanation of these facts is to be found in the peculiar characteristics of commercial banking. Relative to their equity capital, commercial banks have extremely large deposit liabilities that are due

---

[26] Fama (1977) has pointed out that this result is due to the fact that commercial banks arbitrage between short-term municipal bonds and short-term taxable bonds. He also suggests that commercial banks arbitrage between longer-term municipal bonds and longer-term taxable bonds, implying that the proportionate yield differential between such bonds (of equivalent risk) should be the corporate tax rate. We do not accept this argument. But, if the argument is correct, it strengthens our basic conclusions that the average nominal subsidy rate has been underestimated and that commercial banks derive no special advantage (at the margin) from holding municipal bonds.

[27] Data on commercial bank holdings of corporate and foreign bonds were provided by the Federal Reserve. In every year since 1955, the value of commercial bank holdings of foreign and corporate bonds was less than 1 percent of the total assets of insured banks (members of the Federal Deposit Insurance Corporation). Since the category of foreign and corporate bonds includes corporate bonds of all maturities, we may safely conclude that commercial bank holdings of long-term corporate bonds are essentially zero.

TABLE 26

The Distribution of Commercial Bank Holdings of Municipal Bonds by Term to Maturity

	Percentage Distribution by Maturity			
Date	Under one year	One to five years	Five to ten years	Over ten years
31 December 1960	13.4	35.6	28.9	22.1
31 December 1961	19.7	31.9	24.0	24.4
31 December 1962	19.0	33.3	22.1	25.6
30 June 1963	15.5	34.1	24.2	26.2
31 December 1963	18.2	31.3	24.4	26.1
30 June 1964	13.7	31.7	25.2	29.2
31 December 1964	14.5	29.0	25.0	31.5
30 June 1965	10.6	29.3	24.7	35.4
31 December 1965	10.5	27.1	25.0	37.4
30 June 1966	10.9	24.0	24.3	40.8
31 December 1966	14.2	21.6	24.2	40.0

Source: Federal Reserve Bank of Cleveland, *Economic Review*, April 1967.

either on demand or on very short term. The value of these deposit liabilities is fixed in terms of money. The values of bank assets, however, are not fixed in terms of money. When market interest rates fluctuate, so do the market values of many bank assets. This is particularly so for long-term bonds, both corporate and municipal. Hence, given the nature and size of its deposit liabilities, a bank undertakes substantial risk whenever it holds a long-term bond rather than a shorter-term bond or loan. The yield differential in favor of the long-term bond relative to the shorter-term bond or loan must compensate the bank for this higher risk. (Again, this is an implication of the theory of equalizing differences.) Otherwise, the bank will not choose to hold the long-term bond. For municipal bonds, the yield differential in favor of longer-term bonds is sufficient that commercial banks are willing to accept the higher risk associated with longer term to maturity. For corporate bonds, the yield differential in favor of intermediate or long-term bonds relative to short-term bonds and commercial paper is not sufficiently great to compensate banks for the higher risk. Hence, commercial banks choose not to hold longer-term taxable bonds. The market for such bonds is restricted to nonbanks, largely pension funds and life insurance companies, which do not face the same risk situation as banks.

Since commercial banks hold no significant amount of longer-term corporate bonds, the yield differential between such bonds and longer-term municipal bonds is not determined by their nominal tax rate. The implicit nominal subsidy rate provided to municipal governments by the exemption on their longer-term borrowings is less than the corporate tax rate. Nevertheless, commercial banks enjoy no special advantage from investing in longer-term municipal bonds relative to other assets they may choose to hold. For commercial banks, the yield differentials between municipal bonds of various maturities and other assets that they choose to hold are the equalizing differences that compensate for the differences in tax status, risk, and other relevant characteristics that distinguish the yields on different assets.

Besides commercial banks, the other important holders of municipal bonds are fire and casualty insurance companies and individual households. Unfortunately, less detailed and less accurate information is generally available concerning the portfolios of these investors than is available for commercial banks. Fire and casualty insurance companies are subject to the same nominal corporate tax rate as commercial banks. However, since these companies are generally less restricted in their investment practices than banks, they can invest in tax shelters (other than municipal bonds) that reduce their effective marginal tax rate. For example, they can and do hold substantial amounts of common and preferred stock. Thus, the effective marginal tax rate for fire and casualty insurance companies is probably lower than for commercial banks. A survey of the financial statements submitted to the New York superintendent of insurance by the twenty-five largest fire and casualty insurance companies (or their largest subsidiaries) for business done in 1970 reveals the following facts. For twenty-one of these companies, at least one of the following conditions was satisfied: either (1) holdings of taxable corporate bonds were a small fraction (less than 5 percent) of total bond holdings; or (2) federal income taxes paid were small or negative. Either of these two conditions is consistent with the theory of equalizing differences. If corporate bond holdings are negligible, then the investor is not indifferent between taxable corporate bonds and tax-exempt municipal bonds. If the corporate tax rate is not effective, then the yield differential between corporate and municipal bonds need not be equated to this tax rate. For the four out of twenty-five companies that did not satisfy either of the above conditions, special circumstances were responsible either for the high level of taxes or for the characteristics of the company's bond portfolio.[28] Thus, when all factors are taken into account, the behavior of these twenty-five large insurance companies is consistent with the theory of equalizing differences.

Little is known about the maturity structure of municipal bonds held by fire and casualty insurance companies. It is likely, however, that the holdings of these insurance companies are less heavily concentrated in the short end of the maturity spectrum than are the holdings of commercial banks. For one thing, commercial banks hold virtually all of the very short-term municipal obligations, leaving little for insurance companies or any other investor. Further, while insurance companies do have large short-term liabilities in the form of unearned premiums, the ratio of such liabilities to capital and reserves is much lower than the deposit-capital ratio of commercial banks. Hence, fire and casualty insurance companies do not have as strong an incentive as banks to hold very short-term municipal bonds. For these companies, the higher yields that are available on intermediate and long-term tax-exempt bonds are probably sufficient inducement to hold such bonds and to leave the very short-term market to commercial banks.

The latest information on the municipal bonds held by individual households comes from the *Survey of Financial Characteristics of Consumers* in 1962.[29] The survey indicates that municipal bond holdings are heavily concentrated at the upper end of the income and wealth distribution. Even for the highest-income households, however, municipal bonds are a relatively small part, only 5 percent, of total wealth. For these same households, corporate bonds constituted only one-half of 1 percent of total wealth. Moreover, total holdings

---

[28] In the case of Home Insurance, the company realized an extraordinary capital gain that accounted for the abnormally high level of federal tax payments. In preceding years, federal tax payments were very close to zero. In the case of Fireman's Fund, federal income taxes incurred in 1970 were about 8 percent of net income, but income taxes incurred in the preceding year were about minus 7 percent of net income. The average experience of this company is that it pays very little income tax. In the case of the Hartford Insurance Group, one company, the Hartford Accident and Indemnity Co., paid very little federal tax in 1970, and another, the Hartford Fire Insurance Co., paid about 20 percent of its net income in federal tax in 1970. This tax payment, however, was an unusual event, arising out of the company's very large investment income (perhaps related to its merger with ITT). In 1969, the Hartford Fire Insurance Co. paid very little federal tax (even though it had substantial net income). Finally, in the Travelers Insurance Group, one company, the Travelers Indemnity Co., paid very little tax, while another, the Travelers Insurance Co., paid a substantial amount of federal tax, apparently related to this company's large life insurance operations.

[29] See Projector and Weiss (1966).

of fixed interest assets by these households were more than out-weighed by their fixed interest debt. These facts indicate that the wealthy households that hold municipal bonds are not choosing at the margin between municipal bonds and taxable corporate bonds. As will be discussed more extensively in the next chapter, the relevant marginal choice for these households is between municipal bonds and equity assets such as common stocks and real estate. Further, the analysis in the next chapter indicates that, when account is taken of favorable tax treatment afforded to equity assets, the effective nominal marginal tax rate facing wealthy households is far less than the official marginal tax rate of these households. Evidence from a variety of sources indicates that the effective marginal tax rate for the house-holds that hold the bulk of municipal bonds is no greater than 36 percent and may be as low as 30 percent. This suggests that indi-vidual households derive no special advantage, at the margin, from holding municipal bonds rather than the other assets they also choose to hold.

Summary

In this chapter, we have examined the size of the nominal subsidy enjoyed by municipal borrowers as a result of the right to issue tax-exempt bonds. The nominal subsidy rate is the proportionate differ-ential between the nominal yield that municipal governments would have to pay on taxable bonds and the nominal yield they pay on tax-exempt bonds. Our findings are as follows: First, on long-term bonds of about twenty-year maturity, the nominal subsidy rate is at least 32 percent. This figure represents the proportionate yield differential between new issues of publicly offered long-term corporate bonds and comparably rated issues of long-term municipal bonds. This figure does not take account of the fact that many municipal bonds would have to be issued in the private placements market or of other char-acteristics of municipal bond issues that would tend to increase the yields on taxable municipal bonds above those on publicly offered corporate bonds. For this reason, as well as others, 32 percent is probably an underestimate of the true borrowing advantage enjoyed by municipalities on bonds of twenty-year maturity. Second, the nominal subsidy rate varies significantly with term to maturity. The subsidy rate on bonds with one-year maturities is close to the cor-porate tax rate, presently 48 percent. As term to maturity is length-ened, the subsidy rate gradually declines, reaching 40 percent at five-year maturities, 36 percent at ten-year maturities, 32 percent at twenty-year maturities, and 28 percent for maturities of thirty years and longer. Third, the average nominal subsidy rate on outstanding municipal bonds is at least 35 percent. This average subsidy rate refers to the average of subsidy rates for municipal bonds of different terms to maturity, weighted by the relative importance of different maturities (at original date of issue) in the outstanding stock of municipal bonds. The estimated average subsidy rate of 35 percent is probably an understatement of the true rate for two reasons. First, the subsidy rates for specific maturities are underestimates of the true subsidy rates for those maturities. Second, the relative importance afforded to longer maturities in the relative weighting scheme probably overstates the true relative importance of these longer maturities in the outstanding stock of municipal bonds.

In this chapter, we also considered why the subsidy rate varies with term to maturity. Essentially, the explanation rests on the theory of equalizing differences: For any two assets actually held by an investor, the difference in yield should exactly balance the difference in tax status, risk, and other relevant characteristics. Commercial banks hold substantial amounts of short-term taxable debt and dominate the market for short-term municipal debt. Since the only important difference between these two classes of debt (other than yield) is their tax status, the yield differential between short-term corporate debt and short-term municipal debt is determined by the nominal tax rate of commercial banks, presently 48 percent. Since commercial banks do not hold any significant amount of longer-term corporate bonds, their tax rate is not the effective determinant of the yield differential between corporate and municipal bonds of longer maturities. Indeed, since commercial banks have very large short-term liabilities in relation to equity capital, they are reluctant to hold long-term bonds of any kind, unless the bonds pay a considerable premium relative to shorter-term bonds and loans. This reluctance of banks to hold longer-term bonds accounts, to some extent, for the tendency of yields on municipal bonds to rise as term to maturity is lengthened.

Fire and casualty insurance companies, the other important institutional holders of municipal bonds, do not have the same strong incentive as banks to hold short-term bonds. Nor is it likely that their holdings of municipal bonds are as concentrated at the short end of the maturity spectrum as those of banks. Moreover, the yield differential between longer-term corporate and municipal bonds is not fixed by the official marginal tax rate of fire and casualty insurance companies because the effective marginal tax rate is less than the official tax rate and because such companies either hold very few taxable long-term bonds or pay very little federal tax. Finally, for most individual holders of municipal bonds, the relevant choice is not between municipal bonds and corporate bonds but between municipal bonds and equity assets such as stocks and real estate. In the next chapter it is shown that a nominal subsidy rate of about 30 percent is consistent with substantial holdings of long-term municipal bonds by individual investors who are balancing at the margin the advantages of municipal bonds relative to equity assets.

The conclusions of this chapter will be used in subsequent chapters to analyze the effects of the present exemption and the probable consequences of the taxable bond option. In almost every case, a double degree of protection will be provided against the possibility of overstating the size of the nominal subsidy provided by the exemption. One degree of protection comes from the intentional downward bias of our estimates of the true nominal subsidy rate. A second degree of protection is provided by the manner in which these estimates of the nominal subsidy rate will be used in subsequent analysis.

Specifically, in the analysis of the tax inequity and fiscal inefficiency associated with municipal bonds held by individual households (chapter 5), we assume a 30 percent nominal subsidy rate for these bonds. Since municipal bonds held by individual households probably have longer maturities than the average of outstanding municipal bonds, it is appropriate to use a subsidy rate for these bonds that is somewhat below the average nominal subsidy rate. However, since the evidence of this chapter indicates that 32 percent is probably a lower bound for the subsidy rate on long-term municipal bonds, we may be doubly confident that 30 percent is a downward-biased estimate of the subsidy rate for the municipal bonds held by individual households.

In the analysis of the tax inequity and fiscal inefficiency associated with institutional holdings of municipal bonds (chapter 6), we assume a 35 percent nominal subsidy rate for bonds held by banks and a 33 percent nominal subsidy rate for bonds held by other institutions. Since 35 percent is a lower-bound estimate of the average subsidy rate for all outstanding municipal bonds and since municipal bonds held by banks (and perhaps by other institutions) tend to be concentrated toward the short end of the maturity spectrum where nominal subsidy rates are significantly higher than this average, it follows that the assumed values of the nominal subsidy rates for the municipal bonds held by banks and other institutions are biased in a downward direction.

In the consideration of the effectiveness of the subsidy provided by the exemption relative to that which would be provided by a tax-able bond option (chapter 8), we assume that the nominal subsidy rate provided by the exemption is only 30 percent. Since the taxable bond option would affect primarily longer-term municipal borrowing, it is appropriate to use a nominal subsidy rate that is less than the average for all outstanding municipal bonds. Again, because 32 percent is a lower-bound estimate of the nominal subsidy rate for long-term municipal bonds, we may be quite confident that 30 percent is a downward-biased estimate of the nominal subsidy rate to use in calculating the relative effectiveness of the exemption in comparison with the taxable bond option.

The only circumstance in which the 35 percent estimate of the average nominal subsidy rate is used in an undiluted fashion is in the calculation of the total fiscal benefit provided to municipal governments by the exemption and the estimation of the overall fiscal efficiency ratio of the exemption (chapter 7). For the latter purpose, the exact value of the average nominal subsidy rate actually makes little difference. The estimated overall fiscal efficiency ratio of the exemption is little affected by using average nominal subsidy rates anywhere in the range of 30 to 40 percent.[30]

Finally, it should be noted that the theoretical explanation provided in this chapter for the observed term structure of the nominal subsidy rate has an important implication for the inequity issue. The basis of this implication is the common-sense presumption that, taking account of risk, yield, tax status, and all other relevant characteristics of different assets, the total benefit that an investor derives from the last dollar invested in any one asset must be the same as the total benefit from the last dollar invested in any other asset actually held by that investor. In other words, at the margin, an investor derives no special advantage from any one asset he holds relative to any other asset he holds. Since the individuals and institutions that hold tax-exempt municipal bonds also typically hold a variety of other assets, it follows that they gain no special advantage, at the margin, from municipal bonds relative to these other assets. In this sense, no inequity results from marginal holdings of municipal bonds by any investor. In subsequent discussion of the inequity issue, however, numerical estimates of the magnitude of the tax inequity generated by

---

[30] As will become apparent in chapter 7, the estimate of the average nominal subsidy rate affects the estimate of the total financial benefit of the exemption to municipal governments and also the estimated cost of the exemption to the federal government. The estimate of the difference between the cost of the exemption and its benefits to municipal governments, however, does not directly use the average nominal subsidy rate.

the exemption will be derived without regard to this principle. Rather, this principle will be held in reserve in order to provide added assurance that the numerical estimates of the tax inequity generated by the exemption are upward-biased estimates of the true magnitude of this inequity.

5

Individual Holders of Municipal Bonds: Tax Equity and Fiscal Efficiency

The case in favor of the taxable bond option relies heavily on the argument that the present exemption results in both fiscal inefficiency and tax inequity, as measured by the "windfall gain" accruing to holders of tax-exempt municipal bonds. This argument has its greatest logical force for the tax-exempt municipal bonds held directly by individual taxpayers. This is because there is little doubt about who ultimately benefits from the windfall gain associated with municipal bonds held directly by individuals; it accrues to the individuals who presently hold those bonds. In contrast, the determination of the ultimate beneficiaries of the windfall gain associated with municipal bonds held by banks, insurance companies, and other institutions requires a more complicated analysis of tax incidence and tax shifting. These complexities will be discussed in detail in the next chapter. For the present, we will focus attention on the arguments of fiscal inefficiency and tax inequity where they have their greatest logical force: for tax-exempt municipal bonds that are held directly by individuals.

The magnitude of the issues under consideration in this chapter is indicated by the standard estimate of the windfall gain accruing to individual holders of municipal bonds (W^H). For 1976, the standard estimate of this windfall is about \$1.1 billion. This estimate is based on the formula,

$$W^H = (\bar{t}^H - t^m) \cdot i^c \cdot M^H,$$

where $\bar{t}^H$ is the average marginal tax rate of households with municipal bonds, t^m is the implicit nominal tax rate paid by holders of municipal bonds (by accepting lower interest rates), i^c is the nominal yield on corporate bonds, and M^H is the value of municipal bonds held directly by individuals. For 1976, M^H was \$81 billion, i^c was 9 percent, and t^m (as measured by the proportionate yield differential between long-term corporate bonds and long-term municipal bonds of average quality) was 27 percent. If we use the frequently cited estimate of $\bar{t}^H = 42$ percent it follows that, in 1976, W^H was $1.1 billion.

In this chapter we advance arguments that demonstrate the inappropriateness of the standard estimates of both the fiscal inefficiency and the tax inequity associated with individual holdings of tax-exempt municipal bonds. We conclude that under the conditions most favorable for the standard analysis, namely, a zero inflation rate, the appropriate upper-bound estimate of fiscal inefficiency and tax inequity is not $1.1 billion but actually something less than $160 million. Moreover, we argue that as the inflation rate rises the appropriate upper-bound estimate of inefficiency and inequity declines. Indeed, at a 6 percent inflation rate, we conclude that the present tax exemption is fiscally *efficient*; that is, elimination of the exemption would increase the tax revenue of the Treasury by less than it would increase the borrowing costs of state and local governments. This result stands in sharp contrast to the standard estimate of fiscal inefficiency that shows a pronounced tendency to rise as the inflation rate rises.

To establish this general conclusion, we pursue two independent lines of analysis. First, we point out that the standard estimates are too high because they rely on nominal yields for corporate bonds, which reflect high anticipated rates of inflation. Under noninflationary conditions, the only conditions under which the standard analysis may be correctly applied, nominal yields on corporate bonds would be much lower than they have been in recent years. This fact alone would reduce the estimated windfall gain by a factor of one-half to one-third. Second, we argue that the usual estimates of the average marginal tax rate of individual holders of municipal bonds ($\bar{t}^H$) are too high because they fail to take adequate account of the shifting into alternative tax shelters that would take place if tax-exempt bonds were not available.

Inflation and the Bias of the Standard Estimate

The reasons for the upward bias of the standard estimate of tax inequity may be seen by comparing the formula for the standard measure of the windfall gain accruing to individual holders of tax-exempt municipal bonds,

$$W^H = (\bar{t}^H - t^m) \cdot i^c \cdot M^H,$$

with the correct formula,

$$W^{He} = (\bar{t}^{He} - t^{em}) \cdot r^c \cdot M^H,$$

where $\bar{t}^{He}$ is the effective real tax rate of households that have municipal bonds, t^{em} is the real implicit tax rate paid by holders of municipal bonds, r^c is the real yield on taxable bonds, and M^H is the value of municipal bonds held directly by individual households. It is apparent that two factors account for the difference between the standard measure of windfall gain (W^H) and the true measure (W^{He}): (1) divergences between the nominal yield on taxable bonds (i^c) and the real yield on such bonds (r^c); and (2) divergences between the nominal tax rate differential $(\bar{t}^H - t^m)$ and the real tax rate differential $(\bar{t}^{He} - t^{em})$. In this section, we focus on the first of these factors; that is, on the upward bias of the standard estimate of windfall gain that is induced by using nominal yields rather than real yields.

To indicate the extent of this upward bias, we first estimate what the windfall gain from individual holdings of municipal bonds would be at a zero inflation rate. This is a useful exercise for two reasons. First, the nominal tax rates $\bar{t}^H$ and t^m, if measured correctly, should equal the real tax rates $\bar{t}^{He}$ and t^{em} at a zero inflation rate. Since i^c will equal r^c at a zero inflation rate, it follows that the standard estimate of the windfall gain (W^H) should equal the true estimate (W^{He}) at a zero inflation rate. Second, evidence presented in chapter 3 and evidence presented later in this chapter establish that the real tax rate differential $(\bar{t}^{He} - t^{em})$ declines and ultimately becomes negative as the inflation rate rises. Since the real yield on taxable bonds (r^c) remains approximately constant, it follows that the true measure of windfall gain (W^{He}) falls as the inflation rate rises. Therefore, the standard estimate of the windfall gain (W^H) at a zero inflation rate is an upper-bound measure of the true windfall gain at all positive inflation rates.

The evidence in chapter 3 indicates that at a zero inflation rate the nominal and real yields on long-term taxable bonds probably would not exceed 3.3 percent. Assuming that the standard estimates of $\bar{t}^H = 42$ percent and $t^m = 27$ percent would apply under noninflationary conditions, it follows that at a zero inflation rate the standard estimate of the windfall gain accruing to households in 1976 would be $W^{He} = \$400$ million. This estimate is obtained by multiplying the difference between 42 percent and 27 percent by the amount of taxable income that would have been received on $81 billion of bonds with a nominal yield of 3.3 percent. This value for W^H is considerably less than the inflated estimate of $W^H = \$1.1$ billion that is derived using a nominal yield of 9 percent on taxable bonds. The standard estimate is inflated because the nominal yield of 9 percent that prevailed in 1976 consisted of an inflation premium of about 6 percent added to an underlying real yield of about 3 percent.

This example illustrates the magnitude of the upward bias that results simply from the use of nominal yields rather than real yields. The entire excess of the standard estimate of $W^H = \$1.1$ billion (based on a nominal yield on taxable bonds of 9 percent) over the correct estimate of $W^{He} = \$400$ million (based on a real yield on taxable bonds of 3.3 percent) is due to the upward bias induced by the use of nominal yields. The extent of this bias is indicated by the ratio of $1.1 billion to $400 million. Thus, solely because of the use of nominal yields that reflect the impact of inflation, the standard estimate of tax inequity and fiscal inefficiency is exaggerated by a factor of almost three.

The standard estimate of tax inequity and fiscal inefficiency is also exaggerated because the assumed differential between the nominal tax rates ($\bar{t}^H - t^m$) is greater than the differential between the real tax rates ($\bar{t}^{He} - t^{em}$) that are relevant for the true measure of the windfall gain. To establish this fact, we first examine the evidence that $\bar{t}^H$ (the effective marginal tax rate for households that hold municipal bonds) is substantially less than the standard estimate of 42 percent. Then we discuss how the difference between the real tax rates $\bar{t}^{He}$ and t^{em} varies with the rate of inflation and why the windfall gain accruing to households with municipal bonds is actually negative, even at moderate rates of inflation.

The Average Marginal Tax Rate: Evidence from Tax Returns

A precise estimate of the inequity resulting from individual holdings of municipal bonds depends on our having an appropriate value for the average marginal tax rate of individual holders of municipal bonds ($\bar{t}^H$). In this section, we use data from the tax returns of individual taxpayers to calculate an appropriate value for $\bar{t}^H$. We start with the maximum sensible estimate of $\bar{t}^H$, an estimate that is constructed on the assumption that present holders of municipal bonds shift to taxable bonds and pay tax on their additional taxable interest income at the marginal rates appropriate for their income class. We then adjust the estimate of $\bar{t}^H$ to take account of the features of the tax system that permit individual taxpayers to reduce their effective marginal tax rates to well below the official marginal tax rates.

Before proceeding to the numerical determination of $\bar{t}^H$, it is essential to determine the correct conceptual definition. Conceptually, $\bar{t}^H$ is the benchmark rate from which a measure of the inequity owing to exemption can be calculated. The key to this definition is that we wish to measure the inequity owing to the exemption, not to other provisions of the tax system. Thus, the appropriate value of $\bar{t}^H$ is the actual average marginal rate at which holders of municipals would pay taxes under the current federal tax system if not for the exemption. This rate is lower than the official tax rate on ordinary income because taxpayers may use tax shelters other than municipal bonds.

It might be argued that because the officially published tax rates indicate the rates at which individuals in different income classes ought to pay tax, $\bar{t}^H$ should be calculated using these officially published rates, and no correction should be made for the reduction in effective tax rates made possible by other provisions of the tax code. There are four reasons why this position is not tenable. First, much of the divergence between effective tax rates and official tax rates results from long-standing provisions of the Internal Revenue Code that have been repeatedly affirmed by congressional action. Therefore, it is arguable that effective tax rates provide a more appropriate measure than official tax rates of the general social consensus on the taxes that individuals in different income classes ought to pay. Second, if official tax rates were made fully effective through appropriate changes in tax laws and regulations, there would be a substantial increase in tax revenue. This increase in revenue would permit a significant overall reduction in tax rates. Unquestionably, the average marginal tax rate of holders of municipal bonds would be affected by this tax rate reduction. Third, if all tax shelters other than tax-exempt municipal bonds were eliminated, there would be a massive increase in the demand for these bonds. This would drive down the yield on municipal bonds relative to the yield on corporate bonds and, therefore, increase the implicit nominal tax rate paid by holders of municipal bonds. This increase in t^m would have to be taken account of in calculating the inequity resulting from individual holdings of municipal bonds. Fourth and most important, in examining the effects of the tax-exempt status of municipal bonds, the appropriate question to ask is the marginal question: What are the effects of the exemption, holding all other features of the tax system constant? Unless the question is posed in this way, we would incorrectly attribute to the exemption effects that are really due to other features of the tax system and would predict effects of larger magnitude from eliminating the exemption than would actually occur.

It follows that the appropriate value of $\bar{t}^H$ for the calculation of the inequity resulting from individual holdings of municipal bonds is the value that reflects the opportunities taxpayers have to reduce their effective marginal tax rates below their official marginal tax rates. To estimate this value of i^H, it is useful to start with an upper-bound estimate that assumes that individuals would not take advantage of opportunities for reducing tax payments. This upper-bound estimate is constructed on the assumption that if the exemption were eliminated present holders of municipal bonds would hold taxable bonds and pay tax on their interest income at the maximum marginal rates applicable on their present tax returns.[1] Two facts are essential to this calculation: knowledge of the distribution of individual holdings of municipal bonds by income class, and knowledge of the maximum marginal tax rates presently applicable to different income classes.

The *Survey of Financial Characteristics of Consumers* for 1962 provides the most recent published information on holdings of municipal bonds by individual households.[2] The percentage distribution of municipal bondholdings, by income class, is reported in column 1 of Table 27.[3] The latest published information on marginal tax rates for individuals in different income classes comes from the Internal Revenue Service's *Statistics of Income for 1973*. From the data reported therein, it is possible to infer the maximum marginal tax rate appropriate for different income classes (see column 2 of Table 27).[4]

The upper-bound estimate of the average marginal tax rate for all individual holders of municipal bonds is 54 percent. This is the figure reported at the end of column 2 of Table 27. This tax rate is obtained by taking a weighted average of the marginal tax rates in column 2, where the weights are the percentages of municipal bonds held by individuals in each income class, as indicated by the figures in column 1.

This estimate of $i^H = 54$ percent must be corrected for the fact

---

[1] Some present holders of tax-exempt municipal bonds would be forced into higher tax brackets if the exemption were eliminated. This effect is ignored in the discussion that follows.

[2] It would be desirable to have a more recent source of information on municipal bondholdings by individual households, but unfortunately no such source is available.

[3] To correct for the increase in income since 1962, the income levels of the 1962 survey have been multiplied by a factor of two.

[4] This inference was made in the following manner: Table 3.13 of the IRS *Statistics of Income* gives information on the number of returns in each adjusted gross income class that paid tax at each marginal rate. Starting at the maximum marginal rate of 70 percent and working down, it is possible to determine the number of returns in each adjusted gross income class for which the maximum tax rate was any given rate. The marginal tax rate for the adjusted gross income class is assumed to be a weighted average of the maximum marginal rates, where the weights are the fractions of returns in that class which have a given maximum marginal rate.

TABLE 27

Average Official and Effective Marginal Tax Rates
(percent)

Adjusted Gross Income Class	Percentage of Municipal Bonds Held by Individuals (1)	Official (Maximum) Marginal Tax Rate (2)	Effective Marginal Tax Rate (3)
$ 0–30,000	7	25	20
30–50,000	4	37	33
50–100,000	13	50	39
100–200,000	50	55	44
Over $200,000	26	63	46
Weighted average		54	42

Source: Column 1 is from Projector and Weiss (1966). Column 2 is from the Internal Revenue Service, *Statistics of Income: Individual Income Tax Returns, 1973* (October 1976), table 3.13. Column 3 is based on calculations described in the text.

that taxable bonds are not the best alternative to tax-exempt bonds. If prevented from holding tax-exempt bonds, households would not shift entirely to taxable bonds but would take advantage of all other opportunities for minimizing their tax payments. An estimate of the reduction in effective tax rates that taxpayers can achieve may be determined from the empirical relationship between adjusted gross income and income taxes paid, as reported in the *Statistics of Income*. Specifically, we can calculate the average tax rate for each income class by taking the ratio of total taxes paid by that class to its total adjusted gross income. This operation yields the schedule of effective average tax rates by income class. The estimated effective *marginal* tax rates are derived from the schedule of effective *average* tax rates. These marginal rates, for tax data from 1973, are reported in column 3 of Table 27. These effective marginal tax rates are well below the official marginal tax rates reported in column 2. As a result, the estimate of the average marginal tax rate for holders of municipal bonds is reduced from 54 percent (column 2), to 42 percent (column 3).

This estimate of $t^H = 42$ percent still possesses some upward bias. One reason for this bias is that true economic income is generally greater than reported adjusted gross income. The difference is due in part to underreporting of income for tax purposes. It is also due to the special way in which adjusted gross income is defined for tax purposes. In particular, adjusted gross income is defined to include only one-half of realized long-term capital gains. For the high-income individuals who are the predominant holders of municipal bonds, such capital gains form an important part of economic income. When the excluded half of long-term capital gains is added back into adjusted gross income, the estimate of $\bar{t}^H$ drops to 36 percent.

A number of previous studies indicate that even this estimate of the average effective marginal tax rate for municipal bondholders may be too high. Estimates of effective tax rates prepared for two Brookings Institution studies (Goode 1976 and Pechman 1977) indicate that, if account is taken of all sources of divergence between adjusted gross income and total economic income, the average effective tax rate for present holders of municipal bonds is probably no greater than 33 percent. The basis for this estimate is given in Tables 28 and 29.

TABLE 28

AVERAGE AND MARGINAL EFFECTIVE TAX RATES, BASED ON GOODE'S STUDY
(percent)

Income Class (thousands of dollars)	Average Effective Tax Rate	Marginal Effective Tax Rate for Adjacent Income Classes
10–15	10.3	
		17.7
15–20	12.4	
		20.5
20–25	14.2	
		22.2
25–50	17.4	
		33.0
50–100	25.2	
		36.2
100–150	29.6	
		31.7
150–200	30.2	
		30.6
200–500	30.4	
		31.0
500–1,000	30.7	
		31.8
Over 1,000	31.4	

SOURCE: Average effective tax rates from Goode (1976), table A-11, p. 309. Marginal effective tax rates are calculated from the average effective tax rates.

"Total income" is defined as the sum of adjusted gross income, the excluded portion of net realized capital gains, and other tax preference items as defined by the Tax Reform Act of 1969, such as excludable sick pay and moving expenses. The effective tax rates for each total income class indicate the fraction of total income that is paid in federal income tax. The effective tax rates in Table 28 differ slightly from those in Table 29 because the former are based on the tax code of 1973 and the latter are based on the tax code of 1976.

The effective tax rates reported in the Goode and Pechman studies are average tax rates rather than marginal tax rates. From the average effective tax rates in two adjacent income classes, however,

TABLE 29

AVERAGE AND MARGINAL EFFECTIVE TAX RATES, BASED ON
PECHMAN'S STUDY
(percent)

Income Class (thousands of dollars)	Average Effective Tax Rate	Marginal Effective Tax Rate for Adjacent Income Classes
10–15	8.9	
		17.0
15–20	11.2	
		20.2
20–25	13.2	
		21.5
25–50	16.5	
		35.0
50–75	23.9	
		37.9
75–100	27.9	
		36.6
100–150	30.5	
		36.5
150–200	32.2	
		33.2
200–500	32.7	
		29.9
500–1000	31.2	
		25.9
Over 1,000	27.9	

SOURCE: Average effective tax rates from Pechman (1977), table C-11, pp. 349–50. Marginal effective tax rates are calculated from the average effective tax rates.

it is possible to calculate the marginal effective tax rate linking the two classes.[5] The results of these calculations are also reported in Tables 28 and 29. The highest marginal effective tax rate is 37.9 percent. No other rate exceeds 37 percent. Indeed, for the highest income levels, marginal effective tax rates are lower than for moderately high income levels. The appropriate weighted averages of the marginal effective tax rates indicate that the estimate of $\hat{t}^H$ implied by the Goode study is only 31.5 percent and the estimate of $\hat{t}^H$ implied by the Pechman study is 33.3 percent. These estimates are slightly sensitive to the assumed distribution of municipal bond holdings by income class. However, there is no reasonable assumption about this distribution that would result in an estimate of $\hat{t}^H$ of greater than 33 percent for the Goode study or of greater than 35 percent for the Pechman study. These results strengthen the conclusion that the average marginal effective tax rate for households with municipal bonds is no greater than 36 percent.

Further support for this conclusion is provided by the U.S. Treasury in the very document that sets forth the justification for President Carter's proposal for a taxable bond option: *The President's 1978 Tax Program: Detailed Descriptions and Supporting Analyses of the Proposals.* Chart I-B-1 in this document shows Office of Tax Analysis estimates of effective individual tax rates as a percentage of expanded income. This chart is reproduced here as Figure 3. The effective tax rate is almost level at 30 percent for the two top income classes. This indicates that the marginal effective tax rate for these upper-income households that account for the bulk of individual holdings of municipal bonds is almost exactly 30 percent. Indeed, as was true of the marginal effective tax rates derived from the Goode and Pechman studies, the marginal effective tax rate linking the two highest income classes in the Treasury study (30.2 percent) is lower than the maximum marginal effective tax rate (34.6 percent). The appropriate weighted average of the marginal effective tax rates indicated by the Treasury study implies an estimate of $\hat{t}^H$ of less than 32 percent.

Further, it should be noted that the observed relationship be-

---

[5] These marginal tax rates are calculated as follows: First, it is assumed that the average level of income in each income class corresponds to the midpoint of the income class, with $2 million the average income for those with incomes of over $1 million. Second, the average amount of tax paid by the average individual in each class is estimated by multiplying the average effective tax rate by the average level of income for each class. Third, the marginal tax rate connecting two income classes is calculated by dividing the increase in total tax between the two classes by the difference between the average income levels of the two classes.

114

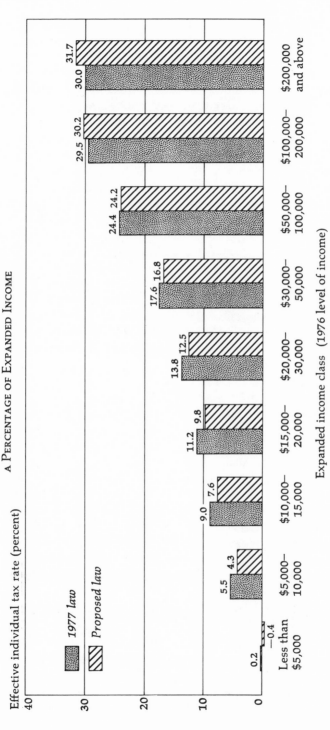

FIGURE 3

TAX REFORM PROGRAM: INDIVIDUAL TAXES AS
A PERCENTAGE OF EXPANDED INCOME

Effective individual tax rate (percent)

1977 law

Proposed law

Expanded income class (1976 level of income)

SOURCE: Department of the Treasury, *The President's 1978 Tax Program: Detailed Descriptions and Supporting Analyses of the Proposals,* January 30, 1978, chart I–B–1, p. 14.

115

tween income and taxes paid does not reflect complete freedom of taxpayers to choose the form in which they receive their income. Even high-income individuals receive a significant part of their income as "ordinary income" (wages and salaries, interest, rents, and dividends), which is difficult to shelter from income taxes. As a result, they pay higher taxes than they would pay if they could freely choose the form of their income. If the exemption were eliminated, however, holders of municipal bonds would have complete freedom to choose an alternative form of income (ordinary income, or capital gains, or consumption services from durable goods), and they would generally be able to achieve lower effective tax rates than those indicated by the empirical relationship between income and taxes paid.

When all of this evidence is put together, we may be confident that an estimate of $\bar{t}^H = 36$ percent slightly overstates the true value of the average marginal tax rate that would actually be paid by households that presently hold municipal bonds. Use of this estimate of $\bar{t}^H$ contributes a slight upward bias to the calculated value of the windfall gain (W^H) accruing to households with municipal bonds.

To complete the calculation of W^{He}, at a zero inflation rate, it is essential to determine an appropriate value for t^m, the nominal implicit tax rate paid on municipal bonds held directly by individual households. In 1976, the proportionate nominal yield differential between long-term taxable bonds and long-term tax-exempt bonds of average quality was 27 percent. The evidence in chapter 3 indicates that this yield differential was slightly higher than the corresponding yield differential in years with lower inflation rates. On the other hand, the evidence in chapter 4 indicates that the average proportionate yield differential between taxable and tax-exempt bonds of all maturities is at least 35 percent. Taking account of the fact that households probably hold a somewhat larger share of longer-term municipal bonds than do institutions, we can plausibly assume that the proportionate yield differential for the average maturity held by households is at least 30 percent. This figure is probably a downward-biased estimate of t^m, a factor contributing to an upward bias in the estimate of the windfall gain accruing to households with municipal bonds.

Using the estimate of $\bar{t}^H = 36$ percent and $t^m = 30$ percent, we may calculate that the value of W^{He} in 1976, under noninflationary conditions, would have been $160 million. This figure is derived by multiplying the difference between $\bar{t}^H = 36$ percent and $t^m = 30$ percent by the amount of taxable interest income that would have been earned on the $81 billion of municipal bonds held by households if these bonds had had a taxable nominal and real yield of 3.3 percent.

It should be emphasized that $160 million is probably an overestimate of the true windfall that would have been enjoyed by households with municipal bonds under noninflationary conditions. There are four reasons why this is so. First, the evidence presented in this chapter indicates that 36 percent is a slightly upward-biased estimate of the average marginal effective tax rate for households with municipal bonds. Second, the evidence in chapter 4 suggests that 30 percent may be too low an estimate for the implicit tax rate paid by municipal bondholders. Third, the theoretical argument developed in chapter 4 established that, at the margin, no investor enjoys any windfall gain from municipal bonds of any maturity relative to other assets he actually holds; the present estimate overstates the true windfall because it implicitly assumes that households in high tax brackets enjoy a windfall gain on their entire holdings of municipal bonds, not just on inframarginal holdings. Finally, as we shall show, the estimate of $W^H = \$160$ million is appropriate only for noninflationary conditions. As the inflation rate rises, the true measure of the windfall gain accruing to households with municipal bonds declines. Hence, the figure of $160 million is an upper-bound estimate of the tax inequity and fiscal inefficiency that results from individual holdings of tax-exempt municipal bonds at all positive inflation rates.

The Average Marginal Tax Rate: An Alternative Estimate

The estimate of $\bar{t}^H$ derived in the preceding section was based on information from the tax returns of individuals. An alternative estimate may be derived by first examining the assets into which present holders of municipal bonds would be likely to shift if the tax exemption were eliminated and then ascertaining the tax revenue likely to be collected from the income generated by these assets. This alternative estimate of $\bar{t}^H$ provides a check on the estimate derived in the preceding section and also provides a method for determining the effects of different rates of inflation on the value of $\bar{t}^H$. It is thus valuable for estimating the fiscal consequences of eliminating the exemption in an inflationary economy.

In order to construct the alternative estimate of $\bar{t}^H$, it is essential to know how the wealth presently invested in municipal bonds would be distributed among alternative assets if the tax exemption were eliminated. Unfortunately, direct evidence on the nature of these portfolio readjustments is not available. Thus, we shall assume that, if the tax exemption were eliminated, present holders of municipal bonds would distribute the wealth invested in these bonds to other assets in the fractions in which those other assets are presently held in their portfolios. The data in the *Survey of Financial Characteristics of Consumers* suggest the following distribution for wealth presently invested in municipal bonds: taxable bonds, 5 percent; common stocks, 60 percent; other equity assets, 25 percent; consumer durables, 10 percent.[6]

The next step in calculating the alternative estimate of i^H is to determine the amounts of income each of these alternative assets would yield and the amount of tax that would be paid on this income. For taxable bonds, nominal income per dollar of investment is given by the nominal yield, i^e. This nominal yield is assumed to equal the fixed real yield of 3.3 percent plus the rate of inflation, π. This nominal income is taxed as "ordinary income." Earlier analysis indicated that 54 percent is an *upper bound* estimate of the marginal effective tax rate on ordinary income for the average individual holder of municipal bonds. Given the opportunities for sheltering even ordinary income through underreporting or by purchasing discount bonds, convertible debentures, and other securities with some tax advantage, it is doubtful that the effective marginal tax rate on ordinary income exceeds 50 percent. Thus, taxes paid per dollar invested in taxable bonds would probably be no more than $\tau_b = (0.50) \cdot (0.033 + \pi)$.

For common stocks, the situation is somewhat more complicated. Common stocks yield dividends, which are taxable as ordinary income, and capital gains, which are subject to more favorable tax treatment. Evidence collected by Fisher and Lorie (1977) indicates that over the postwar period the real yield on common stocks has averaged 7.4 percent per year, with about half of this real yield made up of dividends. For the high-income individuals who hold municipal bonds, however, evidence from tax returns suggests that the reported dividend yield is only about 2 percent. This dividend yield is taxed at the rate appropriate for ordinary income, which is probably about 50 percent. Thus, taxes paid on the dividend yield per dollar invested in common stocks would be $\tau_d = (0.50) \cdot (0.02)$.

The rest of the yield on common stock accrues in the form of capital gains. The rate at which capital gains accrue is assumed to be the real capital gains rate of 5.4 percent (7.4 percent minus 2 percent),

---

[6] These percentages are approximations. Taxable bonds include all fixed interest assets—except municipal bonds—less all fixed interest debts. Common stocks include stocks that are held indirectly through interests in trusts and estates. Consumer durables include the value of the individual's home. Other equity assets are in a residual category that includes investment real estate and interests in businesses and partnerships.

plus the rate of inflation, π. The tax law provides that upon realization, long-term capital gains (in excess of $25,000 per taxpayer per year) are taxed at one-half of the rate applicable for ordinary income. In addition, the half of long-term capital gains that is excluded from adjusted gross income is treated as a tax preference item at a rate of 15 percent. Therefore, when account is taken of the fact that the levy on tax preferences does not apply to all holders of municipal bonds, 30 percent is a plausible upper-bound estimate of average tax rate on realized long-term capital gains.

Realized capital gains, however, are only a small fraction of the capital gains that accrue in any year. A recent study by David concludes that the ratio of realized to accrued gains has been only about 16 percent.[7] Presumably, this ratio will increase somewhat as a result of the 1976 tax law changes that eliminated the "step-up-in-basis-at-death." However, David's estimates indicate that, even under the assumption that all capital gains are realized at death for tax purposes, the ratio of realized to accrued capital gains would rise to only 34 percent.[8] Applying this ratio to the tax rate of 30 percent on realized capital gains implies an effective tax rate on accrued capital gains of only 10 percent.[9] Therefore, taxes paid on accrued capital gains per dollar invested in common stocks are estimated to be $\tau_g = (0.10)(0.054 + \pi)$.

Equity assets other than common stocks yield very little in the form of ordinary income; virtually all of the yield comes in the form of capital gains. In particular, depreciation allowances are generous

---

[7] See David (1968), chapter 4, especially pp. 93–103.

[8] David's results indicate that if the "step-up-in-basis-at-death" were eliminated the ratio of realized (reported) capital gains to accrued capital gains would rise from 16.0 percent to 33.7 percent. See, specifically, rows 7 and 8 of table 4-22 in David (1968).

[9] Because taxation on realization rather than accrual reduces the effective tax rate on income from common stocks, some tax reformers have suggested that some procedure for "constructive realization" of accrued capital gains be incorporated into the tax system. This would have the effect of moving the tax system closer to taxation on accrual rather than realization, thereby increasing the effective tax rate on common stocks. The effect of this "reform," however, would be to extend the double taxation of savings to savings held in the form of common stocks. Many economists who support the idea of an expenditure-based tax (rather than an income-based tax) argue that this double taxation of savings is undesirable. The implication of this argument is that the opportunities for tax deferral that are presently enjoyed on unrealized capital gains on common stocks should be extended to all sorts of income earned on assets. In recent years, Congress has moved further in this direction by permitting more generous and more elaborate retirement accounts. Taxes on all income earned on assets held in such accounts (including interest, dividends, and capital gains) are deferred until the assets are withdrawn.

to such a degree that high-income individuals who own rental property report virtually no rental income for tax purposes. If we assume that the yield on equity assets other than stocks is the same as that on stocks but that it all comes in the form of accrued capital gains, it follows that the taxes paid per dollar invested in these assets are given by $\tau_e = (0.10) \cdot (0.074 + \pi)$.

Finally, consumer durables yield most of their "income" in the form of consumption services that are not subject to tax. Occasionally, when consumer durables are resold, they yield taxable capital gains. However, the principal potential source of such gains is owner-occupied housing, and the tax treatment of capital gains on principal residences is so favorable that the effective tax rate on all income from consumer durables is effectively zero.

Given the above estimates, we may now calculate the taxes that would be paid per dollar presently invested in tax-exempt municipal bonds, τ. The value of τ is a weighted average of the taxes paid per dollar invested in the four assets, taxable bonds (τ_b), common stocks ($\tau_s = \tau_d + \tau_g$), other equity assets (τ_e), and consumer durables, where the weights are the fractions of wealth presently invested in municipal bonds that would be allocated to each of these assets. Thus, the formula for τ is:

$$
\begin{aligned}
\tau &= 0.05\,\tau_b + 0.60\,(\tau_d + \tau_g) + 0.25\,\tau_e + 0.10\,(0) \\
&= (0.05) \cdot [(0.5) \cdot (0.033 + \pi)] + (0.60) \cdot [(0.5)\,(0.02)] + \\
&\quad (0.60) \cdot [(0.1)\,(0.054 + \pi)] + (0.25) \cdot [(0.1)\,(0.074 + \pi)] \\
&= 0.012 + (0.11) \cdot \pi.
\end{aligned}
$$

This formula says that at a zero inflation rate, 1.2 cents would be paid each year on each dollar presently invested in municipal bonds. As the inflation rate rises, the amount of taxes collected would rise. In particular, at a 10 percent inflation rate taxes per dollar of investment would be 2.3 cents.

It should be noted that the formula that determines τ was derived on the assumption that the real yields on various assets (particularly common stocks and other equity assets) are not affected by changes in the expected rate of inflation. The recent performance of the stock market, however, suggests that the real yield on common stocks declines as the expected rate of inflation rises.[10] By failing to take account of this effect of higher expected inflation rates, the formula for τ overstates its true value at high expected inflation rates.

---

[10] This point was forcefully made by Lintner (1975). For empirical analyses of the relation between inflation and returns on common stocks, see Fama and Schwert (1977) and Nelson and Schwert (1977).

For this reason, there is an upward bias to the measures of the tax inequity and fiscal inefficiency that result from individual holdings of municipal bonds at high expected inflation rates.

Since τ is measured as a tax rate on wealth, it is not directly comparable to the tax rates $\bar{t}^H$, t^m, $\bar{t}^{He}$, and t^{em} that are measured as tax rates on income. In order to make the comparison, it is necessary to convert from units of wealth to units of income. To determine the correct conversion factor, it is important to keep in mind the purpose for which the conversion is being made. Ultimately, we wish to measure the tax inequity and fiscal inefficiency resulting from individual holdings of tax-exempt municipal bonds. To do so, we must compare the taxes that municipal bondholders would have paid on alternative assets that would have been held if tax-exempt municipal bonds were not available with the amount of the subsidy that municipal governments enjoyed from being able to issue tax-exempt bonds. In the absence of the subsidy, municipal governments would have borrowed by issuing taxable bonds. The real subsidy that municipal governments enjoy for each dollar of tax-exempt bonds they issued is equal to the real yield they would have had to pay on taxable bonds (r^c) multiplied by the real subsidy rate they enjoyed on tax-exempt bonds. This real subsidy rate is the same as the real implicit tax rate paid by municipal bondholders $[t^{em} = (r^c - r^m)/r^c]$, namely, the proportionate differential between the real yield on taxable bonds (r^c) and the real yield on tax-exempt municipal bonds (r^m). Therefore, the real subsidy enjoyed by municipal governments on each dollar of tax-exempt borrowing is $\sigma = t^{em} \cdot r^c = r^c - r^m$. The tax inequity and fiscal inefficiency resulting from each dollar of tax-exempt municipal bonds held by households are equal to the difference between τ and σ. We can express the total tax inequity and fiscal inefficiency resulting from the stock of municipal bonds held by households (M^H) as

$$W^{He} = (\tau - \sigma) \cdot M^H.$$

Alternatively, we may define $\bar{t}^{He} \equiv \tau/r^c$ and write the formula for W^{He} in the more standard form,

$$W^{He} = (\bar{t}^{He} - t^{em}) \cdot r^c \cdot M^H.$$

The interpretation of $\bar{t}^{He}$ in this formula is that it is the real effective tax rate that municipal bondholders would have paid on the income they would have earned on alternative assets, stated as a fraction of the real interest income they would have received on taxable bonds. The computation of $\bar{t}^{He}$ is based on the assumption that municipal bondholders would shift primarily into other assets with much lower effective tax rates than taxable bonds rather than shifting entirely into taxable bonds. Nevertheless, it is essential to measure $\bar{t}^{He}$ as the ratio of taxes that would be paid (on the assets that would actually be held) to income that would be received on taxable bonds because in the absence of the exemption municipal governments would issue taxable bonds. The implicit subsidy they receive on tax-exempt bonds, therefore, must be judged relative to what their borrowing costs would be if they issued taxable bonds.

At a zero inflation rate, τ is estimated to be 1.2 percent. The real yield on taxable bonds (r^e) is no more than about 3.3 percent. Hence, the implied value of $\bar{t}^{He}$ at a zero inflation rate is 36 percent, equal to the ratio of 1.2 percent to 3.3 percent. This estimate corresponds to the estimate of the average marginal effective tax rate of municipal bondholders ($\bar{t}^H$) derived in the previous section. Since the estimate of $\bar{t}^{He}$ has a somewhat different conceptual basis from the estimate of $\bar{t}^H$, it would be misleading to place too great an emphasis on the exact correspondence of these two tax rates. Nevertheless, the close correspondence between the two estimates strengthens the contention at the end of the previous section that the tax inequity and fiscal inefficiency resulting from individual holdings of tax-exempt municipal bonds with zero inflation is at most $160 million. This estimate also sets an upper bound on the true measure of tax inequity and fiscal inefficiency at positive inflation rates, an upper bound that is far less than the standard estimate of $1.1 billion.

Inequity and Fiscal Inefficiency at Positive Inflation Rates

It has been repeatedly stated in this chapter that the windfall gain accruing to individual holders of municipal bonds at a zero inflation rate is an upper-bound measure of the tax inequity resulting from the exemption. The main reason for this, as established in chapter 3, is that the real implicit tax rate on individually held municipals (t^{em}) rises as inflation rises. The correct measure of tax inequity resulting from individual holdings of municipal bonds is also affected by the way in which the effective real tax rate of these individuals ($\bar{t}^{He}$) varies with the rate of inflation. Given the results of the preceding section, we will now show that, as the inflation rate rises, t^{em} rises faster than $\bar{t}^{He}$. This implies that the correct measure of tax inequity declines as the inflation rate rises. Indeed, at rates of inflation of 4 to 6 percent (which seem likely to prevail over the next few years), we will show that the tax inequity correctly attributable to individual holdings of municipal bonds is *negative*! We will discuss the economic rationale for this seemingly paradoxical result and consider its implications for the question of the social benefit to be derived from the elimination of the exemption.

In the preceding section, we developed an expression for τ, the taxes that would be paid per dollar presently invested in tax-exempt municipal bonds if the exemption were eliminated: $\tau = 0.012 + (0.11)$ $\cdot \pi$. This formula indicates that as the inflation rate rises, the tax paid per dollar would also rise. This is because a higher inflation rate implies greater nominal capital gains on common stocks and other equity assets and a greater nominal yield on taxable bonds. The extent of this increase in tax revenue is indicated by column 1 of Table 30, which shows the values of τ for inflation rates between 0 and 6 percent. As previously explained, τ is measured as a tax rate on wealth, not as a tax rate on income. To convert from τ to $\bar{t}^{He}$, it is necessary to divide τ by the real yield on taxable bonds, $r^c = 3.3$ percent. The values of $\bar{t}^{He}$ thus computed, for inflation rates between 0 and 6 percent, are reported in column 2 of Table 30.

The analysis in chapter 3 established that the real effective tax rate implicitly paid by holders of tax-exempt municipal bonds (t^{em}) rises as the inflation rate rises. This fact is reflected in the values of t^{em} given in column 3 of Table 30. These values are calculated on the assumption that the implicit nominal tax rate paid by holders of tax-exempt municipal bonds, $t^m = (i^c - i^m)/i^c$, is constant at 30 percent,

TABLE 30

Estimates of Net Fiscal Gain from Elimination of the Exemption

Expected Inflation Rate (percent)	τ (1)	$\bar{t}^{He}$ (2)	t^{em} (3)	Net Fiscal Gain (millions of dollars) (4)
0	0.0120	0.36	0.30	160
1	0.0131	0.40	0.39	27
2	0.0142	0.43	0.48	−134
3	0.0153	0.46	0.57	−294
4	0.0164	0.50	0.66	−428
5	0.0175	0.53	0.76	−615
6	0.0186	0.56	0.85	−775

NOTE: τ = taxes paid per dollar presently invested in tax-exempt municipal bonds if the exemption were eliminated. $\bar{t}^{He}$ = average marginal tax rate of individuals holding municipal bonds. t^{em} = real effective tax rate implicitly paid by holders of municipal bonds. Calculations are described in the text.

independent of the inflation rate; and on the assumption that the real yield on taxable bonds is constant at $r^c = 3.3$ percent. Given these assumptions, the values of t^{em} are determined by the formula:

$$t^{em} = (i^c/r^c) \cdot t^m = [(0.033 + \pi)/(0.033)] \cdot (0.30).$$

We now have all of the essential ingredients for calculating the tax inequity resulting from individual holdings of tax-exempt municipal bonds,

$$W^{He} = (\bar{t}^H - t^{em}) \cdot r^c \cdot M^H.$$

The values of $\bar{t}^{He}$ and t^{em} are given by the entries in columns 2 and 3 of Table 30, respectively, and r^c is assumed to equal 3.3 percent. For the stock of municipal bonds held by individuals in 1976 ($M^H = \$81$ billion), the estimates of the windfall gain for inflation rates between 0 and 6 percent are given in column 4. Specifically, at a zero inflation rate, the windfall gain is estimated to be $160 million. (This is the upper-bound estimate of the windfall gain at all positive inflation rates that was discussed extensively in the preceding section.) At a 2 percent inflation rate, the windfall gain is already wiped out and the estimated windfall "gain" is actually negative. As the inflation rate rises, the estimated windfall gain becomes more negative, reaching a figure of minus $775 million at an inflation rate of 6 percent.

The finding of a negative windfall gain is a startling and counter-intuitive result that should not be accepted without careful scrutiny. In this regard, the crucial issue is not the precise value of the estimated windfall gain given in column 4 of Table 30. Plausible changes in the parameters that underlie these estimates could change the estimated windfall gain at a 6 percent inflation rate from minus $775 million to minus $500 million or minus $1.1 billion. But it is difficult to find plausible parameter changes that imply that the windfall gain is positive at an inflation rate of 6 percent, or even 4 percent. This means that under the inflationary conditions that are likely to prevail in the future, the tax inequity correctly attributable to individual holdings of tax-exempt municipal bonds is likely to be negative. It also means that the potential fiscal benefit from elimination of the exemption is likely to be negative; that is, the gain in tax revenue to the Treasury from elimination of the exemption is less than the increase in the borrowing costs of state and local governments.

These results appear paradoxical because they seem to violate the commonsense presumption that no one would presently hold tax-exempt municipal bonds unless he could thereby reduce his taxes by more than his loss of income from lower interest rates. This common-sense presumption, however, is directly relevant only to the choice between taxable bonds and tax-exempt bonds. These two types of bonds share the same basic economic characteristics, and the facts show that for present holders of municipal bonds the benefits of the exemption far outweigh the reduction in before-tax yield. This is demonstrated by the calculations that show the real effective rate of tax implicitly paid by holders of municipal bonds at an inflation rate of 6 percent to be $t^{em} = 85$ percent, while the real effective rate of tax they would pay on taxable bonds would be $t^{ec} = 141$ percent.[11]

The difference between t^{ec} and t^{em}, however, is not what is relevant for calculating the fiscal inefficiency and tax inequity resulting from the exemption. Present holders of municipal bonds would not shift any significant portion of their wealth into taxable bonds if the exemption were eliminated. Instead, they would increase primarily their holdings of common stocks and other equity assets. These assets do not share the same economic characteristics as taxable and tax-exempt bonds. The total yield on common stocks and other equity assets is greater than the yield on bonds, but this advantage is counterbalanced by greater risk and the disadvantage that investors in common stocks become locked into particular investments in order to avoid paying tax on accrued but unrealized capital gains.[12]

The disadvantages of the lock-in effect and of high risk explain how it is possible for the effective rate of tax on municipal bonds to exceed the effective tax rate on the portfolio of alternative assets. Effective tax rates are only one of the factors that affect the relative attractiveness of different assets. In equilibrium, the net advantage of holding various alternative assets must be equalized at the margin. If the disadvantages of the lock-in effect and of high risk are sufficiently strong, equilibrium will require that the implicit tax rate on municipal bonds exceed the tax rate on alternative investments.

The evidence indicates that at a zero inflation rate the equilibrium value of t^{em} is less than $\bar{t}^{H}$. As the inflation rate rises, however, the disadvantages associated with assets other than tax-exempt municipal

---

[11] The value of t^{ec} comes from Table 9. It is based on the assumption that holders of tax-exempt municipal bonds are, on average, in the 50 percent nominal tax bracket. The value of t^{em} comes from Table 11. It is based on the assumption that $t^{m} = 30$ percent, the nominal implicit tax rate for municipal bonds of longer maturity.

[12] In order to enjoy the tax advantages of equity assets, investors must hold them for substantial periods of time. This permits investors to build up unrealized capital gains that are not taxed until the asset is sold. The disadvantage of this procedure is that, once an investor has built up a substantial amount of unrealized capital gains, he cannot shift his wealth to other assets without paying tax on these gains. This is the "lock-in effect."

bonds increase. This effect is very strong for taxable bonds where the entire increase in nominal yield is taxed as ordinary income. For equity assets, inflation has a less severe effect because the increase in nominal yield is taxed as a capital gain. The disadvantage suffered by holders of equity assets, however, is greater than the amount indicated by the effective tax rate on long-term capital gains. To achieve this low tax rate, holders of equity assets must maintain a low ratio of realized to accrued capital gains, and hence they must avoid buying and selling stock as frequently as they might like. Therefore, to maintain the "equalizing difference" between municipal bonds and alternative investments as the inflation rate rises, the implicit effective tax rate on municipal bonds (t^{em}) must rise relative to the effective tax rate on alternative assets ($\bar{t}^{He}$).

It should be emphasized that the situation just described is not peculiar to the tax treatment of municipal bonds. It is precisely the situation that economists expect to arise whenever the tax rate on a heavily taxed activity is raised to a prohibitive level. The activity in question is the receipt of income from fixed interest securities. At a 6 percent inflation rate, the real effective tax rate on this activity for holders of long-term municipal bonds is about 85 percent. At this tax rate, a great deal of tax revenue is generated in the form of reduced borrowing costs for state and local governments. The elimination of the exemption would increase the real effective tax rate on fixed interest securities to 141 percent. At this effectively prohibitive tax rate, little tax revenue will be generated because present holders of municipal bonds will not shift to any significant extent into taxable bonds. Instead, they will shift primarily into equity assets where the effective tax rate is even lower than 85 percent. As a result of this shift, government tax revenues will decline and so, obviously, will tax payments. This reduction in tax payments, however, does not signify that taxpayers are better off. They suffer the inconvenience of shifting from their most preferred activity to a less preferred activity. The loss associated with this inconvenience is greater than the gain from lower tax payments.

The Economic Significance of the Windfall Gain

The fact that the estimated windfall gain to holders of tax-exempt municipal bonds is negative at rates of inflation of 4 to 6 percent raises the issue of what the estimated windfall gain really measures. By definition, the windfall gain accruing to individual holders of municipal bonds is equal to the additional tax revenue that the government would collect from these individuals if the exemption were eliminated. Therefore, the estimated windfall gain measures the potential fiscal benefit to the government (all units combined) from eliminating the exemption. It also measures the tax advantage presently accruing to holders of municipal bonds.

The windfall gain does not measure, however, the total advantage of the tax exemption to present holders of municipal bonds. This is because it focuses exclusively on taxes and neglects the real economic disadvantages associated with investments in equity assets. When account is taken of these economic disadvantages, the loss to holders of municipal bonds from elimination of the exemption necessarily exceeds the estimated windfall gain. Furthermore, the excess of the total loss to individual holders of municipal bonds over the estimated windfall gain indicates a deadweight social loss, since it measures a loss to individuals that is not counterbalanced by a gain in revenue to the government.

At a zero rate of inflation, the estimated windfall gain is $160 million. This means that all government units would enjoy a combined fiscal benefit of this amount as a result of elimination of the exemption. Present holders of municipal bonds will pay for this benefit and, in addition, will incur the inconvenience of shifting to alternative assets. The increase in tax payments by present holders of municipal bonds is a gain in tax equity and is appropriately regarded as a social benefit. But the additional inconvenience, which provides no revenue to the government, is a social loss. Therefore, the total social benefit from elimination of the exemption is smaller than the fiscal gain to the government.

At a 6 percent rate of inflation, the estimated windfall gain is minus $775 million. This estimate indicates that if the exemption were eliminated, all government units would suffer a combined fiscal loss of $775 million. Present holders of municipal bonds would reduce their tax payments by an equal amount. This reduction in tax payments does not imply, however, that holders of municipal bonds would gain from the elimination of the exemption. They could have enjoyed these tax benefits by shifting to alternative assets when the exemption was available. The fact that they choose not to do so indicates that the real economic disadvantages of these alternative assets outweigh their tax benefits. It follows that present holders of municipal bonds must lose as a result of elimination of the exemption; the real disadvantages suffered from shifting to alternative assets must be greater than the reduction in taxes measured by the negative windfall. Since the disadvantages suffered by holders of municipals in excess of their reduced tax burden are of no benefit to anyone, this constitutes a social deadweight loss.

When the inflation rate is high, the estimated windfall gain (W^{He}) declines and ultimately is negative. This implies that both the fiscal benefit to the government and the gain in tax equity from elimination of the exemption are negative. It is also the case that the cost imposed on holders of municipal bonds from elimination of the exemption rises as the inflation rate rises. Since the government derives no benefit from this imposed cost, the net social benefit derived from it is also negative.

Summary

In this chapter, we have examined the arguments of fiscal inefficiency and tax inequity as they relate to tax-exempt municipal bonds held directly by households. We have focused primarily on the effects of outright elimination of the exemption, rather than the more limited proposal of the taxable bond option. As explained in chapter 1, this procedure is useful because the gains in fiscal efficiency and tax equity that would be achieved by the taxable bond option are bounded above by what would be achieved by outright elimination of the exemption.

We showed, first, that the standard estimates of the tax inequity and fiscal inefficiency associated with individual holdings of municipal bonds are seriously biased in an upward direction. The source of this bias is the use of nominal yields in the standard estimate of the windfall gain to holders of municipal bonds, when the theoretically correct estimate should use real yields. Under current inflationary conditions, this error alone results in an upward bias of the standard estimates of tax inequity and fiscal inefficiency by a factor of almost three to one.

Second, the point was made that the theoretically correct estimate of the windfall gain at a zero rate of inflation provides an upper bound for the tax inequity and fiscal inefficiency resulting from individual holdings of municipal bonds at all positive inflation rates. The appropriate value for this upper-bound estimate depends on the real effective tax rate of present holders of municipal bonds. This tax rate should reflect all of the opportunities for tax avoidance that the present tax system provides, excluding tax-exempt municipal bonds. Evidence from a variety of sources indicates that 36 percent is an upper-bound estimate of this real effective tax rate, implying that the upper-bound figure for the tax inequity and fiscal inefficiency resulting from individual holdings of municipal bonds is $160 million, far less than the standard estimate of about $1.1 billion.

The third major point of this chapter concerned the effect of inflation on the true measure of tax inequity and fiscal inefficiency. As the inflation rate rises, this measure declines. At an inflation rate near 2 percent, the tax inequity and fiscal inefficiency attributable to individual holdings of tax-exempt municipal bonds reach zero. Above this break-even inflation rate, the gain in tax revenue to the federal Treasury from elimination of the exemption is less than the increase in borrowing costs to state and local governments. This net fiscal loss implies a *reduction* in tax equity from elimination of the exemption. Furthermore, though the net fiscal loss accrues as a tax reduction to present holders of municipal bonds, it is more than burned up by the costs these individuals suffer by shifting to alternative assets with lower effective tax rates but greater real economic disadvantages than municipal bonds. Thus, the fiscal loss to the government and the resulting reduction in tax equity actually understate the total cost to society of eliminating the exemption.

On the basis of the analysis offered in this chapter, we reach two general conclusions. First, though the standard arguments concerning the fiscal inefficiency and tax inequity resulting from individual holdings of tax-exempt municipal bonds are conceptually correct in a non-inflationary economy, the standard estimates of the magnitude of these defects are seriously overstated. The correct estimate is around $160 million rather than $1.1 billion. Second, under the inflationary conditions that are likely to prevail, the standard analysis is totally inappropriate. The correct analysis shows that the fiscal inefficiency and tax inequity resulting from individual holdings of municipal bonds will be negative. Elimination of the exemption would result in a net social loss rather than a net social gain.

6

Institutional Holders of Municipal Bonds: Efficiency and Equity

Financial institutions have for many years dominated the market for tax-exempt municipal bonds. In 1976 two-thirds of all municipals were held by such institutions. Among them, commercial banks were the most important, with 63 percent of all institutional holdings of municipal bonds. Fire and casualty insurance companies followed with 23 percent of institutional holdings, and the remaining 14 percent was distributed among life insurance companies, state and local government retirement funds, mutual savings banks, savings and loan associations, and brokers and dealers. Given the importance of institutional holders of municipal bonds, particularly commercial banks, it is apparent that a comprehensive analysis of the tax inequity and fiscal inefficiency arising out of tax-exempt municipal bonds should take careful account of the special characteristics of institutional holders of such bonds.

For understandable reasons, the dominant institutional holders of municipal bonds are taxable corporations, generally subject to a nominal marginal tax rate of 48 percent. In the standard analysis of the tax inequity and fiscal inefficiency resulting from the exemption, these corporations are treated the same way as individual holders of municipal bonds with nominal marginal tax rates of 48 percent. By holding municipal bonds, these corporations escape paying tax at this marginal rate and pay only at the implicit nominal tax rate on municipal bonds, equal to 27 percent in 1976.[1] The difference between

---

[1] This implicit tax rate is the proportional yield differential between long-term corporate bonds and long-term municipal bonds. The yield differential for short-term bonds was significantly greater. Since institutions are particularly important as holders of short-term municipals, the implicit tax rate paid by the institutions was actually significantly greater than 27 percent. The evidence supporting this point was examined in chapter 4.

the implicit tax these corporations do pay and the tax they "should" pay measures the "windfall gain" to institutional holders of tax-exempt municipal bonds and constitutes the standard estimate of the tax inequity and fiscal inefficiency resulting from these institutional holdings. For 1976, this standard estimate of the windfall gain accruing to taxable institutions as a result of the exemption was $3.2 billion; for commercial banks alone, the standard estimate of the windfall gain was $2.0 billion.

In this chapter, we will argue that this standard estimate is not correct for two fundamental reasons. First, and most important, unlike individuals, institutional holders of tax-exempt municipal bonds cannot be viewed as the ultimate beneficiaries of any windfall gain resulting from the present exemption. Instead, when we consider institutional holdings of municipal bonds, we must analyze the question of tax incidence; that is, we must determine who ultimately captures the windfall gains associated with institutional holdings of tax-exempt municipal bonds. We will argue that the ultimate beneficiaries of any windfall gains accruing on institutional holdings of municipal bonds are widely diffused throughout the population, with some slight concentration toward the lower end of the income distribution. Therefore, no clear-cut tax inequity results from institutional holdings of municipal bonds. Moreover, as we have previously argued, without the finding of tax inequity the argument of fiscal inefficiency loses much of its force.

Second, we will focus on the magnitude of the fiscal inefficiency resulting from institutional holdings of tax-exempt municipal bonds and show that the standard estimate of $3.2 billion significantly overstates the potential net gain to government units from elimination of the exemption. The standard estimate ignores both the tax revenue indirectly generated by institutional holdings of tax-exempt municipal bonds and the alternative tax avoidance opportunities available to institutional holders of municipal bonds. Taking account of these factors, we will conclude that the potential budgetary gain from elimination of the exemption is no more than $1 billion.

The General Question of Tax Incidence

The analysis of tax incidence is one of the most discussed subjects in the theory of public finance. It seeks to determine who ultimately bears the burden of any particular tax or captures the benefit of any particular subsidy. The analysis of tax incidence is particularly important in discussing the effects of taxes that are nominally levied on business enterprises and other institutions. This is so because no business enterprise *ultimately* bears the burden of any tax or captures the benefit of any subsidy. Ultimately, the incidence of any tax or subsidy must fall on some individual, who may be the owner of the enterprise, a customer of the enterprise, or someone who supplies a factor of production (such as labor).

The implicit assumption that appears to underlie the standard analysis of the tax inequity resulting from municipal bonds is that the windfall gain accruing on institutional holdings of tax-exempt bonds is captured by the people who own equity in these institutions. It is also implicitly assumed that the burden of the increased taxes generated by elimination of the exemption would fall on the owners of this equity.[2] A moment's reflection, however, reveals that these assumptions may not be valid. Consider, for example, a new tax on gasoline of ten cents per gallon, nominally levied on service stations' sales of gasoline. At least in part, this tax would be passed forward to gasoline purchasers in the form of higher prices. To some extent, it might also be passed backward to suppliers of gasoline and, ultimately, to owners of crude oil. It is clearly not the case, however, that this tax would be borne in any substantial measure by the owners of service stations. We shall argue that similar considerations apply in the case of the increase in taxes that would be collected from institutional holders of municipal bonds if the exemption were eliminated. The burden of these taxes would not fall on the owners of equity in these institutions but would be passed forward to customers (such as holders of bank loans) or passed backward to suppliers of inputs (such as bank depositors).

In considering the likely incidence of the taxes generated by elimination of the exemption, it is important to note that institutional holdings are predominantly held by two types of institutions, commercial banks and fire and casualty insurance companies. This concentration of municipal bondholdings implies that the subsidy inherent in the present exemption is not a general subsidy to a wide range of business enterprises but a specific subsidy to two particular industries.

---

[2] Most studies of the exemption and of the taxable bond option do not explicitly consider the question of tax incidence. They implicitly assume that taxable corporations are the ultimate taxpayers and that 48 percent is the rate at which corporations should pay tax. Break and Pechman (1975) do consider the question of tax incidence. They assume that the windfall benefits of institutional holdings of tax-exempt municipal bonds are distributed to the stockholders of such institutions. Specifically, they assume that the benefits are distributed among individuals in the same manner as dividend income. They do not, however, present any justification for this assumption.

Similarly, the tax resulting from elimination of the exemption would not be a general tax on a broad range of business enterprises but a tax directed specifically at two principal industries, commercial banking and fire and casualty insurance. Thus, the theory of tax incidence relevant to our present concerns is the theory of the incidence of taxes on specific industries rather than the theory of the incidence of general taxes on business profits.

Three general principles from the theory of tax incidence are of special relevance. First, a tax levied on a competitive industry producing under conditions of constant long-run marginal cost will be borne by the customers for that industry's output. As a result of the tax, the scale of the industry will contract somewhat, but the return per unit of equity capital will remain constant at the "normal rate of return," with input prices and output prices adjusting to "pay" for the tax. Minor divergences from the conditions of competition and constant long-run marginal cost lead to only minor divergences from the conclusions that customers bear the burden of any tax. Second, even in the case of monopoly, a tax will be borne partly by the customers and partly by the equity owners. Conversely, a subsidy will accrue partly to customers and partly to equity owners, but a subsidy will also lead to a more efficient level of production by inducing the monopolist to expand its scale of operation. Third, the incidence of a tax will fall generally more heavily on the owners of factors that are specific to the taxed industry and on consumers who lack good short-run substitutes for the taxed industry's output. Highly mobile factors and customers with good substitutes will not bear much of the burden of the tax.

The Incidence of a Tax on Commercial Banks

Commercial banks are the most important holders of tax-exempt municipal bonds. In order to analyze the tax inequity associated with these holdings, we must first infer something about tax incidence by examining the economic characteristics of the banking industry in the United States. On the basis of this evidence, we argue that customers of banks, rather than the owners of bank equity, capture most of the benefits of any tax windfall accruing on bank holdings of tax-exempt municipal bonds and would bear most of the long-run and short-run burden of the additional taxes collected as a result of elimination of the exemption. In the following section we argue that as a group bank customers are not especially advantaged by the tax system and that there would be no gain in tax equity from increasing the tax burden on this group through elimination of the exemption.

There are more than 14,000 commercial banks in the United States. These banks compete aggressively with each other and with the large number of other financial institutions that provide similar services. By every standard measure of industrial concentration, commercial banking is not an industry with heavy concentration in a few top firms. Although entry into the banking business is controlled by the official agencies that issue bank charters, it is relatively easily effectuated either by securing a new bank charter or by buying out the equity of an already existing bank. The lack of concentration and the freedom of entry suggest that the commercial banking industry satisfies many of the essential characteristics of a competitive industry.[3] Furthermore, the evidence shows that the return to equity capital invested in commercial banking is approximately equal to the normal return to equity capital of its risk class prevailing in the economy as a whole. Any attempt to tax specifically the return on equity capital in commercial banking is likely to result mainly in a displacement of equity capital from commercial banking and into more remunerative activities rather than in a reduction in the return to equity below its normal rate.

To see why, consider the special nature and function of the equity capital of commercial banks. In most industries, equity capital consists of plant and equipment that is specific to the production of that industry's output. For this reason, the owners of equity capital are likely to bear at least part of the short-run burden of any increase in taxes on the industry where their capital is employed.[4] The equity capital of commercial banks, however, does not primarily take the form of specialized plant and equipment. Only a small fraction of bank capital is accounted for by physical assets (such as bank premises), and many of these assets could easily be transferred to alternative uses (such as general office space). The bulk of bank capital is financial capital that performs the function of providing the margin of solvency for the bank. This margin of solvency permits a bank to absorb losses on its loans and on the value of its securities without

---

[3] For the purposes of the present discussion, it is not essential that commercial banking be a perfectly competitive industry. The question is whether it is sufficiently competitive that the standard analysis of tax incidence for a competitive industry is applicable. For a survey of the relevant literature, see Greenbaum (1967).

[4] In the long run, as capital owners have the opportunity to move their capital out of a taxed industry (through not reinvesting as capital depreciates), the main burden of increased taxation will be shifted to the customers for the industry's output or to other factors of production that lack substitute employment.

going bankrupt. If the return to equity capital in commercial banks were forced below the normal return for capital of its risk class, this capital could easily be shifted to alternative uses. For this reason, it is unlikely that the burden of increased taxation of commercial banks would be borne to any significant extent by the owners of bank equity.[5]

In order to pin down the incidence issue more precisely, let us examine the two principal markets in which banks sell their services. In the loan markets, where banks "sell" credit, they compete on a local, national, and international basis with other banks, with non-bank financial institutions, and with direct credit market instruments. There can be little doubt that these credit markets are highly competitive. In the deposit market, where banks "sell" deposits, competition is somewhat less extensive; only banks are legally permitted to sell the services of demand deposits. (Time deposits, however, can be issued by savings and loan associations, which compete vigorously with banks for these funds.) The deposit business of an individual bank is limited to a single state and, in some cases, to a single county or even a single branch. The interest rates that banks may pay to depositors are controlled by government regulation (Regulation Q). Nevertheless, there is substantial evidence that commercial banks do effectively compete for deposit business by offering services and gifts to depositors "free of charge."[6]

Not only is commercial banking reasonably competitive in its output markets; it also seems to produce its output under conditions approximating constant long-run marginal cost. There is some evidence that large banks are more efficient than small banks, but these scale economies are not enormous.[7] (Moreover, to the extent that there are any scale economies from overall expansion of the banking system, these scale economies reinforce our argument.) The essential point is that there are not decreasing returns to scale. Hence, if the scale of the commercial banking industry is forced to contract as a result of heavier effective taxation, there will be no significant reduction in the marginal cost of providing bank services. Under these con-

---

[5] This does not mean that the owners of bank equity will bear no burden, but most of the burden would be shifted, even in the short run, to bank customers.

[6] Klein (1974) finds that the hypothesis that bank customers derive in services the full value of forgone interest on their deposits is to be accepted over the hypothesis that they derive nothing.

[7] The presence of increasing returns to scale strengthens our argument. If there are scale economies, then, since the taxable bond option would reduce the size of the banking industry, it may result in a loss of economic efficiency.

ditions, the burden of increased taxation will fall on the consumers of bank services rather than on the equity owners of the banks.

It is worth emphasizing that this conclusion does not depend upon banking being a *perfectly* competitive industry. To the extent that the return to equity capital constitutes monopoly returns (because of the industry structure or regulation) rather than the normal return to capital and risk taking, some of the incidence would fall on the equity owners. Our case is simply that an examination of characteristics of the industry reveals a significant degree of competition, a relatively constant marginal cost of providing bank services, and conditions in which capital can flow easily into or out of the industry. Under these conditions, one can expect that an increase in the effective tax rate on municipal bonds would result mainly in an increase in charges on bank loans and a reduction in interest paid and services provided on bank deposits.

Elimination of the tax exemption or introduction of a taxable bond option with a high (40 to 50 percent) direct subsidy rate would significantly increase the effective tax rate on the profits of commercial banks. The standard estimate of the windfall gain from the exemption indicates that, if the exemption were eliminated, taxes paid by commercial banks in 1976 would have risen by $2 billion. This amounts to approximately 30 percent of the after-tax profits of commercial banks. This tax could easily be passed through to customers; for example, it would require an increase of only around one-fourth of 1 percent in the spread between loan rates and deposit rates to replace the $2 billion of bank profits lost through elimination of the exemption.

The general diagnosis of the consequences for commercial banks of the elimination of the exemption is supported by three pieces of factual evidence. The first is simply ordinary observation of the way in which prices respond to changes in economic circumstances. Consider rental housing. It is generally known that recent increases in property taxes and increases in heating costs created by the energy price hikes have not been absorbed by the owners of rental housing but have been passed through to tenants in the form of higher rents. Furthermore, rental housing is an industry in which capital is relatively specific to a given use for a long time. Therefore, this is an industry where one ought to see the short-run burden of increased taxes and increased operating expenses borne to a relatively greater extent by the owners of equity capital. The observation that a substantial amount of shifting onto customers occurs in the rental housing industry suggests that an even greater amount of such shifting is likely to occur in the commercial banking industry, where equity capital is very mobile.

The second piece of evidence comes from the data on bank income, expenses, and profits during the past twenty-five years, as reported in Table 31. Column 1 reports the ratio of bank operating income to total bank deposits. This ratio has risen over time primarily because of the increases in interest rates on bank loans and securities. Column 2 reports the ratio of bank operating expenses (including interest paid on deposits) to total bank deposits. This ratio has risen over time because the interest rates paid on deposits and the expenses incurred to provide services to depositors have risen. Column 3 reports the ratio of after-tax bank profits to bank operating income. This ratio has declined over time, indicating that the increase in bank income generated by high interest rates on loans and securities is not being captured in bank profits but, rather, is being transferred to depositors. Column 4 reports the ratio of after-tax bank profits to bank capital, a measure of the rate of return on bank capital. This ratio increases by about 2 percent in the years following 1968 because of a change in officially mandated accounting practices. Aside from this accounting change, the measure of the nominal rate of return to the owners of bank capital shows remarkable constancy. In the face of rising inflation rates, this constancy of the nominal rate of return implies that the real rate of return on bank capital was declining, a fact consistent with the observed decline in the real rate of return on the capital of nonfinancial corporations.[8]

The significance of the data in Table 31 is that they show that changes in economic conditions that affect bank income or cost are not borne by the owners of bank capital but are passed through to bank customers. The dramatic change faced by banks during the past twenty-five years has been the enormous increase in nominal market interest rates induced by higher anticipated rates of inflation. This increase has permitted banks to charge higher interest rates on their loans and hence to increase the amount of operating income per dollar of deposits (column 1). This increase in operating income, however, has not resulted in a great swelling either of bank profits as a fraction of income or of return to capital. The competition between banks, on the one hand, and among banks, other financial institutions, and the

---

[8] The relative constancy of accounting profits may reflect the well-known tendency of accounting procedures to understate fluctuations in true economic profits. Nevertheless, the basic story that is told by the figures in Table 31 remains intact. The increase in the general level of market interest rates has not led to a massive increase in the rate of return on bank equity capital.

TABLE 31

BANK INCOME, EXPENSES, AND PROFITS
(percent)

			Ratio of		
Year	Income to deposits (1)	Expenses to deposits (2)	After-tax profits to income (3)	After-tax profits to capital[a] (4)	After-tax profits to capital (Canadian banks) (5)
1952	2.9	1.8	20.1	7.9	6.4
1953	3.1	1.9	18.8	7.7	11.3
1954	3.2	2.0	22.7	9.2	15.5
1955	3.3	2.1	18.2	7.7	7.3
1956	3.7	2.3	16.9	7.6	9.3
1957	4.0	2.6	17.0	8.0	8.9
1958	4.0	2.6	20.0	9.3	8.5
1959	4.4	2.9	15.4	7.8	7.3
1960	4.7	3.0	18.7	9.7	8.3
1961	4.5	3.0	18.0	9.0	9.4
1962	4.7	3.3	16.4	8.4	7.5
1963	4.9	3.5	15.9	8.5	8.3
1964	4.9	3.6	15.2	8.3	7.5
1965	5.1	3.8	14.9	8.4	9.9
1966	5.5	4.1	13.7	8.5	8.0
1967	5.5	4.2	14.4	9.2	8.9
1968	5.9	4.5	13.4	9.3	7.1
1969	7.0	5.5	14.8	11.5	11.4
1970	7.2	5.7	14.3	11.6	11.9
1971	6.8	5.5	14.4	11.2	14.1
1972	6.5	5.4	14.0	10.8	17.0
1973	7.8	6.5	12.3	11.2	14.5
1974	9.2	7.9	10.4	11.2	12.6
1975	8.6	7.4	10.9	10.5	16.1

[a] This ratio increases by about 2 percent after 1968 because of a change in accounting practices.

SOURCE: Federal Deposit Insurance Corporation, *Bank Operating Statistics*, various issues; and the *Bank of Canada Review*, various issues.

direct credit markets on the other has induced banks to pass the increased income resulting from higher interest rates through to their customers in the form of higher interest rates on deposits or greater bank services, implying greater costs per dollar of deposit (column 2). These actions on the part of commercial banks were not compelled by the regulatory authorities, who set only the maximum interest rates that banks may pay on deposits. It seems probable that banks would act with at least equal alacrity to pass on to their customers the increased tax burden that would result from elimination of the tax exemption for interest on municipal bonds.

The third piece of evidence comes from the rate of return to capital of Canadian banks. This rate of return may be calculated, as it is for American banks, by taking the ratio of after-tax bank profits to bank capital (see column 5 of Table 31). During the last few years, the return to capital in Canadian banks has been higher than that in U.S. banks. This may be because of different accounting practices, a different economic structure of the banking industry, or differences in general economic conditions. The important point is that the higher rate of return to capital of Canadian banks is not dependent on their more extensive use of tax-exempt municipal bonds. Indeed, in Canada, the interest on bonds issued by local and provincial governments is not exempt from taxation. This suggests that the availability of tax-exempt bonds is not essential to maintaining the profitability of American banks because, as we have shown, the burden of increased taxes resulting from elimination of the exemption would be borne not by the owners of bank capital but by the customers of banks.

It would be misleading to assert that the evidence just cited is unassailable or that it conclusively proves that not even a small part of the tax burden resulting from elimination of the exemption would be borne by the owners of bank equity. The essential point of this section is simply that economic theory, common sense, and the available actual evidence all support the view that the bulk of this tax burden will fall on the customers of commercial banks.

The Equity of a Tax on Commercial Banks

Having identified the groups who will suffer the burden of an increase in the effective tax rate on bank profits—holders of bank deposits and bank loans—we can now discuss the implications of such a tax increase for the question of tax equity. As we have previously argued, this question of tax equity is of vital importance. Unless it can be shown that the increase in the effective tax rate on commercial banks resulting from elimination of the exemption (or from the taxable bond option) would improve tax equity, there is no strong reason for favoring this particular form of tax increase. It becomes simply one of the many ways in which additional tax revenue could be raised, and the raising of additional tax revenue, by itself, generates no social benefit.

Holders of demand deposits can be expected to bear an important part of the tax burden resulting from elimination of the exemption or from introduction of the taxable bond option. Virtually all business firms and households have demand deposits. Furthermore, there are no good alternatives to demand deposits as a means of payment for many transactions. For this reason, virtually all holders of demand deposits are likely to suffer some increase in the price they pay for the services of these deposits as a result of elimination of the exemption. For firms, the price increase is likely to take the form of an increase in compensating balances. For individuals, there is likely to be some increase in minimum balances or in service charges, or some reduction in the ancillary banking services that are "freely" provided to bank depositors.

For holders of demand deposits, therefore, the tax will operate like a very general sales tax, with essentially neutral implications for tax equity. In fact, the *Survey of Financial Characteristics of Consumers* indicates that demand deposits form a smaller fraction of the portfolios of high-income households than of low-income households. The relevant figures are given in column 1 of Table 32. These figures suggest that an increased tax on demand deposits is likely to be slightly regressive in its incidence.

Holders of time deposits must be divided into two classes: ordinary depositors and owners of large certificates of deposit (CDs).

TABLE 32

DISTRIBUTION OF HOLDINGS OF DEMAND DEPOSITS, BANK SAVINGS
ACCOUNTS, AND BANK DEBT AS A PERCENTAGE OF PORTFOLIO

Household Income in 1962	Demand Deposits (1)	Bank Savings Accounts (2)	Bank Debt (3)
Less than $3,000	6.8	20.4	21.0
$3,000–$5,000	3.5	14.3	34.0
$5,000–$7,500	5.6	14.1	83.3
$7,500–$10,000	3.9	11.2	69.9
$10,000–$15,000	4.5	13.9	59.2
$15,000–$25,000	4.6	9.8	35.1
$25,000–$50,000	3.6	4.9	20.1
$50,000–$100,000	3.7	4.1	8.2
$100,000 and over	2.6	1.1	7.4

SOURCE: Projector and Weiss (1966).

140

There is substantial evidence that owners of large CDs shift easily into alternative credit market instruments whenever the yield on their CDs falls below the yield on these alternative instruments.[9] Holders of ordinary time deposits also shift in response to yield differentials but to a significantly lesser extent. This suggests that it will be the holders of ordinary time deposits, rather than the owners of large CDs, who will bear the burden of the reduction in interest paid on deposits occasioned by elimination of the exemption.

For holders of ordinary time deposits, the potential regressivity of the incidence of effective tax burden resulting from elimination of the exemption is even more striking than for holders of demand deposits. The figures for the fraction of the portfolio invested in bank savings accounts, by income class, are reported in column 2 of Table 32. These figures show that time deposits are a far more important investment for low-income households than for high-income households. This suggests that low-income households will bear a disproportionate share of the increased tax burden falling on holders of bank time deposits.

With respect to holders of bank loans, it is difficult to come to any clear-cut conclusion concerning tax equity. The figures for bank debt as a fraction of the portfolio are given in column 3 of Table 32. These figures show a lower fraction of debt for households at the upper end of the income distribution, suggesting regressivity in the incidence of the tax burden on bank borrowers.[10] Most bank loans are made to businesses, however, not to households, and it is not clear who ultimately bears the burden of increased loan costs to businesses. Of course, not all bank customers would passively accept an increase in loan rates. Some loan customers could easily obtain credit from nonbank financial institutions or could borrow through the direct credit markets. By and large, these customers will tend to be big firms that are already well known in the credit markets. These loan customers will either continue to pay favorable interest rates or will shift their borrowing out of the banking system and into alternative credit markets. These customers will bear little of the burden of higher loan charges induced by elimination of the exemption. The customers who will bear the burden are those who lack good alternatives to

---

[9] This is the widely discussed phenomenon of "disintermediation." It occurs when the interest rates paid by banks and other financial intermediaries fall significantly below the interest rates on short-term, easily negotiable instruments that are traded on the direct credit markets.

[10] The figures are for total debt, not for debt owed to banks. This makes the inference drawn from these figures subject to some question.

bank credit: primarily lower-income individual borrowers and smaller businesses.

On the whole, therefore, we should expect no gain in tax equity resulting from the increase in taxes induced by elimination of the exemption or introduction of the taxable bond option. The bulk of the tax burden can be expected to fall on the customers of commercial banks rather than their equity owners. Further, among bank customers, those who will bear the greatest burden will be those who have the poorest alternatives to bank deposits and bank credit. These customers include virtually all holders of demand deposits, holders of ordinary time deposits, and the small businesses and individual borrowers who are dependent on bank credit. The available evidence indicates there is a slight concentration of these customers toward the lower end of the income distribution, implying that elimination of the exemption would be a slightly regressive form of taxation and hence would not increase tax equity.

The Fiscal Effect of a Tax on Commercial Banks

Without the argument of improved tax equity, the potential fiscal gain from increasing the effective tax rate on commercial banks has relatively little significance. For later discussion of the overall fiscal effects of elimination of the exemption or introduction of the taxable bond option, however, it is important to undertake a correct analysis of the "windfall gain" presently resulting from municipal bondholdings of commercial banks. In this section, we show that the standard analysis ignores three important factors in arriving at an estimate of this "windfall": (1) the tax revenues presently collected from the ultimate beneficiaries of the windfall gain; (2) opportunities for banks to reduce their effective tax rates below the nominal corporate tax rate of 48 percent on at least some of their assets; and (3) the fact that the implicit tax rate on many shorter-term municipals is significantly greater than the 27 percent nominal tax rate appropriate for longer-term bonds. Once these factors are properly accounted for, we will show that the correct estimate of the windfall gain is close to $480 million rather than the standard estimate of $2 billion.

The first problem with the standard estimate is that it neglects the tax revenue collected from the ultimate beneficiaries of the gain nominally accruing to commercial banks. These beneficiaries include recipients of bank loans who benefit from lower interest rates on their loans. Interest paid on bank loans is a deductible expense for both individuals and businesses. Hence, part of the interest saving is captured by the government, because income tax deductions for interest expense are smaller. The beneficiaries of the windfall also include holders of interest-bearing bank deposits who benefit from higher interest rates on their deposits. Interest income is taxable for both individuals and businesses. Hence, part of the benefit of higher interest rates paid on bank deposits is captured by the government in higher taxes.

It is difficult to determine precisely the marginal tax rate at which the government effectively collects tax from the ultimate beneficiaries of the windfall accruing on commercial bank holdings of municipal bonds. For businesses, this tax rate is probably somewhat below the nominal corporate tax rate of 48 percent. For individual borrowers and holders of bank deposits, the marginal tax rate may be under 30 percent. All things considered, an estimate of 25 percent is probably not too high. This estimate implies that only 75 percent of the windfall gain that normally accrues on commercial bank holdings of municipal bonds is actually captured by the ultimate beneficiaries of this windfall. The rest is collected as tax revenue by the government. For this reason, the standard estimate of the windfall must be written down from $2 billion to no more than $1.5 billion.

The second problem with the standard estimate is that it assumes that the marginal tax rate for commercial banks is the corporate tax rate of 48 percent. There is substantial evidence that the effective tax rate for commercial banks is significantly below 48 percent. Direct analysis of the tax avoidance opportunities open to banks, undertaken in previous studies, has indicated that commercial banks do have important tax avoidance opportunities other than municipal bonds.[11] Additional evidence on this issue comes from the accounting data of commercial banks collected by the Federal Deposit Insurance Corporation. The relevant data for the years 1969 through 1974 are presented in Table 33. Column 1 reports the total operating income of commercial banks, before tax. Column 2 reports income from interest on municipal bonds. Column 3 reports income from sources other than municipal bonds, calculated by subtracting column 2 from column 1. Column 4 reports the provision for federal income taxes made by insured commercial banks. Column 5 gives the ratios of the entries in column 4 to the entries in column 3. The entries in column 5 are consequently a measure of the average effective tax rate on that part of bank profits that is not shielded from federal taxation through hold-

---

[11] For a discussion of the tax avoidance opportunities of commercial banks, see Bedford (1975) and Kimball (1977).

TABLE 33

COMMERCIAL BANK INCOME AND FEDERAL TAXES PAID
(millions of dollars)

Year	Operating Income before Tax (1)	Income from Municipal Bonds (2)	Income from Sources Other than Municipal Bonds (1)−(2) (3)	Provision for Federal Income Taxes (4)	Average Effective Tax Rate on Income in Column 3 (4)÷(3) (5)
1969	6,728	2,215	4,513	1,288	0.29
1970	7,126	2,620	4,506	1,620	0.36
1971	6,713	3,127	3,586	1,367	0.38
1972	7,251	3,494	3,757	1,289	0.34
1973	8,707	3,865	4,842	1,336	0.28
1974	9,251	4,454	4,797	1,357	0.28

SOURCE: Federal Deposit Insurance Corporation, *Bank Operating Statistics*, various issues.

ings of municipal bonds. The average of these estimated tax rates is 32 percent.

This average is probably too low an estimate for the marginal effective tax rate facing commercial banks. One reason is that the total provision for income taxes (federal, state, and local) is generally about 10 percent less than total income taxes actually paid.[12] Assuming that the ratio of provisions for income taxes to taxes actually paid is the same for federal and for state and local taxes, the estimate of the average effective tax rate for commercial banks rises from 32 to 35 percent. Further, this is an estimate of the average effective tax rate, not the marginal effective tax rate. This average effective tax rate reflects the optimal use of all of the tax avoidance opportunities available to commercial banks. Since many of these tax avoidance opportunities (such as reserve funds for loan losses) have quantitative limits or are not easily expandable at the margin, the marginal effective tax rate for commercial banks undoubtedly exceeds the average

---

[12] The FDIC reports "total applicable income taxes" as well as "provision for federal income taxes" and "provision for state and local income taxes." Total applicable income taxes average about 10 percent higher than total provisions for income taxes, but total applicable income taxes are not broken down into federal as distinct from state and local.

144

effective tax rate. This fact is of special importance in evaluating the fiscal effects of elimination of the exemption. Since tax-exempt municipal bonds are the most important tax shelter used by commercial banks, elimination of this shelter would require banks to make increasing use of less desirable alternative shelters, thereby forcing up the effective tax rate paid by commercial banks. With elimination of the exemption, the marginal effective tax rate would probably reach the nominal corporate tax rate of 48 percent.

The appropriate tax rate to use in calculating the windfall gain presently accruing to commercial banks from their holdings of tax-exempt municipal bonds lies somewhere between this maximum marginal effective tax rate of 48 percent and the present marginal effective tax rate of perhaps 36 percent. A reasonable middle-ground estimate of this average marginal effective tax rate for commercial banks is 42 percent. Using this figure rather than the 48 percent tax rate employed in the standard estimate and taking account of the taxes already being paid by the ultimate beneficiaries of the windfall enjoyed by banks reduces the estimated windfall from $2 billion to $1.1 billion.

The third problem with the standard estimate is that it is based on the erroneous assumption that the implicit rate presently paid on such bonds is equal to the 27 percent proportionate yield differential between long-term corporate bonds and long-term municipal bonds that prevailed in 1976. In 1976 the municipal bond market was still feeling the effects of the New York City financial crisis. For this reason, the yield differential was unusually small relative to the standard of the entire 1967–76 decade. A better estimate for the normal long-term yield differential is 30 percent. More important, the yield differential for shorter-term bonds is significantly greater than the yield differential for long-term bonds. The evidence presented in chapter 4 indicates that the average proportionate yield differential for bonds of all maturities is at least 35 percent.[13]

This 35 percent estimate of the implicit tax rate must be compared with the average marginal effective tax rate of commercial banks to produce a revised estimate of the windfall gain. The difference between the two tax rates is now only 7 percent (42 percent minus 35

---

[13] The evidence presented in chapter 4 indicates that 35 percent is probably a lower-bound estimate of the average proportionate nominal yield differential for all municipal bonds. Evidence presented in chapter 4 also indicates that commercial banks invest more heavily in shorter-term municipal bonds than do other investors. Since the proportionate yield differential between municipal bonds and corporate bonds is greatest for short-term bonds, it is likely that the proportionate yield differential for those municipal bonds that are held by commercial banks is greater than 35 percent.

percent). This difference must be multiplied by the amount of taxable interest income that commercial banks would have earned on the $102 billion invested in municipal bonds in 1976. This yields an estimated windfall gain associated with commercial bank holdings of municipal bonds of $640 million. Taking account of the taxes paid by the ultimate beneficiaries of this windfall, the estimate must be reduced by one-quarter, yielding a final estimate of the windfall gain associated with commercial bank holdings of municipal bonds of only $480 million rather than $2 billion.

Further, the analysis developed in chapter 4 suggests that $480 million is probably a significant overestimate of the windfall gain associated with commercial bank holdings of municipal bonds. In that chapter, it was noted that the proportionate yield differential between high-grade, short-term taxable instruments and high-grade, short-term tax-exempt instruments was very close to the corporate tax rate of 48 percent. This is to be expected because the only significant differences between these two classes of instruments are tax status and yield. The yield differential is, therefore, the "equalizing difference" that exactly balances the tax advantage of high-grade, short-term tax-exempt instruments for the predominant holder of such instruments, commercial banks. It follows, therefore, that there is no windfall gain to commercial banks from holding such bonds.

It appears that commercial banks would enjoy a windfall gain if they held longer-term municipal bonds. This is so because the proportionate yield differential between longer-term municipal bonds and longer-term corporate bonds is only about 30 percent, significantly less than the corporate tax rate of 48 percent. But commercial banks hold virtually no long-term corporate bonds.[14] Therefore, it is inappropriate to measure the special advantage to banks from long-term municipal bonds by comparing the proportionate yield differential between long-term corporate bonds and long-term municipal bonds with the corporate tax rate. All that can legitimately be said is that yield advantage in favor of longer-term corporate bonds is *less* than the equalizing differential that would induce banks to hold long-term

---

[14] Long-term corporate bonds accounted for less than 1 percent of total commercial bank assets in 1976. Taking account of the fact that some of these holdings may have been of deep discount bonds (which benefit from some advantages of capital gains taxation) and that other bonds may have been held as speculative investment (in anticipation of a reduction in the general level of interest rates), it is reasonable to conclude that commercial banks held virtually no long-term corporate bonds for general investment purposes. In contrast, longer-term municipal bonds constituted about 9 percent of commercial bank assets.

taxable bonds as well as long-term tax-exempt bonds. Indeed, this evidence is consistent with the general theoretical presumption that at the margin commercial banks derive no special advantage from municipal bonds relative to any other asset they actually choose to hold. This suggests that the estimated windfall gain of $480 million overstates the special advantage derived from commercial bank holdings of municipal bonds.

Nonbank Holdings of Municipal Bonds

So far, the discussion in this chapter has focused on commercial banks as the dominant institutional holder of municipal bonds. This emphasis is justified because commercial banks account for 63 percent of all institutional holdings of municipal bonds and because the analysis for commercial banks carries over to the other important institutional holder of municipal bonds, fire and casualty insurance companies, which accounted for 23 percent of institutional holdings of municipal bonds in 1976.

Fire and casualty insurance companies share all the essential economic characteristics of commercial banks: the industry is competitive; the number of companies is large; and entry is relatively easy. Since the industry uses no highly specialized factors of production that have a rising supply price to the industry as a whole, there is good reason to believe that the long-run marginal cost of providing fire and casualty insurance is constant or declining. The equity capital of these insurance companies plays a role similar to that of the equity capital of commercial banks; it provides the ultimate contingency reserve to absorb extraordinary underwriting losses. This equity capital is largely financial capital that could easily be shifted to alternative employments in the face of any decline in its expected rate of return in the insurance business.

Elimination of the exemption or introduction of the taxable bond option with a high subsidy rate would increase the effective tax rate on fire and casualty insurance companies. The standard estimate of the windfall gain that would be captured as a result of elimination of the exemption is $720 million. The economic characteristics of the industry, however, imply that the burden of this increase in taxes would not be borne to any substantial extent by the owners of equity capital in fire and casualty companies, even in the short run. Rather, it is the policyholders who would ultimately bear the burden through increases in their premiums.

It is well known that insurance rates differ widely among classes of policyholders, across states, and even within metropolitan areas. These differences reflect differences in the cost of writing insurance. In particular, if teenage boys have a greater risk of auto accidents than married men, and if personal injury awards in auto accident cases are higher in California than in Iowa, then personal liability coverage for teenage boys in California will be more expensive than the same coverage for married men in Iowa. Further, if something happens that changes the expected cost of writing a certain type of policy, such as an increase in personal injury awards or an increase in hospital costs, the consequences of this change are promptly passed along to policyholders through changes in premiums. If insurance rates are controlled, adjustment is achieved by refusing to write policies that are expected to be unprofitable. Thus, the owners of equity capital who put their capital at risk earn the normal rate of return for the risk they bear. This normal return is enforced by the operation of the economic system, through the freedom of movement of equity capital into and out of the insurance industry.

It is clear that the benefits of lower premiums on fire and casualty insurance are very broadly distributed among different income classes. For this reason, it is difficult to argue that there is any significant tax inequity resulting from the windfall gain on holdings of municipal bonds by fire and casualty insurance companies, or that there would be any gain in tax equity by increasing the effective tax rate on holders of fire and casualty policies.

As with commercial banks, it should be recognized that the standard estimate of the potential gain in tax revenue from fire and casualty insurance companies, $720 million, is too high. The effective marginal tax rate for fire and casualty insurance companies (like that for commercial banks) is lower than the nominal corporate tax rate of 48 percent. Evidence concerning the tax reduction opportunities available to fire and casualty insurance companies may be obtained from the reports that these companies submit to various state insurance agencies. The annual reports of the New York State superintendent of insurance are especially useful. Table 34 reports the data from the 1971 annual report on the financial condition and operation of the ten largest fire and casualty insurance companies. These data show that these companies do not pay large fractions of their net income as federal income tax. The largest proportion of income paid in federal income tax is the 20 percent reported by the Hartford Fire Insurance Company. This proportion, however, reflects the extraordinary capital gains this company realized in 1970 (probably associated with its merger with ITT). In 1969, federal income taxes incurred by the

Hartford Fire Insurance Company were only 2 percent of reported net income. Similarly, while the Continental Insurance Company incurred federal income taxes equal to 16 percent of net income in 1970, in 1969 it incurred federal income taxes of less than 3 percent of net income.

Taking account of the operations of subsidiaries, all ten of the largest fire and casualty insurance companies made extensive use of tax-exempt municipal bonds in order to reduce the size of the federal income tax payments. It is apparent, however, that this was not the only tax reduction opportunity utilized by these companies. All ten also held extensive amounts of common and preferred stock. These stock holdings confer a substantial tax benefit because long-term capi-

TABLE 34

FINANCIAL DATA FROM TEN LARGE FIRE AND CASUALTY INSURANCE COMPANIES FOR 1970

(millions of dollars)

Company	U.S. Government Obligations	Tax-Exempt Bonds	Corporate Bonds	Stocks	Net Income	Federal Income Tax
State Farm Mutual Auto	316	1,007	147	314	81.6	2.6
Allstate	21	1,129	69	832	64.7	2.2
Continental Insurance	30	67	79	802	70.9	11.2
Travelers Indemnity	26	658	234	164	− 23.3	0.0
Aetna Casualty & Surety	28	573	429	403	104.7	0.0
Hartford Fire Insurance	14	90	70	640	96.1	18.9
Hartford Accident & Indemnity[a]	32	556	181	348	− 13.4	− 13.5
Liberty Mutual	132	554	463	136	− 45.5	0.0
Insurance Company of North America	95	352	171	790	55.8	0.5
Continental Casualty	47	266	101	366	35.5	1.2
Fireman's Fund	20	200	83	486	27.6	2.3

[a] The Hartford Accident and Indemnity Co. is a subsidiary of the Hartford Fire Insurance Co.

SOURCE: *New York Insurance Report*, 1971, all assets valued at market prices, figures rounded to the nearest million.

tal gains are taxed at a lower rate than ordinary corporate income and, more importantly, because taxation can be deferred until gains are realized. Moreover, because of the 85 percent deduction for dividends received from another corporation, the effective tax rate on such dividends is only 7.2 percent (0.48×0.15).

Because fire and casualty insurance companies can and do make extensive use of the tax reduction opportunities afforded by stocks, an opportunity not open to commercial banks, it is reasonable to suppose that their effective marginal tax rate is at most the 42 percent effective marginal tax rate assumed for commercial banks. Further, since the average nominal subsidy rate on municipal bonds has been estimated to be at least 35 percent, it is plausible to assume that the nominal subsidy rate for municipal bonds held by fire and casualty insurance companies is at least 33 percent.[15] The reduction in the estimate of the effective marginal tax rate for fire and casualty insurance companies (from 48 percent to 42 percent) and the increase in the estimated implicit tax rate on the municipal bonds held by these companies (from 30 percent to 33 percent) imply that the estimate of the windfall gain associated with the municipal bonds held by these companies must be reduced from $720 million to no more than $310 million. This is still an overestimate of the true windfall because it neglects not only the increased tax deductions that businesses would be able to take in the face of increased insurance costs but also the theoretical presumption that fire and casualty insurance companies gain no special advantage, at the margin, from holding tax-exempt municipal bonds relative to any other asset they choose to hold.

Commercial banks and nonlife insurance companies together accounted for 86.3 percent of institutional holdings of municipal bonds in 1976. The remaining 13.7 percent was distributed as follows: life insurance companies, 3.0 percent; state and local government general funds, 3.7 percent; state and local government retirement funds, 2.4 percent; other corporations, 2.0 percent; mutual savings banks, 1.4 percent; savings and loan associations, 0.7 percent; and brokers and

---

[15] In chapter 4 it was established that 35 percent is probably a lower-bound estimate of the proportionate nominal yield differential for municipal bonds of average maturity. The fact that very short-term municipal bonds are held preponderantly by commercial banks suggests that the differential applicable for bonds held by fire and casualty insurance companies may be somewhat less than the average differential. Since a 35 percent differential has been assumed for the municipal bonds held by commercial banks and a 30 percent differential has been assumed for the municipal bonds held by individuals, it follows that the assumption of a 33 percent differential for the municipal bonds held by nonbank institutions preserves an upward bias for the total estimated fiscal inefficiency resulting from municipal bonds.

dealers, 0.5 percent. The 6.1 percent held by state and local government general and retirement funds clearly gives rise to no tax inequity or fiscal inefficiency. This leaves the 7.6 percent held by life insurance companies, mutual savings banks, savings and loan associations, brokers and dealers, and other corporations. The same considerations relevant for commercial banks and nonlife insurance companies are also relevant for these holdings of municipal bonds. In particular, to the extent that there is any windfall gain associated with these holdings, it is captured primarily by the customers of these institutions, who are widely spread throughout the population. For this reason, it is difficult to argue that any tax inequity results from these holdings. Further, the effective marginal tax rates for these institutions are generally lower than the effective marginal tax rates for commercial banks and nonlife insurance companies. Therefore, the potential gain in tax revenue from increasing the effective tax rate on the customers of these institutions through elimination of the exemption is probably no greater than $85 million.[16]

Fiscal Inefficiency and Inflation

An estimate of the total fiscal inefficiency resulting from institutional holdings of municipal bonds may be obtained by adding together the estimates for the specific classes of institutions. The total estimated fiscal inefficiency is $875 million—$480 million from commercial banks, $310 million from fire and casualty insurance companies, and $85 million from other institutions. This estimate is far less than the standard estimate of $3.2 billion because it takes account of three essential facts that are neglected in the standard estimates: (1) The proportionate nominal yield differential between taxable bonds and tax-exempt bonds of the average maturities held by institutions is greater than the proportionate yield differential for long-term bonds that is used in the standard estimate. (2) The effective marginal tax rate for institutional holders of municipal bonds is generally somewhat less than the official marginal tax rate of 48 percent. (3) Some of the purported windfall associated with institutional holdings of municipal bonds accrues as taxable income to the ultimate beneficiaries of this windfall, and taxes are presently collected on this income.

Further, it should be emphasized that $875 million is probably

---

[16] This figure is derived by taking the ratio of municipal bonds held by these institutions to municipal bonds held by fire and casualty companies, and then multiplying by the estimated $310 million of windfall gain associated with tax-exempt muncipal bonds held by fire and casualty companies.

an overestimate of the fiscal inefficiency associated with institutional holdings of municipal bonds. In constructing this estimate, it was assumed that the average proportionate yield differential between taxable and tax-exempt bonds is 35 percent for the maturities held by commercial banks and 33 percent for the maturities held by other institutions. The evidence in chapter 4 indicates that 35 percent is a lower-bound estimate of the proportionate yield differential for municipal bonds of average maturity and that institutions (particularly commercial banks) hold bonds which have greater than average yield differential. Moreover, the theory of equalizing differences discussed in chapter 4 implies that, at the margin, institutions derive no special advantage from holding municipal bonds relative to the other assets they choose to hold. It follows that the spread between the effective tax rate of an institution and the proportionate yield differential between taxable and tax-exempt bonds overestimates the advantage that institutions derive from the average dollar invested in municipal bonds.

The estimated fiscal inefficiency resulting from institutional holdings of municipal bonds of $875 million reflects the conditions that prevailed in 1976, in particular the volume of municipal bonds held by various institutions and the nominal yield of 9 percent on taxable bonds. The analysis in chapter 3 established that this nominal yield of 9 percent consisted of an underlying real yield of about 3 percent and an expected rate of price inflation of about 6 percent. Different expectations about the future inflation rate would have implied different values of the nominal interest rate and, hence, different estimates of the fiscal inefficiency associated with institutional holdings of municipal bonds.

The effect of different expected inflation rates on the estimated fiscal inefficiency associated with institutional holdings of municipal bonds is indicated in Table 35. This table is constructed on the assumption that the equilibrium real yield on taxable bonds is 3.3 percent, the upper-bound estimate suggested by the evidence in chapter 3. For each value of the expected rate of inflation, it is assumed that the nominal yield on taxable bonds is equal to the equilibrium real yield of 3.3 percent, plus the expected rate of inflation. The estimate of the fiscal inefficiency at each expected inflation rate is derived by taking the ratio of this nominal yield to the nominal yield of 9 percent that prevailed in 1976 and multiplying it by the estimated fiscal inefficiency of $875 million for 1976.[17]

---

[17] Proportionality holds exactly, provided that the effective marginal tax rate for institutional holders of municipal bonds and the implicit (nominal) tax rate

TABLE 35

Maximum Fiscal Inefficiency from Institutional Holdings of Tax-Exempt Municipal Bonds

Expected Inflation Rate (percent)	Nominal Yield on Corporate Bonds (percent)	Fiscal Inefficiency (millions of dollars)
0	3.3	321
1	4.3	418
2	5.3	515
3	6.3	613
4	7.3	710
5	8.3	807
6	9.3	905

Note: The nominal yields are obtained by adding the expected rate of inflation to a real yield of 3.3 percent. The estimates of fiscal inefficiency are derived by multiplying $875 million by the ratio of the nominal yield in column 2 to the 9 percent nominal yield on corporate bonds in 1976.

The estimated fiscal inefficiency associated with institutional holdings of tax-exempt municipal bonds rises as the inflation rate rises. If no inflation is expected, the fiscal inefficiency is only $321 million, whereas if 6 percent inflation is expected, the estimated fiscal inefficiency is $905 million. These estimates show a very different pattern from that indicated by the estimates of the fiscal inefficiency associated with individual holdings of tax-exempt municipal bonds reported in Table 30. For individuals, the maximum estimated fiscal inefficiency of $160 million occurs at a zero expected rate of inflation. As the expected inflation rate rises, fiscal inefficiency declines, reaching minus $775 million at an expected rate of inflation of 6 percent. This difference between the behavior of the fiscal inefficiency attributable to institutional holdings and that attributable to individual holdings reflects the fact that individual holders have a much broader range of alternative tax reduction opportunities than do institutional holders.

on municipal bonds are not affected by changes in the nominal yield on taxable corporate bonds. Probably neither of these conditions is met exactly, but the error made from assuming that they are is not very large. This procedure is justified because, given the quantities of municipal bonds held by various institutions, the fiscal inefficiency associated with these bonds should be almost proportional to the nominal yield on taxable bonds.

Summary

In this chapter we have examined the issues of fiscal inefficiency and tax inequity as they relate to tax-exempt bonds held by institutions. In the standard analysis, institutional holders of tax-exempt bonds are treated as individuals subject to a 48 percent tax rate. Based on this rate and a 27 percent implicit tax rate on municipals, the standard estimate of the fiscal inefficiency and tax inequity associated with institutional holdings of municipal bonds is $3.2 billion. Even ignoring the equity issues associated with inflation discussed in chapter 3, we have shown in this chapter that the standard analysis is not correct for two fundamental reasons.

First, and most important, unlike individuals, institutional holders of tax-exempt bonds cannot be viewed as the ultimate beneficiaries of any windfall gain resulting from the present exemption. The dominant institutional holders of municipal bonds, commercial banks and insurance companies, operate in industries with considerable competition among firms, face approximately constant costs, and have highly mobile capital. These conditions indicate that it is the customers of these institutions, rather than the owners of the equity, who capture the gains resulting from exemption and who would pay the increased taxes resulting from elimination of the exemption. The implication for tax equity of such an increase in taxes paid by customers is, at best, that there would be no gain in tax equity from eliminating the exemption. For commercial banks, the greatest burden would fall on those customers who have the poorest alternatives to bank deposits and bank credit. Those customers include virtually all holders of demand deposits, holders of ordinary time deposits, and small businesses and individual borrowers dependent on bank credit. There is a slight concentration of these customers toward the lower end of the income distribution, implying that elimination of the exemption would be a slightly regressive form of taxation. For insurance companies and other institutional holders, the effects of elimination of the exemption would be widely diffused throughout the economy, with no clear-cut gain in equity.

Second, the standard estimate of fiscal inefficiency of $3.2 billion significantly overstates the potential net budgetary gain to all government units combined from elimination of the exemption. This is so because the standard estimate ignores the tax revenue that is indirectly generated by institutional holdings of tax-exempt municipal bonds, the alternative tax avoidance opportunities that are available to institutional holders of municipal bonds, and the fact that the yield differential for shorter maturities is significantly greater than the implicit tax rate calculated for twenty-year maturities. Taking account of these factors, we found that the potential budgetary gain from elimination of the exemption in 1976 was no more than $875 million. Under non-inflationary conditions, this figure would have been reduced to $321 million. Finally, since there is no inequity generated by institutional holdings of municipal bonds, there is nothing that particularly recommends elimination of the exemption as an equitable and desirable method of raising government revenue.

7

The Fiscal Efficiency of the Exemption and the Fiscal Effects of the Taxable Bond Option

So far, the discussion of fiscal efficiency and tax equity has concentrated on the issue of tax equity and has dealt with the extreme proposal of outright elimination of the exemption. This emphasis was justified because, as pointed out in chapter 1, the fiscal inefficiency of the exemption is of limited importance unless it corresponds to a tax inequity, and because the extreme proposal of elimination sets an upper bound on what could be accomplished by the taxable bond option in the areas of fiscal efficiency and tax equity. The basic conclusion of chapters 3, 4, 5 and 6 is that elimination of the exemption would achieve no significant gain in tax equity (and perhaps even a loss in equity). It follows that there would be no significant gain in tax equity from the taxable bond option.

This conclusion implies that the fiscal effects of the option are of limited significance. The Treasury will incur some financial costs from the direct interest subsidy paid on taxable municipal bonds, but this cost will be largely a transfer to municipal governments. Part of the windfall gain presently accruing to holders of tax-exempt municipal bonds will be recaptured either as tax revenue by the Treasury or as an increased implicit subsidy enjoyed by municipal governments. Yet the recapture of this windfall gain does not indicate any net social benefit; the gain to governments is a loss to the private sector, and the individuals within the private sector who ultimately suffer the loss are not those who unfairly avoid taxes. Nevertheless, the overall fiscal cost of the taxable bond option is a question of some significance because this cost must somehow be financed, whether by higher taxes, by a reduction in other federal expenditures, or by larger deficits. Indeed, the question of the cost of the option has been regarded as an issue of primary importance by the Treasury and has played a major role in the controversy over the option.

The upper bound of the potential net fiscal gain from a taxable bond option is set by the aggregate fiscal inefficiency that is correctly attributable to the exemption. In the two previous chapters, estimates were derived for the fiscal inefficiency associated with individual and institutional holdings of municipal bonds. This chapter combines the two estimates into an aggregate measure of the fiscal inefficiency resulting from the exemption. This measure is useful both because it indicates the high level of efficiency that is presently achieved by the exemption and because it sets an upper bound for the fiscal benefits of the taxable bond option. Proponents of the option assert that, because it would allow municipal governments to benefit from capturing part of this inefficiency, it would actually provide more than one dollar of benefit to municipal governments for every dollar of cost to the U.S. Treasury. This chapter disputes this claim and shows that when all factors are taken into account a 40 percent taxable bond option would probably provide no more than about eighty cents of financial benefit to municipal governments for every dollar of cost to the Treasury.

The Fiscal Inefficiency of the Exemption

The fiscal inefficiency of the exemption is the excess of the loss of tax revenue by the U.S. Treasury over the gain from reduced borrowing costs to municipal governments that issue tax-exempt bonds. Estimates of the magnitude of this fiscal inefficiency for the one-third of municipal bonds held directly by individual households were developed in chapter 5 and summarized in Table 30. Estimates of the fiscal inefficiency associated with the two-thirds of municipal bonds held by institutions were developed in chapter 6 and reported in Table 35. Combining the estimates for individuals and institutions, we obtain the estimates of the overall fiscal inefficiency resulting from the exemption reported in Table 36.

As was true of the estimated fiscal inefficiency associated with individual holdings and with institutional holdings of municipal bonds, the estimate of the total fiscal inefficiency of the exemption is sensitive to the expected rate of inflation. The sensitivity of the aggregate estimate, however, is less than that of two components because the two components move in opposite directions when the expected rate of inflation changes. At a zero expected rate of inflation the total fiscal inefficiency is $481 million, and at a 6 percent expected rate of inflation this total is considerably lower, $130 million.

The fiscal inefficiency of the exemption is the difference between

TABLE 36

THE FISCAL INEFFICIENCY OF THE EXEMPTION
(millions of dollars)

Expected Inflation Rate (percent)	Fiscal Inefficiency from Individuals (1)	Fiscal Inefficiency from Institutions (2)	Total Fiscal Inefficiency (3)
0	160	321	481
1	27	418	445
2	−134	515	381
3	−294	613	319
4	−428	710	282
5	−615	807	192
6	−775	905	130

SOURCE: Column 1 is from Table 30. Column 2 is from Table 35. Column 3 is the sum of columns 1 and 2.

the cost of the exemption to the federal government and the benefit to state and local governments. To judge the importance of this inefficiency, it is useful to compare it with either the cost of the exemption or the benefit of the exemption. The traditional method for conducting this comparison is to look at the "efficiency ratio" of the

TABLE 37

THE EFFICIENCY RATIO OF THE EXEMPTION

Expected Inflation Rate (percent)	Benefit to Municipal Governments (millions of dollars) (1)	Cost to the Federal Government (millions of dollars) (2)	Efficiency Ratio (3)
0	2,864	3,345	0.86
1	3,732	4,177	0.89
2	4,600	4,981	0.94
3	5,468	5,787	0.94
4	6,336	6,618	0.96
5	7,204	7,396	0.97
6	8,072	8,208	0.98

SOURCE: Column 1 is obtained by multiplying an average implicit subsidy rate of 35 percent by a nominal interest rate of 3.3 percent, plus the expected inflation rate, and then multiplying by $248 billion of municipal debt. Column 2 is column 1 plus column 3 of Table 36. Column 3 is the ratio of columns 1 and 2.

exemption, that is, the ratio of the benefit of the exemption to municipal governments to its cost to the Treasury. This comparison is made in Table 37. For each value of the expected rate of inflation, it is assumed that the nominal yield on taxable bonds is equal to a real yield of 3.3 percent plus the expected rate of inflation. The total interest costs that municipal governments would have incurred are the nominal yields multiplied by the $248 billion of municipal debt outstanding in 1976. The benefit to municipal governments from the exemption is equal to the implicit subsidy rate they enjoyed because of the exemption multiplied by the interest cost they would have incurred without the exemption. The average implicit subsidy rate on municipal bonds of all qualities and maturities is assumed to be 35 percent.[1] This assumption about the subsidy rate yields the estimates of the benefits of the exemption to municipal governments reported in column 1 of Table 37. The cost of the exemption to the federal government (column 2) is obtained by adding to column 1 the estimate of the fiscal inefficiency of the exemption given in Table 36.[2] Finally, column 3 calculates the fiscal efficiency ratio of the exemption by taking the ratio of column 1 to column 2.

From the results in Table 37, it is apparent that the exemption achieves its lowest efficiency ratio at a zero expected rate of inflation. But even this efficiency ratio of 86 percent is significantly higher than the efficiency ratio of about 70 percent that is frequently cited by proponents of the taxable bond option. Moreover, as the expected rate of inflation rises, so does the efficiency ratio of the exemption, exceeding 90 percent for expected rates of inflation of 2 percent or more. For the range of inflation rates that have prevailed during the past decade and seem likely to prevail in the future, the efficiency ratio of the exemption is at least 96 percent.

Of course, a 96 percent efficiency ratio is not perfect. There are

---

[1] The evidence presented in chapter 4 indicates that 35 percent is a reasonable lower-bound estimate of the subsidy rate on municipal bonds.

[2] The estimates of the fiscal inefficiency of the exemption take account only of the taxes that are lost from present holders of municipal bonds, not the additional taxes that would be paid by holders of taxable municipal bonds (who do not presently hold tax-exempt bonds) if the exemption were eliminated. However, the evidence on who presently holds taxable bonds indicates that the probable holders of taxable municipal bonds would be tax-exempt or low-tax-bracket individuals and institutions. Further, the estimate of the costs of the exemption also neglects fiscal effects of the increase in the general level of interest rates on taxable bonds that would occur if the exemption were eliminated. This increase in interest rates is an additional fiscal cost of elimination of the exemption. The analysis of this cost for the taxable bond option indicates that it outweighs the additional tax revenue that would be collected from holders of taxable municipal bonds.

still four cents out of every dollar lost by the Treasury that do not accrue as a financial benefit to state and local governments. However, in considering this four cents of fiscal loss, it is essential to keep in mind two vital points: First, fiscal inefficiency is not by itself very important unless it also corresponds to a tax inequity. In the present case, the fiscal inefficiency that results from the exemption at rates of inflation greater than 4 percent is due primarily to the failure to collect greater taxes from the customers of institutions that hold municipal bonds. This loss of tax revenue does not constitute a serious tax inequity. Second, since a decision has been made to subsidize the borrowing costs of municipal governments, the fiscal efficiency ratio of the exemption should be judged relative to the fiscal efficiency of other federal subsidies. Rare indeed is a subsidy program where as much as ninety-six cents out of every dollar of expenditure accrues as a benefit to the ultimate, intended beneficiary of the subsidy. Many subsidy programs have large bureaucracies both within the federal government and within the recipient group, consuming a substantial portion of the costs of the subsidy. Further, the exemption provides an exceedingly desirable form of subsidy to municipal governments. It is essentially free of strings and constraints.

Portfolio Readjustments under the Option

Repeal of the exemption would eliminate the fiscal inefficiency generated by the exemption. Specifically, the gain in tax revenue to the Treasury due to repeal would exceed the financial loss to municipal governments by precisely the amount of the present inefficiency. Proponents of the taxable bond option assert that the option would also result in at least some reduction of the fiscal inefficiency of the exemption. In the case of the option, however, the Treasury would lose while municipal governments gain. The claim is that municipal governments would gain more than the Treasury would lose, because municipal governments would enjoy a reduction in borrowing costs on tax-exempt bonds that continued to be issued under the option, as well as a direct subsidy on taxable bonds. The excess of the benefit of the option to municipal governments over the cost to the Treasury is the net fiscal benefit of the option.

The fiscal inefficiency of the exemption sets an upper bound on the potential net fiscal benefit of the option. This upper bound would be achieved only if the option had the same effect as eliminating the exemption; that is, only if the subsidy rate on taxable bonds were so generous that it induced municipal governments to issue no tax-exempt bonds. A 50 percent subsidy rate would probably come close to this goal. However, most proposals for a taxable bond option have embodied significantly lower subsidy rates. For the purposes of the present discussion, it is useful to consider a taxable bond option with a 40 percent subsidy rate on taxable municipal bonds. This is the long-run level of the subsidy rate in President Carter's proposal.

Under a 40 percent taxable bond option, there would be some replacement of tax-exempt bonds with taxable bonds. The new taxable bonds, however, would not be held only by the individuals and institutions that would reduce their holdings of tax-exempt bonds. In particular, the analysis of chapter 5 indicates that high-tax-bracket individuals who presently hold tax-exempt municipal bonds would not shift to taxable municipal bonds. Instead, they would reinvest the wealth presently held in tax-exempt bonds primarily in equity assets that are accorded far more favorable tax treatment than taxable bonds. On the other side of this portfolio adjustment, there must be low-tax-bracket individuals and institutions that would be willing to give up equity assets and hold additional taxable bonds.[3]

In order to estimate the fiscal effects of a 40 percent taxable bond option, it is necessary to guess at the volume of taxable bonds that would be issued under such an option. In the first few years following the introduction of such an option, the fraction of new issues in taxable form would be abnormally large. This is because it would be necessary for municipalities to adjust the composition of the outstanding stock of municipal bonds to the equilibrium composition that is appropriate for a 40 percent option. Once equilibrium is achieved, the Treasury has guessed that only about one-fourth of the municipal market is likely to go taxable.[4] In terms of 1976 magnitudes, this means about $60 billion of taxable municipal bonds.

---

[3] Changes in the tax structure, such as elimination of the exemption or introduction of the option, will generally affect the demand and supply of equity and debt, causing a sympathetic change in the debt-equity structure of firms in general. We abstract from this effect in our analysis. We assume a fixed supply of equity and let investors' portfolio adjustments reestablish the equilibrium. For discussion of the issues involved, see Miller (1977) and the references therein.

[4] There is little hard evidence on which to base a precise estimate of the volume of taxable municipal borrowing under the option. In *The President's 1978 Tax Program: Detailed Descriptions and Supporting Analyses of the Proposals,* the Treasury concludes, "The new volume of issues of taxable and tax-exempt debt under a 40 percent subsidy is not easy to estimate. It depends not only on what lenders will wish to hold in their portfolios at the new structure of interest rates but also on how quickly they will be able to adjust their portfolios from their current pattern of holdings. A reasonable calculation, based on informed market opinion as well as estimates derived from econometric models, is that after an adjustment period of possibly five years, about 25 percent of State and local bond issues will be in taxable form and 75 percent in tax-exempt form."

This guess at the volume of taxable borrowing is apparently based on the assumption that the institutional demand for tax-exempt bonds would be little affected by a 40 percent taxable bond option. This means that taxable bonds would be issued primarily to replace tax-exempt bonds presently held by individual households that would not find such bonds attractive if the proportionate yield differential between taxable corporate bonds and tax-exempt municipal bonds were increased from 30 percent to 40 percent. It is unlikely that a 40 percent taxable bond option would result in the complete elimination of household demand for tax-exempt municipal bonds. For many households, such bonds would remain as the only fixed-interest investment for which the real tax rate was less than 150 or 200 percent. A plausible assumption is that the household demand for tax-exempt municipal bonds would decline by no more than half as a result of a 40 percent taxable bond option. In terms of 1976 magnitudes, this means that about $40 billion of taxable municipal bonds would be issued to replace the tax-exempt bonds that individual households would no longer desire to hold.

Given this guess at the effect of the option on household demand for tax-exempt municipal bonds, it follows that the total effect of the option on the demand for tax-exempts depends critically on the assumption that institutional demand would be little affected by the option. There are three reasons for making this assumption. First, most of the shorter-term municipal bonds held by institutions already have yield differentials of 40 percent and more, relative to comparable taxable bonds. Presumably, a 40 percent taxable bond option would have little effect on the willingness of institutions to hold such shorter-term bonds. Second, the principal institutional holders of municipal bonds, commercial banks and fire and casualty insurance companies, are subject to the corporate tax rate of 48 percent. As long as the yield differential between taxables and tax-exempts remains less than 48 percent (as it would under a 40 percent option), these taxable institutions would still have an incentive to hold tax-exempt municipal bonds. Third, it is even possible that the institutional demand for tax-exempt bonds might rise as a result of the option. This is because the amount of such bonds that must be held in order to generate a given amount of tax-exempt income rises as the yield per dollar of bonds declines. For example, if commercial banks wish to shield $6 billion of profits from taxation by holding tax-exempt bonds, and if the yield on such bonds is 6 percent, then $100 billion of bonds must be held. If the yield on tax-exempts is only 5 percent, however,

$120 billion of bonds must be held to generate the same $6 billion of tax-exempt income.

There are, of course, arguments on the other side of the issue concerning the effect of a 40 percent option on the institutional demand for tax-exempt bonds. First, commercial banks and fire and casualty insurance companies do have other tax shelters that they would exploit more intensively if the yield on tax-exempt bonds were reduced by the option. Second, on medium-term municipal bonds (maturities of five to ten years), the yield differential, relative to comparable taxable bonds, is only slightly less than 40 percent. This yield differential may be the maximum that is consistent with continued commercial bank demand for such medium-term tax-exempt bonds. Third, as suggested at the end of chapter 6, even for long-term municipal bonds there may be no marginal advantage to banks from holding such bonds, relative to the alternative assets they would choose if tax-exempt municipal bonds were not available. If this is the true situation, then a 40 percent taxable bond option that would increase the yield differential for long-term bonds might well result in a massive decline in the institutional demand for long-term tax-exempt municipal bonds.

From these considerations, it is apparent that any guess about the effect of a 40 percent taxable bond option on volumes of taxable and tax-exempt municipal borrowing is subject to a large margin of error. In this situation, it is useful to make a simple and extreme assumption: the option would have no effect on the institutional demand for tax-exempt bonds. The virtue of this assumption is not its accuracy but its simplicity and the direction of its bias. If there is no change in institutional holdings of tax-exempt bonds, we do not need to worry about the fiscal effects of the change. Also, by assuming that only the household demand for tax-exempt bonds is affected by the option, we tend to understate the financial cost of the option to the federal government but not the benefits to municipal governments. This is because the cost to the federal government is directly dependent upon the volume of taxable bonds issued under the option. The benefits to municipal governments, however, depend on the reduction in net borrowing costs induced by the option, and this reduction should be essentially independent of the volume of taxable borrowing.

One further factor should be accounted for in assessing the volume of taxable borrowing that would take place under the option: the increase in total municipal borrowing that would be stimulated by the higher subsidy provided to municipal governments as a result of the option. For present purposes, however, it is best to ignore this additional borrowing in estimating the option's fiscal effects. Since this additional borrowing would take place in taxable form, the financial cost of the subsidy on it would be very close to the financial benefit enjoyed by municipal governments. Hence, the volume of additional borrowing stimulated by the option does not affect the estimate of the net fiscal benefit of the option.

Fiscal Effects of the Option: A First Approximation

To obtain a first approximation for the fiscal effects of the option, we make the simplifying assumption that a 40 percent taxable bond option would have no effect on the yield on taxable bonds. Specifically, we assume that the real yield on taxable corporate bonds remains constant at 3.3 percent. We also assume that the actual and expected rate of inflation is constant at 5 percent, implying a nominal yield on taxable bonds of 8.3 percent. In the absence of the option, we assume that the implicit nominal subsidy rate (s) on long-term tax-exempt municipal bonds would be 30 percent. Given these assumptions, we wish to calculate the financial benefit that a 40 percent taxable bond option would provide to municipal governments, the financial cost that such an option would have for the federal government, and the net fiscal benefit of the option (that is, the excess of the benefit to municipal governments over the cost to the federal government). These calculations are based on the assumption that the option was in effect in 1976 and that the composition of the outstanding stock of municipal bonds was fully adjusted to the presence of the option.

The financial benefit to municipal governments from the option is the reduction in borrowing costs they would enjoy relative to the situation prevailing under the exemption. This reduction in borrowing costs would accrue not only on taxable bonds subsidized directly by the Treasury but also on the tax-exempt bonds that would still be issued under the option. Issuance of tax-exempt bonds would cost less because municipal governments would reduce the volume of their tax-exempt borrowing until the implicit subsidy enjoyed on tax-exempt bonds was at least as great as the explicit subsidy paid by the Treasury. A crude estimate of the financial benefit of the option to municipal governments may be obtained by assuming that the option would increase the subsidy rate on all municipal bonds from the implicit subsidy rate ($s = 30$ percent) prevailing on long-term bonds under the exemption, to the explicit subsidy rate ($s^* = 40$ percent) that would be provided under the option. The financial gain per dollar of municipal debt is equal to the difference between s^* and s, multiplied by the nominal yield on taxable bonds, assumed to be 8.3 percent. The total financial benefit is the benefit per dollar of municipal debt, multiplied by the $248 billion of municipal debt outstanding in 1976. This crude procedure yields an estimated financial benefit from the option of $2.058 billion.

This estimate of the financial benefit of the option to municipal governments is clearly too high, because the implicit subsidy rate presently enjoyed by municipal governments on bonds of less than twenty-year maturity is significantly greater than 30 percent. On bonds of less than four or five-year maturity, the implicit subsidy rate is probably 40 percent or more. Hence, on these bonds, there would be no financial benefit to municipal governments from a 40 percent taxable bond option. On bonds of five to ten-year maturity, the benefit provided by the option would be very small. Indeed, the evidence cited in chapter 4 indicates that the average implicit subsidy rate on tax-exempt municipal bonds is at least 35 percent. Using an estimate of $s = 35$ percent, rather than $s = 30$ percent, reduces the estimated financial benefit of the 40 percent taxable bond option to half of the previous estimate. Allowing for the fact that the implicit subsidy rate under the exemption is at least 35 percent, we may safely conclude that the financial benefit to municipal governments of a 40 percent taxable bond option would be no more than $1.029 billion.

The direct financial cost of the taxable bond option to the federal government is the direct interest subsidy payments that would have to be made on taxable municipal bonds. For each dollar of taxable bonds, the annual subsidy payment would be 40 percent of the nominal yield on taxable bonds, assumed to be 8.3 percent. We have assumed that the total volume of taxable bonds under the option would be $40 billion. The direct cost of the subsidy on these bonds is, therefore, $1.33 billion.

These direct costs are at least partially offset by the indirect financial benefit of the option to the federal government. This indirect financial benefit consists of three components: additional taxes collected from present holders of tax-exempt bonds when they shift to alternative taxable assets; additional taxes collected from holders of taxable municipal bonds who do not presently hold municipal bonds; and tax revenues lost due to the shifting of tax burdens from institutions to individuals.

We have assumed that institutional holders of tax-exempt bonds would not alter their holdings of such bonds as a result of a 40 percent taxable bond option. It follows that the first part of the indirect financial benefit of the option to the federal government is derived exclusively from individual households that presently hold tax-exempt municipal bonds. The magnitude of this benefit depends on the extent to which these households shift out of tax-exempt municipal bonds as a result of the option and on the taxes they pay on their alternative investments. In the preceding section, we guessed that the amount of shifting under the 40 percent option would be $40 billion. In chapter 5, we estimated the effective tax rate for each dollar shifted from tax-exempt municipals to alternative investments to be $\tau = 0.012 + (0.11) \cdot \pi$.[5] At an inflation rate of 5 percent, $\tau = 0.01725$. This implies that the additional taxes collected by the federal government from present holders of municipal bonds would be $(0.01725) \cdot (\$40 \text{ billion}) = \$650$ million. This figure of $650 million reflects the fact that individuals who presently hold tax-exempt municipal bonds would not shift any substantial portion of their wealth into taxable municipal bonds. Instead, they would increase their holdings of equity assets. To secure these equity assets, they would have to persuade other individuals and institutions to give up equity assets that they presently hold and instead hold taxable municipal bonds.

The second component of the indirect financial benefit of the option to the federal government includes the additional taxes paid by these other individuals and institutions who will ultimately hold the $40 billion of taxable municipal bonds issued to replace tax-exempt municipal bonds presently held by high-tax-bracket individuals. The amount of these additional taxes depends on the difference between (1) the tax rate presently paid by these individuals and institutions on their present holdings of equity assets and (2) the tax rate they would pay on their holdings of taxable municipal bonds. Most taxable municipal bonds would probably be absorbed by pension funds, life insurance companies, and other tax-exempt or very-low-tax-rate institutions. On these bonds, the additional tax revenue accruing to the Treasury would be essentially zero. For other likely purchasers of taxable municipal bonds, the tax rate differential is probably no more than 10 percent. Hence, if as much as $15 billion of an estimated $40 billion of taxable municipal bonds ended up in the hands of taxable investors (a high estimate), the additional tax revenue accruing to the Treasury would be only $125 million. This is probably an overestimate.

The third component of indirect fiscal benefit to the federal gov-

---

[5] Recall that τ is defined as the tax rate on a dollar of wealth, not the tax rate on the income earned on that dollar of wealth.

ernment is negative—that is, it is a cost. Part of the benefit of the option to municipal governments comes from reducing the windfall presently associated with institutional holdings of tax-exempt municipal bonds. The ultimate beneficiaries of this windfall presently pay tax on it; hence, any reduction in the windfall will reduce the amount of tax collected by the Treasury. For commercial bank holdings of municipal bonds alone, this loss would amount to about $100 million.[6] Adding in the fire and casualty insurance companies increases this indirect loss to something more than $100 million.

It is apparent that the second and third components of indirect benefit and cost are both small and almost exactly cancel out. It is convenient to assume that they do cancel. This implies that the indirect fiscal benefit of the option to the federal government is equal to the $700 million of additional taxes that would be collected from present individual holders of tax-exempt municipal bonds when they shift to alternative taxable investments. Subtraction of this indirect benefit from the direct cost of the option of $1.33 billion yields a first approximation of the net cost of the option to the federal government of $630 million.

The net fiscal benefit of the option to all government units combined is the excess of the benefit to municipal governments over the net cost to the federal government. This is estimated to be $399 million, or $1.029 billion of benefit minus $630 million of cost.

Another way of comparing the benefits and costs of the option is by calculating the benefit-cost ratio. That ratio is 1.63 to 1, the ratio of $1.029 billion to $630 million. This indicates that the option would provide $1.63 of benefit for every dollar of cost. While this benefit-cost ratio is low relative to the benefit-cost ratio of more than four to one suggested by proponents of the option, it is still sufficiently high to make the option appear attractive from a fiscal viewpoint.[7] However, it should be remembered that this benefit-cost ratio is based on a first approximation of the option's fiscal consequences and has to be modified to take account of the fiscal effects of the change in interest rates induced by the taxable bond option.

---

[6] An increase in the implicit subsidy rate from 35 to 40 percent implies that banks would pay an additional $420 million in implicit tax on their holdings of municipal bonds. Assuming that the tax rate for the ultimate beneficiaries of the windfall presently enjoyed by banks is 25 percent, the loss of these taxes due to the reduction in the windfall would amount to $105 million.

[7] The assertion of a four-to-one benefit-cost ratio for the 40 percent taxable bond option is made by the U.S. Treasury in *The President's 1978 Tax Program: Detailed Descriptions and Supporting Analyses*.

The Fiscal Effects of Higher Interest Rates

It is generally recognized that the taxable bond option will result in some increase in the general level of yields on taxable bonds. This increase will be required in order to induce the market to absorb a larger volume of taxable bonds. Proponents of the option usually argue that the required increase in taxable yields will be small. In a background paper prepared for the Twentieth Century Fund Task Force on the Municipal Bond Market, Forbes and Peterson (1976) conclude that "the increase in taxable [interest] rates with a 40 percent interest subsidy would be on the order of 10 to 15 basis points."[8] This conclusion is apparently based on a study by Fortune (1973*b*).

It is beyond the scope of this study to evaluate the accuracy of Forbes's and Peterson's prediction. It is relatively easy, however, to use this prediction to calculate the fiscal effects of the increase in interest rates that would be induced by the option. This has not been done before. For the purpose of this calculation, we assume that all taxable yields would increase by 10 basis points, that is, by one-tenth of 1 percent.

Any increase in the general level of taxable yields increases the financial cost of the taxable bond option. The most important source of increased cost is the increase in the interest the federal government must pay on its own debt. With $470 billion of federal debt outstanding in 1976, an increase of 10 basis points (0.1 percent) in the interest rate on all taxable debt would have meant an increase of $470 million in the total annual cost of servicing the national debt.[9] The federal government would have recovered part of these increased interest payments in the form of increased taxes. However, since the average marginal tax rate of holders of U.S. government obligations probably does not exceed 25 percent, the net cost of the interest rate increase would have been at least $340 million.[10]

An increase in the general level of interest rates also has a cost to the federal government through its effect on corporate bonds. Corporations write off their interest expense against a 48 percent cor-

---

[8] See Twentieth Century Fund Task Force on the Municipal Bond Market (1976).

[9] The increase in the interest rate on U.S. obligations would probably be less than the increase in the interest rate on corporate bonds. However, since the figure of 10 basis points is itself a very crude estimate, refinements of this estimate to take account of differences between different types of bonds do not seem worthwhile.

[10] A tax rate of 25 percent is probably a significant overestimate. The evidence from the tax return data reported by the Internal Revenue Service indicates that there must be a great deal of interest income that is never reported. The effective tax rate on nonreported interest income is, of course, zero.

porate tax rate. Holders of corporate bonds (including many tax-exempt institutions) have marginal tax rates that average far less than 48 percent, probably less than 20 percent.[11] An increase of 10 basis points in the interest rate paid by corporations on their $330 billion of outstanding debt in 1976 would have reduced corporate taxes by about $160 million. Taxes collected from holders of corporate bonds would have risen by only about $70 million. This means that the federal government would have suffered a net loss of tax revenue of about $90 million.

Under a 40 percent taxable bond option, an increase of 10 basis points in the general level of taxable yields would mean an increase of 6 basis points in the net interest rate paid by municipal governments. Given an outstanding stock of $248 billion of municipal bonds in 1976, this means an increased interest expense for municipal governments of about $150 million. Further, on the $60 billion of subsidized taxable bonds that would be issued under the option, the federal government would have to pay an increased interest subsidy of 4 basis points, implying an increased subsidy cost of $24 million.

Finally, there is the effect of an increase in the general level of interest rates on tax revenues that is generated by borrowing and lending between individual households (including that done indirectly through financial intermediaries). The evidence on assets and liabilities of individual households indicates that debtors tend to have higher marginal tax rates than lenders. Moreover, both common sense and the factual evidence of tax returns indicate that individuals are more assiduous in deducting interest paid than in reporting interest received.[12] This implies that any increase in the general level of interest rates is likely to reduce the tax revenue generated by borrowing and lending between individual households. The magnitude of this effect is exceedingly difficult to determine.

For those fiscal effects of the interest rate increase for which it is possible to assign numerical values, the total estimated financial cost of a 10 basis point increase is $600 million. To obtain the total cost of the taxable bond option, this $600 million should be added to the

---

[11] The average tax rate for holders of corporate bonds is probably lower than that for U.S. government bonds. Low-tax-rate institutions are relatively more important in the market for corporate bonds than in the market for U.S. government bonds. There is probably more underreporting of interest received from corporate bonds than of interest received from government bonds.

[12] In 1973 total deductions of interest paid by those who itemized their deductions exceeded slightly the total interest income reported by all individual tax returns. It is essentially impossible to rationalize this fact, except by assuming that there is massive underreporting of interest income.

previously estimated net cost of $630 million, resulting in a total cost of $1.23 billion. This compares with the estimated benefit of the option of $1.029 billion, leaving a net fiscal benefit from the option of minus $199 million. The adjusted benefit-cost ratio of the option is 0.84 to 1, equal to the ratio of $1.029 billion to $1.230 billion. In other words, the option provides only eighty-four cents of benefit for each dollar of cost.

Inflation and the Benefits and Costs of the Option

So far, the estimates of the benefits and costs of the taxable bond option have been constructed on the assumption that the expected rate of inflation is 5 percent. This is a useful assumption since it seems unlikely that the rate of inflation will fall much below 5 percent for the foreseeable future. Nevertheless, it is instructive to examine how estimates of the benefits and costs of the taxable bond option would be affected by different assumptions about the expected rate of inflation.

We should expect that both the benefits and the costs of the taxable bond option would increase with increases in the expected rate of inflation. This is because both the benefits and the costs are positively related to the nominal yield on taxable bonds. Therefore, the net fiscal benefit of the option (the excess of benefits over costs) should be less sensitive to changes in the expected rate of inflation than are the benefits and costs taken separately.

Table 38 summarizes the relevant facts concerning the effects of various expected inflation rates on the estimated benefits, costs, and net fiscal benefit of the option. This table is constructed in the following manner: The estimate of benefits to municipal governments (column 1) assumes that the average implicit subsidy rate under the exemption is 35 percent and that this would be increased to 40 percent under the option. The 5 percent difference in subsidy rates is multiplied by the nominal yield on taxable bonds (equal to the real yield of 3.3 percent plus the expected inflation rate) and then multiplied by the $248 billion of municipal bonds outstanding in 1976. The direct costs of the option (column 2) are calculated by multiplying a 40 percent subsidy rate by the nominal yield on taxable bonds and then by the $40 billion of taxable bonds assumed to be issued under the option. The indirect financial benefit of the option to the federal government (column 3) includes the three items discussed in the preceding section. In particular, the amount of additional taxes that would be collected from households that shift out of municipal bonds is deter-

TABLE 38

Benefits and Costs of a 40 Percent Taxable Bond Option at Different Expected Inflation Rates
(millions of dollars)

Expected Inflation Rate (percent)	Financial Benefit to Municipal Governments (1)	Direct Cost to Federal Government (2)	Indirect Benefit to Federal Government (3)	Cost of Interest Rate Increase (4)	Total Cost of Option (5)	Net Fiscal Benefit of Option (6)	Ratio of Benefits to Cost (7)
0	409	528	480	600	648	−239	0.63
1	533	688	524	600	764	−231	0.70
2	657	848	568	600	880	−223	0.75
3	781	1,008	612	600	996	−215	0.78
4	905	1,168	656	600	1,112	−207	0.81
5	1,029	1,328	700	600	1,228	−199	0.84
6	1,153	1,488	744	600	1,344	−191	0.86
7	1,277	1,648	788	600	1,460	−183	0.87
8	1,401	1,808	832	600	1,576	−175	0.89

Note: The calculations are described in the text.

mined by a tax rate of $\tau = 0.012 + (0.11) \cdot \pi$, where π is the expected inflation rate. This tax rate is multiplied by the assumed \$40 billion reduction in tax-exempt municipal bonds held by individual households. The second and third components of indirect financial benefit and cost are assumed to cancel out. The estimated cost of the increase in interest rates (column 4) is based on the assumption that this increase is always 10 basis points, independent of the expected rate of inflation. This is a reasonable assumption, since the principal holders of taxable municipal bonds will probably be life insurance companies and pension funds and other effectively tax-exempt institutions. For these institutions, the relevant consideration ought to be the real yield on taxable bonds, and for these institutions a 10 basis point increase in nominal yield is a 10 basis point increase in real yield, regardless of the expected inflation rate. The total cost of the option reported in column 5 is equal to column 2, minus column 3, plus column 4. The net fiscal benefit of the exemption reported in column 6 is the difference between column 1 and column 5. The benefit-cost ratio in column 7 is the ratio of column 1 to column 5.

The key feature of Table 38 is that the overall net fiscal benefit of the taxable bond option is negative at every expected inflation rate. The fiscal cost of the taxable bond option always exceeds the fiscal benefit. Hence, the benefit-cost ratio is always less than one. However, it would be misleading to focus too much attention on the precise estimates of the benefit-cost ratio. These estimates are subject to substantial error because the estimates of both benefits and costs of the option are subject to error.

Indeed, all the figures in Table 38 should be viewed with a degree of caution. These figures are based on assumptions concerning the volume of taxable bonds that would be issued under the option, the increase in interest rates that would be induced by the option, the alternative assets into which households would shift if the option were adopted, the implicit subsidy rate that would prevail under the exemption at various expected inflation rates, and so forth. In many cases, it is difficult to judge the accuracy of these assumptions. However, an effort has been made to adopt assumptions that tend to overstate the financial benefit of the option to municipal governments and understate the overall cost of the option. For this reason, we may be quite confident that the net fiscal benefit of the option is not positive, especially at inflation rates within the range of recent experience.

Our estimates of the benefit-cost ratio probably overstate the true benefit-cost ratio for reasons other than those already mentioned. In particular, the estimate of costs completely ignores the cost of administering the taxable bond option. In the beginning, these administrative costs should be relatively small since the option is supposed to operate in an essentially automatic fashion. Only a minimal bureaucracy would be required to run the program within the federal government, and the costs of utilizing the program to municipal governments would be relatively small. But this happy situation would deteriorate if, as many municipal government officials fear, strings and constraints came to be attached to the option. In that case, a federal bureaucracy would be required to administer the strings and constraints, and a municipal bureaucracy would be required to comply with them.

Summary

This chapter has examined the fiscal efficiency of the exemption and the probable fiscal effects of a 40 percent taxable bond option. With respect to the whole issue of fiscal efficiency, the first basic point was that this issue is not very important unless it is also coupled with an issue of tax equity. The fiscal inefficiency of the exemption creates no great harm unless it corresponds to an unfair tax advantage captured by wealthy holders of tax-exempt municipal bonds. Any net fiscal benefit from the taxable bond option is not a very impressive benefit if it is derived by imposing higher effective taxes on individuals who are already paying their fair share of taxes. Since the analysis of previous chapters has shown that no significant inequity results from the exemption, it follows that the fiscal inefficiency of the exemption and the net fiscal benefit of the option, whatever their magnitudes, are not very important.

On the question of the magnitude of the fiscal inefficiency resulting from the exemption, the analysis of this chapter shows that it is quite small, much smaller than suggested by proponents of the taxable bond option. Specifically, the excess of the cost to the Treasury from lost tax revenue over the benefit to municipal governments from reduced borrowing costs due to the exemption is less than $500 million, rather than the $3 billion to $4 billion suggested by proponents of the option. For the inflation rates experienced during the past decade and expected to prevail for the foreseeable future, the benefit-cost ratio of the exemption is at least 96 percent. In other words, the exemption provides at least ninety-six cents of financial benefit to municipal governments for every dollar of cost to the federal government. Judged by the standards of other federal subsidy programs, this is a considerable accomplishment, particularly for a program that is essentially lacking in strings and constraints.

The high fiscal efficiency of the exemption indicates that there is very little latitude for the taxable bond option to generate any net fiscal benefit. Neglecting the fiscal effects of higher interest rates induced by the option, we find that the net direct fiscal benefit of a 40 percent taxable bond option (the excess of the financial benefit of the option to municipal governments over its cost to the federal government) is only about $400 million. When account is taken of the fiscal effects of higher interest rates, the net fiscal benefit of the option drops to minus $199 million. The benefits of the option are less than its costs. Indeed, at a 5 percent inflation rate, the option would provide only about eighty-four cents of benefit to municipal governments for each dollar of its cost, and this estimate ignores any of the bureaucratic costs of running the option program.

Finally, it should be noted that the estimates of the fiscal effects of the taxable bond option are based on a variety of assumptions that in some cases are little more than guesses. Therefore, specific numerical estimates of the benefits and costs of the option should be viewed with caution. Nevertheless, since most of the questionable assumptions are biased toward overstating the option's benefits and understating its costs, we are confident that the net fiscal benefit of the option is negative. Moreover, since any net fiscal benefit from the option would result primarily from heavier taxes imposed on the customers of banks and insurance companies, we may conclude that, whatever the option would provide in terms of a fiscal benefit, it would not provide a social benefit.

8

The Effectiveness and Economic Efficiency of the Taxable Bond Option

Proponents of the taxable bond option make two main points concerning the effectiveness of the option vis-à-vis the present exemption as a means of subsidizing municipal borrowing. First, they argue that during the past decade municipal borrowing costs have risen because the market for tax-exempt bonds has not been able to absorb the increase in the supply of municipal debt without a significant increase in borrowing costs, causing some essential public projects to be abandoned or postponed. The option would have remedied this problem, they argue, by providing a greater direct interest subsidy than the implicit subsidy provided by the exemption. Second, proponents of the option argue that the market for tax-exempt bonds is too narrow to absorb the increases in municipal borrowing that will occur during the next decade without further undesirable increases in borrowing costs. The option would alleviate this problem by allowing the excess pressure in the tax-exempt market to be relieved by the issuance of subsidized taxable bonds.

In this chapter, we examine these arguments. First, we show that the increase in the nominal borrowing costs of municipal governments during the past decade does not indicate any decline in effectiveness of the *real* subsidy provided by the exemption. In fact, the real subsidy provided by the exemption has increased significantly during the past decade and is likely to remain high as long as the inflation rate remains near the level experienced during the past decade. Next, we consider the contention that the market for tax-exempt municipal bonds will· be unable to meet the borrowing requirements of municipal governments if the supply of municipal bonds continues to expand as it has in the past. We show that, relative to the size of the U.S. economy, the stock of municipal bonds has expanded by only

175

4 percent during the past decade. On the basis of historical evidence, we argue that the tax-exempt market should have no difficulty in absorbing a similar increase in municipal borrowing in the future. Finally, we examine the economic efficiency of the exemption and of the taxable bond option. We point out that any subsidy to municipal borrowing tends to distort the allocation of capital by encouraging municipal governments to undertake public investments that have a lower social rate of return than private investments that compete for the same funds. The greater the subsidy, the greater the distortion, and therefore the greater the loss of economic efficiency. Thus, we conclude that the increase in the subsidy on municipal borrowing that would be induced by the taxable bond option would not be desirable from the standpoint of its effects on the allocation of resources.

Nominal Yields, Real Yields, and the Real Subsidy Rate

There is no doubt that during New York City's financial crisis in 1975 many municipal governments found it increasingly difficult to secure funds by floating tax-exempt bonds. Those governments that did borrow found that their borrowing costs had increased sharply. From 1974 to 1975 the nominal yield on municipal bonds increased by almost a full percentage point, while the yield on taxable corporate bonds increased by only half of a percentage point. This increase in the yield on municipal bonds clearly signified a real increase in municipal borrowing costs.

A cursory glance at the behavior of the nominal yield on municipal bonds during the past twenty-five years might lead one to believe that, while the financial problems of municipal governments were acute in 1975, there has been a chronic problem for approximately a decade. The series on the nominal yield on long-term municipal bonds of average quality reported in column 4 of Table 39 shows that during the past ten years, the nominal yield on these municipal bonds (i^m) has been significantly higher than it was during the preceding fifteen years. But this increase in the nominal yield on municipal bonds reflects higher expected inflation rates in the past decade, not an increase in the real borrowing costs of municipal governments. As we showed in chapter 3, nominal yields on both municipal and corporate bonds have increased during the past decade because of increased inflation, while real yields—in the case of corporate bonds—remained relatively constant.

The real yield on long-term municipal bonds of average quality (r^m) is reported in column 5 of Table 39. This series is derived by

TABLE 39

INFLATION, INTEREST RATES, AND THE IMPLICIT SUBSIDY TO MUNICIPAL
GOVERMENT BORROWING FOR LONG-TERM BONDS OF AVERAGE QUALITY
(percent)

Year	π (1)	i^o (2)	r^o (3)	i^m (4)	r^m (5)	s (6)	s^o (7)
1952	0.0	3.2	3.2	2.2	2.2	30	30
1953	0.2	3.4	3.2	2.8	2.6	18	19
1954	0.3	3.2	2.9	2.5	2.2	22	24
1955	0.1	3.3	3.2	2.6	2.5	21	22
1956	0.6	3.6	3.0	2.9	2.3	18	21
1957	1.3	4.2	2.9	3.6	2.3	15	22
1958	1.7	4.2	2.5	3.4	1.7	19	32
1959	1.4	4.7	3.3	3.7	2.3	20	28
1960	1.5	4.7	3.2	3.7	2.2	22	32
1961	1.4	4.7	3.3	3.6	2.2	23	32
1962	1.3	4.6	3.3	3.3	2.0	29	40
1963	1.3	4.5	3.2	3.3	2.0	27	38
1964	1.3	4.6	3.3	3.3	2.0	28	39
1965	1.4	4.6	3.2	3.3	1.9	28	40
1966	1.7	5.3	3.6	3.9	2.2	27	40
1967	2.0	5.8	3.8	4.0	2.0	31	48
1968	2.5	6.5	4.0	4.5	2.0	31	51
1969	3.2	7.4	4.2	5.7	2.5	22	39
1970	3.9	8.5	4.6	6.4	2.5	25	45
1971	3.9	7.9	4.0	5.6	1.7	29	58
1972	3.8	7.6	3.8	5.3	1.5	31	60
1973	4.3	7.8	3.5	5.2	0.9	33	74
1974	5.9	9.0	3.1	6.2	0.3	31	89
1975	6.6	9.5	2.9	7.0	0.4	25	84
1976	6.3	9.0	2.7	6.6	0.3	27	90
Average							
1952–76	2.3	5.7	3.4	4.2	1.9	25	44
1952–66	1.0	4.2	3.2	3.2	2.2	23	31
1967–76	4.2	7.9	3.7	5.7	1.4	29	64
1972–76	5.4	8.6	3.2	6.1	0.7	29	80

NOTE: π = anticipated rate of inflation; i^o = nominal yield on corporate bonds;
r^o = real yield on corporate bonds; i^m = nominal yield on municipal bonds; r^m =
real yield on municipal bonds; s = nominal implicit subsidy rate for tax-exempt
bonds; s^o = real implicit subsidy rate for tax-exempt bonds.
SOURCE: The data for π are from Table 8, column 4. The data for i^o and i^m are
from Table 5. Column 3 is column 2 minus column 1. Column 5 is column 4 minus
column 1. The calculations for columns 6 and 7 are described in the text. Calculations are based on unrounded data.

subtracting the series for the expected rate of inflation (π) given in column 1 (taken from column 4 of Table 8) from the series for nominal municipal bond yields (i^m) in column 4. It is apparent that r^m was generally lower during the last ten years than it was during the preceding fifteen years. In fact, the average value of r^m for the decade 1967–76 was only 1.4 percent, whereas for the fifteen years from 1952 to 1966 the average value of r^m was 2.2 percent.

In order to understand the reasons for the decline in the real long-term borrowing costs of municipal governments during the last decade, it is necessary to examine what has happened to the long-term subsidy that is implicit in the privilege of issuing tax-exempt bonds of average quality. The size of this implicit subsidy is usually measured by the nominal subsidy rate (s), defined as the proportionate differential between the nominal long-term borrowing costs of municipal governments and the nominal long-term borrowing costs of taxable corporations; that is, $s = (i^c - i^m)/i^c$. This nominal subsidy rate corresponds exactly to the implicit nominal tax rate paid by holders of long-term municipal bonds of average quality (t^m). From the discussion in chapter 3, however, we know that t^m is not a reliable indicator of the real tax rate paid by holders of municipal bonds during periods of inflation. For the same reasons, the nominal subsidy rate (s) is not a reliable indicator of the real subsidy rate enjoyed by issuers of tax-exempt bonds during periods of inflation. To correct for the effects of inflation, it is essential to look at the real effective subsidy rate (s^e) rather than the nominal subsidy rate (s). The real effective subsidy rate corresponds to the real effective tax rate paid by holders of municipal bonds (t^{em}) and is defined as the proportionate differential between the real borrowing costs of municipal governments and the real borrowing costs of taxable corporations; that is, $s^e = t^{em} = (r^c - r^m)/r^c$.

Columns 6 and 7 of Table 39 illustrate the importance of the distinction between the nominal subsidy rate (s) and the real effective subsidy rate (s^e). During the decade 1967–76, s averaged only 29 percent, a slight increase from the average of 23 percent during the preceding fifteen years. In contrast, during the decade 1967–76, s^e averaged 64 percent, a very substantial increase from the average of 31 percent during the preceding fifteen years.

The data presented in Table 39 are relevant for the comparison of long-term municipal and corporate bonds of average quality. From the discussion in chapter 4, however, we know that it is of interest to look at long-term municipal and corporate bonds of the highest quality, because Aaa-rated bonds are probably less clouded by differences

TABLE 40

INFLATION, INTEREST RATES, AND THE IMPLICIT SUBSIDY TO MUNICIPAL
GOVERNMENT BORROWING FOR AAA-RATED LONG-TERM BONDS
(percent)

Year	π (1)	i^o (2)	r^o (3)	i^m (4)	r^m (5)	s (6)	s^o (7)
1952	0.0	3.0	3.0	1.8	1.8	40	40
1953	0.2	3.2	3.0	2.3	2.1	28	30
1954	0.3	2.9	2.6	2.0	1.7	31	35
1955	0.1	3.1	3.0	2.2	2.1	29	30
1956	0.6	3.4	2.8	2.5	1.9	26	32
1957	1.3	3.9	2.6	3.1	1.8	21	31
1958	1.7	3.8	2.1	2.9	1.2	24	43
1959	1.4	4.4	3.0	3.4	2.0	23	33
1960	1.5	4.4	2.9	3.3	1.8	25	38
1961	1.4	4.4	3.0	3.3	1.9	25	37
1962	1.3	4.3	3.0	3.0	1.7	30	43
1963	1.3	4.3	3.0	3.1	1.8	28	40
1964	1.3	4.4	3.1	3.1	1.8	30	42
1965	1.4	4.5	3.1	3.2	1.8	29	42
1966	1.7	5.1	3.4	3.7	2.0	27	41
1967	2.0	5.5	3.5	3.7	1.7	33	51
1968	2.5	6.2	3.7	4.2	1.7	32	54
1969	3.2	7.0	3.8	5.5	2.3	21	39
1970	3.9	8.0	4.1	6.1	2.2	24	46
1971	3.9	7.4	3.5	5.2	1.3	30	63
1972	3.8	7.2	3.4	5.0	1.2	31	65
1973	4.3	7.4	3.1	5.0	0.7	32	77
1974	5.9	8.6	2.1	5.9	0.0	31	100
1975	6.6	8.8	2.2	6.4	−0.2	27	109
1976	6.3	8.4	2.1	5.7	−0.6	28	129
Average							
1952–76	2.3	5.3	3.0	3.8	1.5	28	52
1952–66	1.0	3.9	2.9	2.9	1.9	28	37
1967–76	4.2	7.5	3.2	5.3	1.7	29	73
1972–76	5.4	8.0	2.6	5.6	0.2	30	96

SOURCE: The data for π are from Table 8, column 4. The data for i^o, i^m, and s are from Table 12, columns 1, 2, and 3, respectively. Column 3 is column 2 minus column 1. Column 5 is column 4 minus column 1. Column 7 is the ratio of columns 2 and 3 times column 6. Calculations are based on unrounded data.

TABLE 41

THE IMPLICIT SUBSIDY TO MUNICIPAL BORROWERS FOR NEWLY ISSUED AAA-RATED BONDS
(percent)

Year	s (1)	s^e (2)
1952	41	41
1953	34	34
1954	33	37
1955	31	32
1956	31	37
1957	30	42
1958	29	50
1959	29	41
1960	31	45
1961	27	39
1962	32	45
1963	28	40
1964	31	44
1965	30	44
1966	31	46
1967	36	59
1968	36	59
1969	29	49
1970	28	52
1971	31	64
1972	32	66
1973	36	80
1974	34	100
1975	29	108
1976	31	130
Average		
1952–76	32	55
1952–66	31	41
1967–76	32	76
1972–76	32	97

SOURCE: Column 1 is calculated as column 2, Table 13, minus column 4, Table 40, divided by column 2, Table 13. Column 2 is calculated as column 2, Table 13, minus column 4, Table 40, divided by the quantity column 2, Table 13, minus column 1, Table 40. Calculations are based on unrounded data.

in ratings. Furthermore, especially in looking at the subsidy to municipal borrowing, it is important to look at new issues rather than seasoned issues because of the differential tax treatment of capital gains. In Table 40 we present the same information as in Table 39, except that we utilize data for Aaa-rated, seasoned corporate and municipal bonds. In Table 41, we present the nominal and real subsidy rates using data for Aaa-rated, newly issued corporate bonds. The qualitative results are the same: there has been a substantial increase in s^e and a corresponding decrease in r^m over the past decade. In fact, the Aaa bonds data indicate that the real subsidy has increased even more dramatically than the data for average quality bonds.

The increase in s^e and the corresponding decrease in r^m during the past decade was not a fluke. It reflected the interaction between higher rates of price inflation and the operation of the U.S. tax system. This point has already been explained in connection with the discussion of why the real effective tax rate of holders of municipal bonds (t^{em}) increased during the past decade. It is useful to review this explanation in order to emphasize both why the real effective subsidy rate (s^e) has increased during the past decade and why it is likely to remain high as long as inflation rates remain near the levels experienced during the past decade.

During the past decade, the before-tax nominal yield on long-term corporate bonds of average quality (i^c) rose by about the same amount as the expected rate of inflation (π). This left the before-tax real yield on those corporate bonds ($r^c = i^c - \pi$) during the past five years at nearly the same average level as that experienced during the fifteen years from 1952 to 1966. Because taxes are levied on nominal interest income, however, the after-tax real yield on corporate bonds decreased dramatically for most taxable investors. For example, for an investor with a marginal tax rate of 30 percent, the after-tax real yield on corporate bonds is $r^c - (0.30) \cdot i^c$. During the past five years, this after-tax real yield averaged only 0.7 percent. In contrast, during the fifteen years from 1952 to 1966, the after-tax real yield on corporate bonds for an investor with a 30 percent marginal tax rate averaged 1.9 percent. For investors with marginal tax rates greater than 30 percent, the decline in the after-tax real yield on corporate bonds has been even more dramatic.

The decline in the after-tax real yield on corporate bonds has had a profound effect on the real yield on municipal bonds (r^m). If r^m had remained constant in the face of higher inflation rates (that is, if i^m had increased by the same amount as π), then all taxable holders of corporate bonds would have had a very strong incentive to shift out

181

of taxable corporate bonds and into tax-exempt municipal bonds. Given the existing supplies of corporate and municipal bonds, however, this shift could not be accomplished. Instead, the real yield on municipal bonds was bid down until investors were indifferent between holding taxable corporate bonds and holding tax-exempt municipal bonds. To achieve this equilibrium, r^m fell by about as much as the real after-tax yield on corporate bonds for an investor with a 30 percent marginal tax rate—that is, from 2.2 percent in the fifteen years from 1952 to 1966 to 0.7 percent during the past five years.

Investors with an approximate 30 percent marginal tax rate are important because they are nearly indifferent between taxable long-term corporate bonds and tax-exempt long-term municipal bonds. This border of indifference is determined by the proportionate nominal yield differential between corporate bonds and municipal bonds, that is, by $s = t^m = (i^c - i^m)/i^c$. Investors with marginal tax rates (t) greater than t^m will find municipal bonds more attractive than corporate bonds, and investors whose marginal tax rates are less than t^m will find corporate bonds more attractive. The nominal yield differential is relevant for determining the border of indifference because taxes are levied on nominal interest income. As emphasized in chapter 3, however, nominal tax rates do not correspond to real effective tax rates during a period of inflation. The real effective tax rate on corporate bonds for an investor in the 30 percent nominal tax bracket is $t^{ec} = (0.30) \cdot (r^c + \pi)/r^c$. Clearly, given an approximately constant value of r^c, as π rises, t^{ec} also rises. This implies that the implicit real effective tax rate that this investor would be willing to pay on municipal bonds, $t^{em} = (r^c - r^m)/r^c$, rises to the same extent as the increase in t^{ec}. In fact, the value of t^{em} is equal to the value of t^{ec} for the investor who lies at the border of indifference between municipal bonds and corporate bonds.

The real effective rate of subsidy (s^e) enjoyed by issuers of tax-exempt municipal bonds (s) is equal to the real effective tax rate (t^{em}) paid by holders of these bonds. Therefore, since an increase in the inflation rate increases t^{em}, it also must increase s^e. Moreover, as long as the inflation rate remains high, so also will the real implicit tax rate and hence the real effective subsidy rate. In fact, if inflation persists at the rates experienced during the past decade, it is likely that the real effective subsidy will be greater than the rates indicated in Table 39. First, as we have seen in Tables 40 and 41, subsidies to Aaa-rated borrowers were greater than subsidies to "average quality" borrowers; and, as argued in chapter 4, the Aaa subsidy rate is the more appropriate measure. Second, to some extent, the inflation that was experienced during the past decade was unanticipated. As a result, anticipated nominal yields on taxable bonds were less than they would have been if inflation had been correctly anticipated, and so were the real effective subsidy rates on tax-exempt municipal bonds. Third, the nominal implicit subsidy rate on municipal bonds of average maturity is significantly greater than that on long-term municipal bonds. This means that the real effective subsidy rate for municipal bonds of average maturity is proportionately greater than the real effective subsidy rate for long-term municipal bonds.

The effect of different expected inflation rates on the real effective subsidy rate on municipal bonds (s^e) is indicated in Table 42. The subsidy rates in this table are the values of s^e that would prevail in equilibrium, when nominal yields accurately reflect the expected rate of inflation and when the real yield on taxable bonds is equal to its equilibrium value, assumed to be 3.3 percent. For each expected inflation rate, two values of s^e are given, one for municipal bonds of average maturity and one for long-term municipal bonds. These values of s^e are determined by the formula,

$$s^e = t^{em} = s \cdot (r^c + \pi)/r^c = s \cdot i^c/(i^c - \pi),$$

where $s = (i^c - i^m)/i^c$ is the implicit nominal subsidy rate on municipal bonds, $r^c = 3.3$ percent is the real yield on taxable corporate bonds, $i^c = r^c + \pi$ is the nominal yield on taxable corporate bonds, and π is the expected inflation rate. Using the findings in chapter 4, we assume that the nominal implicit subsidy rate for bonds of average maturity is 35 percent, and for long-term bonds, 30 percent.[1]

It is apparent that the real effective subsidy rate for both average and long-term bonds increases dramatically as the expected inflation rate increases. Given the experience of the past decade, and particularly more recent experience with the actual inflation rate, it seems unlikely that the expected inflation rate will fall below the range of 4 to 6 percent for the foreseeable future. Hence, the values of s^e that are appropriate for expected inflation rates in this range provide lower bounds for the real effective subsidy rates that are likely to be enjoyed by municipal borrowers for the foreseeable future. Specifically, for long-term municipal bonds, the real effective subsidy rate is likely to be at least 66 to 85 percent. For municipal bonds of average maturity, the real effective subsidy rate will be even higher, at least 77 to 99 percent. Indeed, during 1977, high-grade municipal borrowers were able to borrow substantial amounts at interest rates of about 5 per-

---

[1] Table 42 is identical to Table 11 since the real effective subsidy rate is identical to the real implicit tax rate.

TABLE 42

REAL EFFECTIVE SUBSIDY RATES UNDER THE EXEMPTION
(percent)

Expected Inflation Rate (percent)	Real Effective Subsidy Rate	
	Bonds of average maturity	Long-term bonds
0	35	30
1	46	39
2	56	48
3	67	57
4	77	66
5	88	75
6	99	85
7	109	94
8	120	103
9	130	112
10	141	121

SOURCE: Table 11.

cent. Since 5 percent is probably less than the expected rate of inflation in 1977, it follows that these state and local governments were
able to borrow at negative real yields. In other words, they enjoyed
a real effective rate of subsidy in excess of 100 percent.

The Supply of Municipal Bonds and the Prospects for Municipal Borrowing Costs

Another important issue raised by advocates of the taxable bond
option is the purported incapacity of the market for tax-exempt bonds
to absorb the increases in municipal borrowing that are likely to occur
over the next decade without producing substantial increases in municipal borrowing costs. Proponents of the option point to the fact
that the substantial increase in the volume of municipal debt that
occurred during the past decade was associated with a substantial
increase in the borrowing costs of municipal governments (as measured by the nominal yield on municipal bonds). They argue that the
market for tax-exempt bonds will not be able to absorb the similar
increase in the volume of municipal debt projected to occur during
the next decade, because the market for tax-exempt bonds is inherently a limited one, appealing only to high-tax-bracket investors. In

the absence of adequate demand to absorb the projected increase in the supply of municipal bonds at a given level of yields, the yield on municipal bonds will have to rise in order to attract investors with lower and lower tax rates into the market. The result will be both an increase in the borrowing costs of municipal governments and an increase in the gain accruing to high-tax-bracket holders of municipal bonds.

A cursory examination of the facts concerning the growth of municipal debt during the past twenty-five years appears to lend some support to this line of argument. Specifically, column 1 of Table 43 reports the series on the dollar volume of municipal debt (M). These figures reveal that during the decade 1957–66, when the nominal yield on municipal bonds rose by less than 1 percent, the volume of municipal debt rose by 112 percent. In contrast, during the decade 1967–76, when the nominal yield on municipal bonds rose by about 2 percent, the volume of municipal debt rose by 134 percent. If we project a further increase of 134 percent in the volume of municipal debt during the coming decade, past experience appears to suggest that there would have to be a further substantial increase in the nominal yield on municipal bonds.

The crude facts, however, present a very misleading picture of what has happened and what is likely to happen in the market for tax-exempt municipal bonds. As shown in the preceding section, the picture is distorted because the nominal yield on municipal bonds does not correspond to the real yield on municipal bonds. While nominal yields on municipal bonds rose during the past decade, real yields declined.

Another reason for the distortion is that the increase in the dollar value of municipal debt is not a good measure of the increase in the volume of such debt. A large part of the increase in the dollar value of municipal debt has been accounted for by the increase in the general price level. The importance of the increase in the price level is indicated by the series in column 2 of Table 43, which reports the real value of the outstanding stock of municipal bonds, using 1967 as the base year for the price index. During the decade 1957–66, the real value of municipal debt increased by 76 percent, somewhat less than the 112 percent increase in the nominal value of municipal debt. During the decade 1967–76, the real value of municipal debt increased by only 33 percent, far less than the 134 percent increase in the nominal value of municipal debt.

An even better way to look at the size of the outstanding stock of municipal bonds is to compare it with the size of gross national

TABLE 43

Municipal Debt
(billions of dollars)

Year	Municipal Debt in Current Prices (1)	Municipal Debt in 1967 Prices (2)	Ratio of Municipal Debt to GNP (3)
1952	$ 30	$ 38	0.086
1953	35	42	0.095
1954	41	51	0.111
1955	46	58	0.115
1956	49	62	0.119
1957	54	65	0.123
1958	59	68	0.131
1959	65	76	0.138
1960	71	80	0.142
1961	76	84	0.146
1962	81	89	0.145
1963	87	75	0.147
1964	93	100	0.148
1965	100	105	0.145
1966	106	109	0.141
1967	114	114	0.144
1968	123	118	0.143
1969	133	121	0.143
1970	144	124	0.147
1971	162	134	0.153
1972	177	142	0.153
1973	194	146	0.148
1974	213	144	0.151
1975	224	139	0.147
1976	248	145	0.147
Percentage increase			
1957–66	112	76	18
1967–76	134	33	4

Source: The data for column 1 are from Table 6, column 1. Column 2 is column 1 divided by the consumer price index, which is obtained from the *Federal Reserve Bulletin*. Column 3 is column 1 divided by the gross national product, which is obtained from the *Federal Reserve Bulletin*.

product (GNP). The ratio of municipal debt to GNP (column 3 of Table 43) is a relevant number because one would normally expect that the demand for municipal bonds would expand roughly in proportion to GNP, holding the real effective tax rates on alternative securities constant. During the decade 1957–66, this ratio increased by only 18 percent, in comparison with the 76 percent increase in the real value of municipal debt and the 112 percent increase in the nominal value of municipal debt. During the decade 1967–76, the increase in the ratio of municipal debt to GNP was a meager 4 percent.

We now have a more accurate picture of developments that took place in the market for tax-exempt municipal bonds during the past two decades. During the decade 1957–66, the supply of municipal bonds expanded moderately relative to the overall size of the economy. This increase in the relative supply of municipal debt was absorbed with essentially no change in the real yield on municipal bonds, either absolutely or relative to the real yield on corporate bonds. During the decade 1967–76, the supply of municipal bonds grew at the same rate as the economy as a whole. The increase in the real effective tax rate on corporate bonds and other taxable securities that resulted from accelerating inflation forced up the real effective tax rate implicitly paid by holders of municipal bonds. For this reason, the real yield on municipal bonds actually declined during the decade 1967–76.

There is no good reason to believe that the stock of municipal debt will expand any more rapidly in the coming decade than it has since 1967. At most, the growth of the stock of municipal debt should approximately keep pace with the growth of gross national product. The rationale behind this projection is simply that the need of municipal governments to issue bonds is likely to grow less rapidly in the future than it has in the past. During the 1950s and 1960s state and local governments financed a substantial one-time expansion of educational facilities at the primary, secondary, and higher educational levels. Demography dictates that the need for educational facilities will be far less in the coming decade. Since the Department of Health, Education, and Welfare intends to reduce the total number of hospital beds, it is unlikely that new hospital construction will generate much additional municipal borrowing. The experience of New York City has probably convinced most municipal governments that debt financing of current operating expenses is not the road to fiscal salvation. Moreover, the growth of general revenue sharing and of specific grants-in-aid programs has increased the access of municipal governments to other means of finance. Finally, even if the supply of municipal debt were again to grow as rapidly as it did during the period 1957–66, experience indicates that this growth of supply would be absorbed without much change in the real borrowing costs of municipal governments.

The Exemption, the Option, and Economic Efficiency

As long as the expected inflation rate remains high, the exemption will continue to provide a substantial real subsidy to municipal borrowers. Specifically, we have seen in Table 42 that as long as the expected inflation rate remains in the range of 4 to 6 percent the real effective subsidy rate on long-term municipal bonds will be at least in the range of 66 to 85 percent, and the real effective subsidy rate on municipal bonds of average maturity will be at least 77 to 99 percent.

However, although the real effective subsidy rate provided by the exemption is likely to remain high, there is little doubt that it would be even higher under a taxable bond option with a 40 percent direct subsidy rate. Under such an option, the nominal subsidy rate on both taxable and tax-exempt bonds would be at least 40 percent, because municipal governments would choose to issue tax-exempt bonds rather than subsidized taxable bonds only if the implicit subsidy rate provided by the exemption were at least as great as the direct subsidy of 40 percent provided by the Treasury. On the other hand, municipal governments would choose to issue tax-exempt bonds if the subsidy provided by the exemption were greater than the 40 percent direct subsidy.

The 40 percent taxable bond option would have its greatest effect on long-term municipal bonds because the nominal implicit subsidy rate on such bonds under the exemption is only about 30 percent, and it would be raised to 40 percent under the option. For medium-term municipal bonds, the effect of the option would be slight since the nominal implicit subsidy rate on such bonds is already close to 40 percent. For short-term municipal bonds, the option would have no effect because the nominal implicit subsidy rate on such bonds already exceeds 40 percent.

Since the principal effect of a 40 percent taxable bond option would be felt on long-term municipal bonds, it makes sense to concentrate on the effect of the option on such bonds. Under the exemption, the nominal subsidy rate on such bonds (s) is equal to 30 percent. Under the 40 percent taxable bond option, we would have $s = 40$ percent. Using the formula,

$$s^e = s \cdot (r^e + \pi)/r^e = s \cdot i^e/(i^e - \pi),$$

we may calculate the effect of this increase in s on the real effective subsidy rate (s^e) on long-term municipal bonds at different expected inflation rates (π). As before, it is assumed that the real yield on taxable corporate bonds (r^e) is equal to its equilibrium value of 3.3 percent and that the nominal yield on taxable corporate bonds (i^e) is equal to this real yield plus the expected inflation rate. It follows that the real effective subsidy rate on long-term municipal bonds under the 40 percent option is as indicated in Table 44. For comparative purposes, Table 44 also indicates the real effective subsidy rate on long-term municipal bonds under the exemption (as in Table 42).

From Table 44 it is apparent that the 40 percent taxable bond option would significantly increase the real effective subsidy rate on long-term municipal bonds. The magnitude of this increase is greater, the higher the expected rate of inflation. In particular, with the expectation of inflation rates of 4 to 6 percent, the taxable bond option would increase the real effective subsidy rate from the range of 66 to 85 percent to the range of 88 to 113 percent.

The question that must now be asked is whether this increase in the real effective subsidy rate is desirable. On the whole, proponents of the taxable bond option take it for granted that a higher subsidy rate is preferable because it means greater financial assistance to hard-pressed municipal governments. In contrast, economists criticize the

TABLE 44

REAL EFFECTIVE SUBSIDY RATES ON LONG-TERM MUNICIPAL BONDS
(percent)

Expected Inflation Rate	Under a 40 Percent Taxable Bond Option	Under the Exemption
0	40	30
1	52	39
2	64	48
3	76	57
4	88	66
5	101	75
6	113	85
7	125	94
8	137	103
9	149	112
10	161	121

NOTE: The method of calculation is described in the text.

form of financial assistance provided both by the exemption and by the option because it promotes economic inefficiency. This economic inefficiency results from the fact that the subsidy to municipal borrowing encourages municipal governments to undertake public investment projects that earn a lower social return than the private investment projects that would otherwise be financed by the funds borrowed by the municipal governments. The higher the subsidy rate for municipal borrowers, the greater is the incentive to undertake public investment projects that earn a low social return and, hence, the greater is the economic inefficiency resulting from the subsidy. Since the taxable bond option would increase the subsidy rate enjoyed by the municipal borrowers above that provided by the exemption, it would promote greater economic inefficiency than now results from the exemption.

Concern with the economic inefficiency generated by a subsidy to municipal borrowing is not an issue that arises exclusively in connection with the taxable bond option. Indeed, the problem of economic inefficiency has traditionally been one of the most important arguments raised against the exemption.[2] Proponents of the taxable bond option, however, do not raise this argument in their list of criticisms of the exemption. Interestingly, they seem to recognize that whatever the defects of the exemption in terms of economic inefficiency may be, they hold with even greater force for the option.

To understand the general issue of the economic inefficiency resulting from a subsidy to municipal borrowing, it is useful to consider the situation that would prevail if there were no such subsidy. In that case, private investors would face the same cost of financing their investment projects as do municipal governments. Private investors would undertake only those investment projects for which the expected return (corrected for risk) was greater than or equal to the borrowing costs incurred to finance the project. Municipal governments would undertake only those public investment projects where the expected return was at least as great as the costs of finance. Society's scarce capital resources would be allocated in an economically efficient manner.

Now consider what would happen if borrowing by municipal governments were subsidized by the federal government. The sub-

---

[2] As pointed out by Ott and Meltzer (1963), the issue of economic inefficiency figured prominently in early criticisms of the exemption, but it has received relatively less attention in recent years. Ackerman and Ott (1970) have raised the issue of the additional economic inefficiency that would result from the taxable bond option.

sidy would have two effects: a financial effect and a resource allocation effect. The financial effect is simply the lower costs that municipal governments would enjoy on the borrowing they would have undertaken anyway. The resource allocation effect arises because lower borrowing costs would induce municipal governments to undertake additional public investment projects. This resource allocation effect results in a loss of economic efficiency because the private investment projects that are displaced by the additional municipal borrowing have a higher return than the public investment projects that are undertaken as a result of the subsidy. This displacement of private investment is of special concern in the present economic environment, where low rates of industrial capital formation pose a potential threat to the maintenance of an adequate rate of creation of new jobs and to continued economic growth.

It should be emphasized that the financial effect of the subsidy is probably of greatest concern to municipal governments. For understandable reasons, officials of municipal governments would like to receive as much financial assistance as possible (with as few strings attached as possible) from the federal government. The economic objection to any subsidy to municipal borrowing is not that it provides such financial assistance but that it combines general financial assistance with the incentive to distort the efficient allocation of the economy's scarce resources. Other forms of financial assistance, such as general revenue sharing and some specific grants-in-aid, serve the general function of providing help to municipal governments without inducing a loss of economic efficiency.[3]

Unquestionably, a taxable bond option with a 40 percent direct subsidy rate would provide additional financial assistance to municipal governments. Under the conditions that are likely to prevail for at least the next few years, such an option would increase the real effective rate of subsidy on long-term municipal bonds from the range of 66 to 85 percent to the range of 88 to 113 percent. The taxable bond option, however, is only one of many possible ways of providing increased financial assistance to municipal governments. The economic objection to the taxable bond option is that it would combine increased financial assistance with an increase in the economic inefficiency that is already suffered as a result of the distortionary effects of the subsidy provided by the exemption.

---

[3] Some forms of grants-in-aid may also distort the allocation of resources. This is particularly true of matching grants under which municipal governments pay only a fraction of the cost of the subsidized project.

Summary

In this chapter, we have examined the effectiveness of the exemption as a means of subsidizing the borrowing costs of municipal governments. Contrary to what is generally asserted by proponents of the taxable bond option, we have found that the exemption's effectiveness has increased during the past decade and is likely to remain high as long as the inflation rate remains near or above 4 percent. In particular, we estimate that the real effective rate of subsidy enjoyed by municipal governments will be at least 60 percent and probably as high as 70 or 80 percent for the foreseeable future.

We have also examined the contention that the market for tax-exempt municipal bonds will be unable to absorb the increase in municipal borrowing that is likely to occur during the coming decade, particularly if the stock of debt outstanding continues to grow as rapidly as it did during the past decade. We found that during the past decade the stock of municipal debt grew by only 4 percent relative to the economy as a whole and that the increase in debt was absorbed with a substantial decline in the real borrowing costs of municipal governments. During the coming decade, the stock of municipal debt will probably grow no faster than the economy, and the experience of the past twenty-five years indicates that such an increase can easily be absorbed by the market for tax-exempt bonds without any substantial increase in the real borrowing costs of municipal governments.

Finally, we have examined the contention that a taxable bond option with a 40 percent direct subsidy rate would significantly increase the effectiveness of the subsidy on the borrowing costs of municipal governments. We have not disputed this claim; rather, we have asked whether an increase in the real effective rate of subsidy to the range of 88 to 113 percent from the range of 66 to 85 percent is socially desirable. Our answer is that the high rate of subsidy now provided by the exemption already reduces economic efficiency by encouraging municipal governments to undertake public investment projects that have a lower social rate of return than private investment projects. The introduction of the taxable bond option would exacerbate this problem. For this reason, the taxable bond option is not a desirable method of granting additional financial assistance to municipal governments. To the extent that it is desirable to provide such assistance, there are other means available that would not further distort the allocation of society's scarce capital resources.

9

The Stability of Municipal Borrowing Costs

Proponents of the taxable bond option argue that it would reduce the excessive instability that currently characterizes the market for tax-exempt municipal bonds. This instability is reflected in the variability of the nominal borrowing costs of state and local governments and, particularly, in the variability of the implicit nominal subsidy on tax-exempt municipal bonds, $s = (i^c - i^m)/i^c$. It is argued that this instability is produced largely because the exemption isolates the municipal bond market from the general credit market. Because of this isolation, the pressures generated by disturbances to the demand or supply of municipal bonds cannot escape into the general credit market and therefore have a concentrated and pronounced effect on the yield on municipal bonds. In particular, it is argued that since commercial banks are the dominant participants in the market for municipal bonds, changes in monetary policy that affect banks' demand for municipal bonds have a highly destabilizing effect on the market for these bonds.

The taxable bond option is the purported panacea for these ills. The idea is that, under the option, any special pressures in the market for tax-exempt municipal bonds would be relieved through the greater or lesser issuance of subsidized taxable municipal bonds. For example, if contractionary monetary policy reduced bank demand for tax-exempt municipals and threatened to drive up the nominal yield on tax exempts and reduce the implicit nominal subsidy, state and local governments would respond by issuing fewer tax-exempt bonds and more subsidized taxable bonds. As long as the direct subsidy rate on taxable municipal bonds (s^*) was set high enough to induce the issuance of at least some subsidized taxable bonds, the effective nominal subsidy rate on both taxable and tax-exempt municipal bonds would be stabilized at s^*. This is because municipal borrowers would find it in their interest to issue tax exempts exactly up to the point where their net borrowing costs are equal to the net borrowing costs on subsidized taxable bonds. The experience of the past sixty years indicates that a direct subsidy rate of 40 percent would probably be sufficient to achieve this result.

In this chapter, we do not challenge the assertion that the taxable bond option would stabilize the nominal subsidy on municipal bonds. Rather, we attempt to examine the more fundamental question of whether this particular type of "stability" would actually be beneficial either to municipal borrowers or to the economy as a whole. We point out that the standard analysis of the stability issue has focused on nominal borrowing costs and nominal subsidy rates, rather than the more relevant real borrowing costs and real subsidy rates. While the taxable bond option would eliminate fluctuations in the nominal subsidy rate on municipal bonds, it would not necessarily even reduce fluctuations in the real borrowing costs of municipalities or in the real subsidy rate on municipal bonds. Indeed, we show that had the taxable bond option been in effect during the past twenty-five years the real borrowing costs of municipalities and the real subsidy rate on municipal bonds would have been less stable than they were under the exemption. Further, we argue that, even in circumstances in which the taxable bond option would reduce the variability of real borrowing costs of municipalities, this gain in stability for municipal borrowers might not be a good thing for the economy as a whole. This is because the option would not reduce the magnitude of disturbances to the economic system but would only redistribute the effect of these disturbances from municipal borrowers to other borrowers, such as demanders of home mortgages.

Inflation and the Stability of Municipal Borrowing Costs

During any period of substantial price inflation, it is essential to distinguish between nominal interest rates and real interest rates. The importance of this distinction for the analysis of the fiscal inefficiency and tax inequity resulting from the exemption, and for the measurement of the effectiveness of the exemption as a means of subsidizing borrowing by municipal governments, has been amply demonstrated. In previous chapters, we were primarily concerned with the level of the real yield on municipal bonds, with the level of the real subsidy received by the issuers of such bonds, and with the level of the real effective tax rate paid by the holders of such bonds. In discussing the issue of stability, we are not so much concerned with the average level of the real yield on municipal bonds as with the variability of the real yield around its average level.

The standard analysis of the stability issue is also concerned with the variability of the yield on municipal bonds, but the focus is on nominal yields rather than real yields. In periods of inflation, however, the measure of borrowing costs that is relevant to the financial decisions of municipal governments is the anticipated real yield on the bonds these governments issue. In the standard analysis, no mention is made of the phenomenon of inflation or of the distinction between real and nominal yields. The implicit assumption is that we live in a noninflationary economy where nominal yields correspond to real yields and, in particular, where instability of nominal yields indicates similar instability of real yields.[1] As we shall see, in an inflationary environment, instability of nominal yields generally does not give a good indication of the instability of real yields.

In order to understand the sources of instability in the anticipated real yield on municipal bonds ($r^m = i^m - \pi$), it is useful to delineate the three channels through which economic disturbances may affect r^m. This may be accomplished with the aid of the equation,

$$r^m = r^c - s \cdot (r^c + \pi) = (1 - s) \cdot r^c - s \cdot \pi,$$

where $r^c = i^c - \pi$ is the anticipated real yield on taxable corporate bonds, π is the expected rate of inflation, and $s = (i^c - i^m)/i^c$ is the implicit nominal subsidy rate on the anticipated nominal borrowing costs of municipal governments. From this equation, it is apparent that economic disturbances can affect r^m through three possible channels: variations in r^c (holding π and s constant); variations in π (holding r^c and s constant); and variations in s (holding r^c and π constant).

Variations in r^c result from general disturbances to the demand for credit and the supply of credit in the economy as a whole. These disturbances could result from changes in anticipations concerning the profitability of investments in physical capital. They could also result from changes in the supply of credit induced by actions of the monetary authority, or from changes in the demand for credit induced by changes in the magnitude of the government deficit. An important fact about these general credit market disturbances is that the taxable bond option would do nothing to reduce their magnitude.

---

[1] If the nominal yield on taxable corporate bonds were completely stable, the only source of instability in the real borrowing costs of municipal governments would be the instability of the implicit nominal subsidy rate (s). This is the scenario that implicitly underlies the standard analysis of the stability issue.

Variations in π result from anything that alters expectations concerning the future rate of price inflation—changes in the observed rate of price inflation, changes in the announced future policy of the monetary authority, or changes in predictions of the future federal deficits. Whatever may be the factors that account for variations in π, however, there is no reason to believe that the magnitude of these variations would be reduced by the taxable bond option.

Variations in the implicit subsidy rate (s) result primarily from variations in the demand for tax-exempt municipal bonds or variations in the supply of municipal bonds relative to the demand for credit and the supply of credit as a whole. For instance, an increase in municipal borrowing to finance sewage treatment facilities will tend to drive up the yield on municipal bonds relative to corporate bonds and thereby reduce s. A change in tax regulations that increases the availability of tax shelters other than tax-exempt municipal bonds decreases the demand for municipal bonds relative to the demand for bonds in general. This depresses the subsidy rate and increases the real borrowing costs of municipal governments.

The taxable bond option would stabilize the nominal subsidy rate on both taxable and tax-exempt municipal bonds at the level of the direct subsidy rate paid on taxable municipal bonds. In particular, with a 40 percent direct subsidy rate, the anticipated real borrowing costs of municipal governments would be given by:

$$r^{m^\circ} = r^c - (0.6) \cdot (r^c + \pi) = (0.4) \cdot r^c - (0.6) \cdot \pi.$$

In this formula, s no longer appears as a variable because its value is fixed at $s = s^* = 40$ percent. Since s is no longer a variable, it is clear that variations in s can no longer provide a channel through which economic disturbances affect the anticipated real borrowing costs of municipal governments. The other two channels, variations in r^c and variations in π, however, remain open. Hence, the taxable bond option does not insure complete stability of the anticipated real borrowing costs of municipal governments. More important, it is possible that stabilizing the subsidy rate may increase, rather than reduce, the overall instability of r^m.

This theoretical possibility arises because the total variability of r^m depends not only on the variability of r^c, π, and s but also on the covariances between r^c, π, and s. For instance, if increases in r^c are generally associated with increases in s (positive covariance), then the effect of variations in s will tend to offset the effect of variations in r^c, thereby reducing the total variability of r^m. In this circumstance, fixing the value of s will actually increase the variability of r^m. This situation is analogous to that of an automobile traveling over a bumpy road. The springs of the automobile compress and expand, and this action, by itself, should produce a rough ride. But since the springs compress as the car goes over a bump and expand as the wheels hit a rut, the overall effect is to produce a smooth ride. It is theoretically conceivable that variations in the implicit subsidy rate on tax-exempt municipal bonds play a similar role. If so, the taxable bond option would be comparable to elimination of the springs in an automobile. It would provide a more rigid link between the wheels and the frame, but it would not provide a smoother ride.

Factual Evidence on the Stability of Municipal Borrowing Costs

The analysis of the preceding section suggested the theoretical possibility that the taxable bond option might increase, rather than reduce, the instability of the anticipated real borrowing costs of municipal governments. To ascertain whether this theoretical possibility should be taken seriously, it is instructive to examine the experience of the last twenty-five years and to ask the following question: If the taxable bond option, with a 40 percent direct subsidy rate, had been in operation since 1952, would the instability of the anticipated real borrowing costs of municipal governments have been greater or smaller than it was under the exemption?

Table 45 is relevant for answering this question. It reports the yields on long-term taxable and tax-exempt bonds of average quality for the years 1952 to 1976. The entries at the bottom of each column give the mean and the standard deviation of the series in that column for the period 1952–76, for the noninflationary subperiod 1952–66, and for the inflationary subperiod 1967–76. The standard deviation measures the variability of a series and, hence, is a measure of instability.

Column 1 reports the nominal yield on long-term taxable corporate bonds of average quality (i^o). Column 2 reports the nominal yield on long-term tax-exempt municipal bonds of average quality (i^m). The series in column 3 represents the nominal yield on long-term municipal bonds of average quality, if the taxable bond option, with a 40 percent subsidy rate, had been in operation since 1952 (i^{m*}). This series is constructed by assuming that the nominal yield on municipal bonds under this option would have been 60 percent of the yield on long-term taxable corporate bonds of average quality; that is, $i^{m*} = (0.60) \cdot i^o$. The results indicate that the anticipated nominal borrowing costs of municipal governments would have been

TABLE 45

Nominal Yields on Long-Term Corporate and Municipal Bonds of Average Quality
(percent)

Year	i^o (1)	i^m (2)	i^{m*} (3)
1952	3.2	2.2	1.9
1953	3.4	2.8	2.1
1954	3.2	2.5	1.9
1955	3.3	2.6	2.0
1956	3.6	2.9	2.1
1957	4.2	3.6	2.5
1958	4.2	3.4	2.5
1959	4.7	3.7	2.8
1960	4.7	3.7	2.8
1961	4.7	3.6	2.8
1962	4.6	3.3	2.8
1963	4.5	3.3	2.7
1964	4.6	3.3	2.7
1965	4.6	3.3	2.8
1966	5.3	3.9	3.2
1967	5.8	4.0	3.5
1968	6.5	4.5	3.9
1969	7.4	5.7	4.4
1970	8.5	6.4	5.1
1971	7.9	5.6	4.8
1972	7.6	5.3	4.6
1973	7.8	5.2	4.7
1974	9.0	6.2	5.4
1975	9.5	7.0	5.7
1976	9.0	6.6	5.9
1952–76 mean	5.7	4.2	3.4
Standard deviation	2.1	1.4	1.2
1952–66 mean	4.2	3.2	2.5
Standard deviation	0.7	0.5	0.4
1967–76 mean	7.9	5.7	4.7
Standard deviation	1.1	1.0	0.7

NOTE: i^o = nominal yield on taxable corporate bonds; i^m = nominal yield on tax-exempt municipal bonds; i^{m*} = nominal yield on municipal bonds under taxable bond option with a 40 percent subsidy. Calculations and sources of data are described in the text. Calculations are based on unrounded data.

somewhat less variable under the taxable bond option than they were under the exemption.

The question of interest, however, is the variability of anticipated *real* borrowing costs rather than anticipated *nominal* borrowing costs. To calculate anticipated real borrowing costs, it is essential to have a series on the expected rate of inflation, π. For this critical series, we will use the series reported in column 4 of Table 8.[2] Subtracting this series for π from the series for i^e given in column 1 of Table 45, we obtain the series on r^e reported in column 1 of Table 46. Subtracting the series for π from the series for i^m given in column 2 of Table 45, we obtain the series for r^m under the exemption that is reported in column 2 of Table 46. Subtracting π from the series for i^{m*} given in column 3 of Table 45, we obtain the series for r^{m*} under the 40 percent option that is reported in column 3 of Table 46. The figures at the bottom of columns 2 and 3 indicate that the standard deviation of r^{m*} for the period 1952–76 is greater than the standard deviation of r^m for the same period by a factor of 1.14. This implies that the taxable bond option would have *increased* the variability of the anticipated long-term real borrowing costs of municipal governments issuing average quality bonds during this period by 14 percent.

This result demonstrates that the theoretical possibility that the taxable bond option would increase instability of real municipal borrowing costs must be taken seriously.[3] This does not mean, however, that it would *necessarily* increase instability. In fact, during the 1952–66 subperiod, the figures in Table 45 indicate that the option would

---

[2] Table 8 reports three series on the expected rate of inflation for three values of the assumed speed of adjustment of expectations concerning the inflation rate. The qualitative nature of the results discussed in this chapter does not depend on which of these three series is used. The series in column 4 has been chosen for convenience.

[3] We also looked at the instability of real borrowing costs for Aaa-rated borrowers on seasoned and new issues. Presumably, Aaa-rated new issues remove other potential sources of instability and thus give a clearer picture. The relevant figures are:

	r^m (Aaa)	r^{m*} (Aaa seasoned)	r^{m*} (Aaa new)
1952–76 mean	1.4	0.9	1.0
Standard deviation	0.8	0.9	0.9
1952–66 mean	1.8	1.3	1.5
Standard deviation	0.2	0.3	0.3
1967–76 mean	0.9	0.3	0.4
Standard deviation	1.0	1.0	1.0

Clearly, the instability of Aaa-rated real borrowing costs under the option is almost always greater than under the exemption.

TABLE 46

REAL YIELDS ON LONG-TERM CORPORATE AND MUNICIPAL
BONDS OF AVERAGE QUALITY
(percent)

Year	r^o (1)	r^m (2)	$r^{m o}$ (3)
1952	3.2	2.2	1.9
1953	3.2	2.6	1.9
1954	2.9	2.2	1.6
1955	3.2	2.5	1.8
1956	3.0	2.3	1.6
1957	2.9	2.3	1.2
1958	2.5	1.7	0.8
1959	3.2	2.3	1.4
1960	3.3	2.2	1.4
1961	3.3	2.2	1.4
1962	3.3	2.0	1.5
1963	3.2	2.0	1.4
1964	3.3	2.0	1.5
1965	3.3	2.0	1.4
1966	3.6	2.2	1.5
1967	3.8	2.0	1.5
1968	4.0	1.9	1.4
1969	4.1	2.5	1.2
1970	4.7	2.6	1.3
1971	4.0	1.7	0.8
1972	3.9	1.5	0.8
1973	3.5	0.9	0.4
1974	3.1	0.3	−0.5
1975	2.9	0.5	−0.9
1976	2.7	0.3	−0.9
1952–76 mean	3.4	1.9	1.1
Standard deviation	0.5	0.7	0.8
1952–66 mean	3.1	2.2	1.5
Standard deviation	0.3	0.2	0.3
1967–76 mean	3.7	1.4	0.5
Standard deviation	0.6	0.9	0.9

NOTE: r^o = real yield on corporate bonds; r^m = real yield on municipal bonds; r^{m*} = real yield on municipal bonds under a taxable bond option with a 40 percent subsidy. Calculations and data sources are described in the text. Calculations are based on unrounded data.

have slightly reduced the instability of real borrowing costs. For the 1967–76 subperiod, instability would have been increased somewhat by the option. The reason for this difference is the greater variability in anticipated inflation over the latter subperiod than over the earlier one. This suggests that if the rate of inflation remains relatively constant during the next twenty-five years, at or near its present level of 6 percent, the option might improve slightly the stability of anticipated real borrowing costs of municipal governments. If the experience over the past decade is repeated, however, the option can be expected to increase instability.

For the period 1952–76 as a whole, the option would have increased instability to an even greater extent than it would have for the 1967–76 subperiod. This is because the option deals poorly with the transition from a noninflationary economy to an inflationary one. Thus, if over the next twenty-five years we gradually work ourselves back to a noninflationary economy (a goal espoused by virtually all policy makers), the option would probably increase instability. Obviously, the choice between these scenarios is based on speculation about the future. Only one conclusion is justified on the basis of available evidence: There is no strong reason to believe that the taxable bond option would reduce the instability of the anticipated real borrowing costs of municipal governments to any significant degree, and it may actually increase instability.

The Stability of the Real Subsidy Rate

So far, the discussion in this chapter has focused on the stability of the real borrowing costs of municipal governments. For some purposes, however, it may be more relevant to look at the stability of the real subsidy granted to municipal borrowers. The real subsidy rate (ρ) is the proportional differential between the anticipated real borrowing costs of taxable corporations and the anticipated real borrowing costs of municipalities; that is, $\rho = (r^c - r^m)/r^c = (i^c - i^m)/r^c$. Stability of ρ would be a desirable goal if the objective were to achieve a sharing of disturbances to the credit market between the private sector and the public sector. In contrast, stability of r^m would mean that the effect of all disturbances would be concentrated on the private sector.

The channels through which economic disturbances affect ρ are the same as the channels through which these disturbances affect r^m, but the precise impact of a disturbance on ρ is generally different from its impact on r^m. This may be seen by rewriting the formula for ρ as:

$$\rho = s \cdot (r^c + \pi)/r^c = s \cdot (i^c/r^c).$$

The three channels through which disturbances affect ρ are variations in r^c, variations in π, and variations in s. As one would expect, variations in the nominal subsidy rate (s), holding r^c and π constant, result in proportional variations in ρ, with a factor of proportionality of i^c/r^c.

The taxable bond option would stabilize the value of s and thereby close off one of the three channels through which disturbances can affect ρ. In particular, under an option with a 40 percent direct subsidy rate, the formula for ρ would become:

$$\rho^* = (0.40) \cdot (r^c + \pi)/r^c.$$

Clearly, stabilizing s does not completely stabilize ρ, since variations in r^c and variations in π remain as channels through which disturbances may affect ρ. Moreover, as was the case with r^m, there is at least the theoretical possibility that stabilization of s would actually increase the overall instability of ρ.

To judge the empirical relevance of this theoretical possibility, it is useful to compare the stability of ρ during the past twenty-five years under the exemption with the stability that would have been achieved under the 40 percent option. Some facts relevant for this comparison are summarized in Table 47. Column 1 reports the series for s under the exemption. This series is constructed by taking the difference between i^c and i^m, as reported in columns 1 and 2 of Table 45, and dividing by i^c. Clearly, the nominal subsidy rate under the exemption shows some variability. Column 2 of Table 47 reports a series for ρ under the exemption. This series is constructed by taking the ratio of i^c, as reported in column 1 of Table 45, to r^c, as reported in column 1 of Table 46, and multiplying by s, as reported in column 1 of Table 47. Finally, column 3 of Table 47 reports a series for ρ^* under the 40 percent option. This series is obtained by multiplying the ratio i^c/r^c by the factor 0.40.

The standard deviations reported at the bottom of columns 2 and 3 of Table 47 indicate the effect of the option on the stability of the real subsidy rate. For the whole period 1952–76, the standard deviation of ρ^* is 1.24 times greater than the standard deviation of ρ. This indicates that during this period the instability of the real subsidy rate would have been increased by 24 percent as a result of the option. For the inflationary subperiod 1967–76, there is a similar result; the option would have increased the instability of ρ by 42 percent. On the other hand, for the noninflationary subperiod 1952–66, the results indicate that the option would not have increased the instability of the real subsidy rate.

The evidence presented in Table 47 uses data on long-term corporate and municipal bonds of average quality. From the discussion in chapter 4, however, we know that a more appropriate measure of the subsidy to long-term municipal borrowing is probably obtained by using the yield on Aaa-rated, newly issued corporate and municipal bonds. This is because Aaa-rated corporate and municipal bonds are probably more readily comparable than average quality bonds. Furthermore, using newly issued yields avoids the problem of the differential tax treatment of capital gains. In Table 48, column 1, we present the calculations of the real subsidy to long-term municipal borrowing, using Aaa-rated, newly issued corporate bonds and Aaa-rated municipal bonds. We also present in column 2 what the real subsidy would have been under the option. Clearly, the results are very similar to those of Table 47. The option would have increased the instability for the 1952–76 period as a whole by 24 percent, for the 1952–66 subperiod by 60 percent, and for the 1967–76 subperiod by 32 percent.

The conclusions that are justified on the basis of this evidence are similar to the conclusions reached in the discussion of the stability of real borrowing costs. In general, there is no strong reason to believe that the option would reduce significantly the instability of the real subsidy rate on municipal borrowing, and it may actually increase instability.

Stability and Monetary Policy

Proponents of the taxable bond option point to one particular type of disturbance, contractionary monetary policy, as having special significance for instability in the market for municipal bonds. Faced with a contractionary monetary policy, banks are forced to reduce total bank credit. Rather than reduce loans to longstanding customers, banks sell part of their holdings of marketable securities, consisting largely of obligations of the U.S. government and of municipal governments. Since commercial banks play a dominant role in the market for municipal bonds, these sales generally result in increases in the yields on municipal bonds. Increased yields discourage borrowing by municipal governments and may result in postponement or abandonment of some capital expenditures. One of the purported advantages of the taxable bond option is that it would reduce the sensitivity of municipal borrowing to contractionary monetary policy by broadening the market for municipal bonds. During periods of tight money when yields on tax-exempt municipal bonds tend to rise because of

TABLE 47

NOMINAL AND REAL SUBSIDIES ON LONG-TERM MUNICIPAL BONDS
OF AVERAGE QUALITY
(percent)

Year	s (1)	ρ (2)	ρ° (3)
1952	30	30	40
1953	18	19	42
1954	22	24	44
1955	21	22	41
1956	18	21	48
1957	15	22	58
1958	19	32	66
1959	20	28	58
1960	22	32	58
1961	23	32	56
1962	29	40	56
1963	27	38	56
1964	28	39	56
1965	28	40	57
1966	27	40	59
1967	31	48	61
1968	31	51	66
1969	22	39	71
1970	25	45	73
1971	29	58	79
1972	31	60	79
1973	33	74	90
1974	31	89	115
1975	25	84	131
1976	27	90	134
1952–76 mean	25	44	68
Standard deviation	5	21	26
1952–66 mean	23	31	53
Standard deviation	5	8	8
1967–76 mean	29	64	90
Standard deviation	4	19	27

NOTE: s = nominal subsidy rate on municipal bonds; ρ = real subsidy rate on municipal bonds; ρ° = real subsidy rate on municipal bonds under a taxable bond option with a 40 percent subsidy.

SOURCE: Calculations and data sources described in text. Calculations are based on unrounded data.

TABLE 48

REAL SUBSIDIES ON AAA-RATED NEWLY ISSUED LONG-TERM
MUNICIPAL BONDS
(percent)

Year	ρ (1)	ρ^* (2)
1952	41	40
1953	34	44
1954	37	44
1955	32	41
1956	37	48
1957	42	57
1958	50	68
1959	41	57
1960	45	58
1961	39	58
1962	45	57
1963	40	57
1964	44	56
1965	44	58
1966	46	58
1967	55	58
1968	59	64
1969	49	68
1970	52	74
1971	64	83
1972	66	83
1973	80	89
1974	100	116
1975	108	150
1976	130	166
1952–76 average	55	70
Standard deviation	25	31
1952–66 average	41	53
Standard deviation	5	8
1967–76 average	76	95
Standard deviation	28	37

SOURCE: Column 1 is the same as column 2, Table 41, Column 2 is (0.4) $\times$ $[i^e/(i^e - \pi)]$, where i^e is from column 2 of Table 13 and π is from column 4 of Table 8. Calculations are based on unrounded data.

decreased demand on the part of banks, municipal governments would be able to continue borrowing by issuing taxable bonds to all potential demanders of such securities.

One of the difficulties with this argument has already been pointed out. By making the municipal bond market less sensitive to the disturbances created by contractionary monetary policy, the taxable bond option may also increase the sensitivity of this market to other types of disturbances. The total effect of the option might therefore decrease the overall stability of the market for municipal bonds.

The argument that the taxable bond option reduces the sensitivity of municipal borrowing to contractionary monetary policy must confront another important difficulty. By itself, the option does not reduce the overall magnitude of the disturbance created by contractionary monetary policy; it merely redistributes it from municipal borrowers to some other sector of the economy. Specifically, when municipal governments issue taxable bonds to escape the effects of contractionary monetary policy, the funds that they secure with these bonds do not appear out of thin air. Every additional dollar that municipal governments borrow by issuing subsidized taxable bonds displaces a dollar of nonsubsidized private borrowing. Thus, although the option may diminish the sensitivity of municipal borrowing to contractionary monetary policy, it does so only by increasing the sensitivity of the private sector. This raises the question: Why is it desirable to diminish the sensitivity of one sector of the economy simply to increase the sensitivity of some other sector?[4]

The general answer to this question is provided by the principle that monetary policy should be made to work on as broad a front as possible. By operating on a broad front, the effectiveness of monetary policy in achieving its basic macroeconomic objectives is enhanced, and severe disturbances to particular sectors of the economy are avoided. In order to expand the front on which monetary policy operates, it is desirable to redistribute its effects away from those sectors that presently bear the brunt of monetary policy and toward those sectors that are presently most insulated from monetary policy.

The taxable bond option is unlikely to result in this desirable form of redistribution. By insulating municipal borrowers from the effects of contractionary monetary policy, the effect of the option will

---

[4] This point is recognized by at least one proponent of the taxable bond option. Peter Fortune (1973a) notes, "It is possible that the taxable bond option will stabilize the municipal debt market only to introduce greater instability into some other market equally high on the social priority list (e.g., the mortgage market). In such a case there is no *a priori* case for stabilizing the municipal debt market."

be to concentrate the burden of the policy on those sectors of the economy, other than municipal governments, that are most dependent on bank credit. These sectors include residential construction, an industry that is highly sensitive to the availability of mortgage credit and that already bears a disproportionate share of the burden of monetary policy. Increased concentration of the impact of monetary policy on such industries cannot be regarded as a benefit of the option.

It should be emphasized that the logic of this discussion applies not only to the disturbances created by contractionary monetary policy but to other types of disturbances as well. In general, the taxable bond option does not reduce the overall magnitude of disturbances impinging on the economy; it only redistributes the effect of disturbances away from municipal borrowers and toward other sectors of the economy. There is no good reason to believe that such a redistribution is socially desirable. Indeed, when it is recognized that state and local governments can always resort to taxation as a source of finance, an alternative not available to private borrowers, the case for shifting the burden of disturbances from municipal borrowers to private borrowers is further weakened.

Summary

In this chapter we have examined the issue of the stability of the taxable bond option. The standard analysis focuses on nominal yields and argues that the option would stabilize the nominal subsidy to municipal borrowers and would insulate the municipal bond market from the destabilizing effects of monetary policy by giving borrowers access to a broader market. In our analysis, we showed that these conclusions, though not incorrect, are incomplete and misleading.

First, we argued on a theoretical level that while the taxable bond option would eliminate fluctuations in the nominal subsidy rate on municipal bonds it would not necessarily reduce fluctuations in the real subsidy rate. More important, the option would not necessarily reduce fluctuations in the real borrowing costs of municipal governments. We showed that over the past twenty-five years, had the option been in existence, both real borrowing costs and the real subsidy rate would have been more unstable than they actually were under the exemption. We concluded that there is no basis for believing that the option would work to reduce the instability of real borrowing costs or the real subsidy rate.

Second, we looked at the full effect of the reduced impact of monetary policy and other disturbances on the municipal market. We argued that although the municipal bond market would be somewhat insulated from the destabilizing effects of monetary policy the option would have no effect on the overall impact of the disturbance created by contractionary monetary policy. Rather, it would only redistribute the impact from municipal borrowers to other sectors of the economy. Every dollar that municipal governments borrow by issuing subsidized taxable bonds displaces nonsubsidized private borrowing. Thus, the option would diminish the sensitivity of municipal borrowing to contractionary monetary policy only by increasing the sensitivity of the private sector, residential construction in particular.

10
Conclusion

This study has focused on the major issues raised by opponents of the present exemption and proponents of the taxable bond option—the issues of fiscal efficiency, tax equity, effectiveness, and stability. With respect to each of these issues, proponents of the taxable bond option have argued that it would produce a significant improvement over the situation that has prevailed and is likely to continue to prevail under the exemption. These arguments constitute the basic case for the adoption of the taxable bond option. In this study, we have examined the logical and factual basis for these arguments, and our general conclusion is that they are without foundation. The defects of the present exemption have been grossly overstated because of the failure of proponents of the option to account for relevant facts concerning economic conditions in the United States. In every major dimension, the potential benefits of the option are, at best, very small, and in two of the major areas, effectiveness and stability, they may well be negative.

In this chapter, we summarize the facts that lead to these negative conclusions about the potential benefits of the taxable bond option. Before proceeding to this summary, however, we discuss six problems that may arise in connection with the option: (1) The increased subsidy provided by the option may induce an undesirable distribution of benefits, with the greatest benefits going to states and localities that borrow the most, rather than to those that are the neediest. (2) Speculation over changes in the subsidy rate paid on taxable bonds is likely to create instability in the municipal bond market. (3) Some state and local governments may be tempted to abuse the option by borrowing more than they should. (4) The option may complicate our international financial relations by involving foreigners and foreign governments in the municipal bond market. (5) The direct interest subsidy may be used by the federal government to restrict the financial independence of municipal governments. (6) The taxable bond option is a subsidy program with no natural limit, which may ultimately lead to increased federal involvement in the allocation of credit and capital. By themselves, these problems might not constitute overriding objections to the option, if a strong case could be made for it on the major issues of tax equity, fiscal efficiency, effectiveness, and stability. But, since the arguments for the option on these major issues are, at best, very weak, these problems with the option take on added significance.

The Distribution of the Benefits of the Option

As discussed in chapter 7, a taxable bond option with a 40 percent direct subsidy rate would increase the real effective rate of subsidy on longer-term municipal bonds. At a 6 percent inflation rate, the increase in the real effective rate of subsidy would be from about 85 percent under the present exemption to over 110 percent under the option. Clearly, this increase in the subsidy rate on borrowing costs does not benefit all municipalities equally; it benefits only those that borrow, and it provides the most benefit to those that borrow the most. This raises problems of both horizontal and vertical equity between different municipalities.

Horizontal equity applies to municipalities with essentially the same economic conditions: the same levels of income and the same basic needs for public services. It is entirely possible that the residents of two such similar communities will make significantly different decisions about the level of public services they wish to have. Indeed, one of the strengths of the federal system of government is that it permits independent decisions to be made. As long as communities pay for their public services through taxation, no issue of horizontal equity arises; communities that want more public services pay for them and get them. When municipal expenditures are financed by federally subsidized borrowing, however, an issue does arise. A community that decides to borrow little suffers relative to an essentially similar community that decides to borrow a great deal. This is because the costs of the subsidy on municipal borrowing costs are borne by residents of the entire country, but the benefits accrue only to residents of communities that finance public expenditures through borrowing. In practice, a subsidy to municipal borrowing means that financially conservative communities that operate on a pay-as-you-go basis are penalized relative to spendthrift communities.

The problem of vertical equity concerns the distribution of benefits among municipalities in different economic circumstances. If the benefits of a subsidy on municipal borrowing costs accrued largely to the poorest municipalities and to those with the greatest inherent need for public services, the subsidy would probably be regarded as improving vertical equity. But the facts do not indicate that the municipalities that borrow most are, in general, the neediest. Not surprisingly, there is a slight positive relationship between income per capita and borrowing by state governments per capita. As one would expect, communities with high incomes tend to demand high levels of public services and high levels of public borrowing. One of the perverse effects of a subsidy to municipal borrowing costs is that it benefits disproportionately such high-income communities.

The problems with the distribution of the benefits of a subsidy to municipal borrowing are not, of course, specific to the taxable bond option. One of the objections that used to be raised to the exemption was that its benefits were inequitably distributed among municipalities. This criticism has not been emphasized by proponents of the taxable bond option, however, not because the problem has disappeared but because it is recognized that since the taxable bond option increases the subsidy rate on municipal borrowing it also exacerbates the problem of inequitable distribution.

Speculation over Changes in the Subsidy Rate

Under the taxable bond option, the effective nominal rate of subsidy on newly issued municipal bonds, both taxable and tax-exempt, would equal the rate of the direct interest subsidy paid by the Treasury on taxable municipal bonds. If the yield on taxable bonds is held constant, it follows that an increase in the direct subsidy rate will reduce the nominal yield on newly issued tax-exempt municipal bonds. This reduction in yield is required in order to increase the implicit nominal subsidy rate on tax-exempt bonds to the new level of the direct subsidy rate on taxable bonds. Since, from the viewpoint of investors, previously issued tax-exempt bonds are a very good substitute for newly issued tax-exempt bonds, it follows that the yield on previously issued tax-exempt bonds will have to fall by about the same amount as the reduction in the yield on newly issued tax-exempt bonds induced by the increase in the direct subsidy rate on taxable municipal bonds.

The whole argument works in reverse for a decrease in the direct subsidy rate. Thus, changes in the direct subsidy rate are a potential source of instability for the yield on all outstanding and newly issued tax-exempt bonds.

Further instability in the yield on tax-exempt municipal bonds can be produced by speculation over changes in the direct subsidy rate, whether or not such changes actually occur. There are two channels through which such speculation may operate. First, municipal governments themselves may speculate on changes in the direct subsidy rate. If an increase in subsidy rate is anticipated, municipal governments will have an incentive to delay borrowing until the higher subsidy rate is actually introduced. Conversely, if a decrease is anticipated, municipal governments will want to do their borrowing before the subsidy is lowered. Second, private investors will speculate on changes in the direct subsidy rate. If an increase is anticipated, the yield on outstanding tax-exempt bonds will fall because investors expect lower yields in the future. Conversely, if a decrease in the subsidy rate is anticipated, current yields will rise in expectation of higher yields in the future.

The importance of the effect of actual and anticipated changes in the direct subsidy rate is that they add another source of instability in the market for municipal bonds. Once the taxable bond option is introduced, it will become apparent that the direct subsidy rate is not fixed. During periods of financial difficulty, municipal governments will look to increases in the subsidy rate as one means by which their difficulties could be eased. Congress would probably find it difficult to resist the political pressures that would develop for an increase in the subsidy rate in these circumstances. On the other hand, if the subsidy rate rises and if municipal governments issue large amounts of subsidized taxable bonds, the cost of the subsidy is likely to become an increasing concern to the Treasury. This may lead to moves to reduce the subsidy. Intense opposition to such moves from officials in municipal governments is to be expected. Yet as long as Congress has the power either to reduce or to increase the subsidy rate, speculation about congressional action will be a destabilizing influence on the market for municipal bonds.

It should be emphasized that the problem with speculation over changes in the subsidy rate is by no means a remote possibility. Indeed, the proposal that President Carter has submitted to Congress has instability built right into it. Under the Carter program, the subsidy on taxable bonds starts out at 35 percent for the first two years and then jumps to 40 percent. If this program is enacted, then, as the announced moment for the change in the subsidy rate approaches, municipal government officials will become aware of the significant financial gain from delaying any issue of taxable bonds until after the increase in the subsidy rate. Hence, in the months immediately preceding the change, the supply of taxable municipal bonds will dry up; and, after the change takes place, there will be a huge increase in taxable borrowing. It is difficult to discern the social gain from such artificially induced instability.

Abuse of the Option

The taxable bond option is usually presented as an open-ended commitment on the part of the federal government to subsidize automatically some fixed fraction of the borrowing costs of state and municipal governments. This automaticity is frequently cited as one of the advantages of the option relative to other proposals to aid municipal borrowers, such as the proposed urban development bank. In this respect, the option is supposed to function like the exemption. No federal agency decides which municipalities are eligible to take advantage of the option or which public investment projects can be financed by issuing subsidized taxable bonds.

The open-endedness and the automaticity of the option, however, also create the potential for abuse—specific abuse by individual municipal governments that engage in unsound financial practices and general abuse through massive and socially unjustified increases in the total amount of municipal borrowing. To be sure, the potential for specific abuse arises under the exemption as well as under the option. If a municipal government finances its expenditures by borrowing, it receives a subsidy from the federal government. If it finances its expenditures by taxation, it receives no subsidy. Therefore, any subsidy to municipal borrowing provides an incentive to engage in unsound financial practices and to extend municipal borrowing beyond financially prudent levels. The problem with the option is that it creates an even greater incentive for such practices.

The problem of general abuse is related to the issue of economic efficiency discussed in chapter 7. Municipal governments have an incentive to pursue public investment projects up to the point where the marginal rate of return on the last dollar of investment is equal to the real borrowing costs of municipal governments. As the real borrowing costs of municipal governments fall lower and lower relative to the real borrowing costs of private firms, more and more dollars are diverted from private investments with high social return to public investments with lower social return. The result is a loss of economic efficiency: a reduction in the society's total output of goods and services. Unquestionably, some such loss of economic efficiency results from the exemption. Under the exemption, however, market forces limit the amount of this loss. Since the market for tax-exempt bonds is limited, a massive expansion of municipal borrowing would drive down the implicit subsidy provided by the exemption and would drive up the real borrowing costs of municipal governments. This would discourage further expansion of municipal borrowing to fund socially unproductive investments. The danger with the option is that this automatic mechanism would be removed. In principle, municipal governments could issue subsidized taxable bonds to finance whatever projects they want.

It would be misleading to suggest that the problem of massive general abuse of the option is likely to be acute. We have not observed a binge of municipal borrowing during the past decade when the real borrowing costs of municipal governments have decreased substantially. Voters in most states and localities have shown notable reluctance to approve municipal bond issues. Nevertheless, it is relevant to point out the dangers that could be encountered if the inflation rate in the United States rises to the 10 to 12 percent level. At 10 percent inflation, the nominal yield on taxable bonds would probably be something between 13 and 14 percent, and the real yield something between 3 and 4 percent. Under these conditions, a taxable bond option with a 40 percent direct interest subsidy would reduce nominal borrowing costs of municipal governments to between 8 and 9 percent. This would mean that the real borrowing costs of municipal governments would be between minus 1 percent and minus 2 percent. At rates of inflation greater than 10 percent, the real borrowing costs of municipal governments would be even more negative. Distortion of the allocation of resources is likely to result from the real borrowing costs of municipal governments being negative, while real borrowing costs for private firms remain positive at around 3 percent. At some point this distortion is likely to become intolerable.

International Financial Complications

At present, bonds issued by state and local governments are not held to any significant extent by foreigners or foreign governments because the tax exemption does not confer any benefit to foreigners and hence does not compensate for the lower yields paid on municipal bonds. Taxable municipal bonds, however, might well prove attractive to foreign investors. This would be of benefit to municipal governments because it would provide them with a broader market in which to sell their bonds. But, as recent experience in Britain and Canada indicates, large-scale borrowing by local authorities in international markets can contribute to an already difficult balance of payments problem. Moreover, concern with the balance of payments ramifications of municipal borrowing could conceivably become an emotional and political justification for the imposition of federal constraints. These constraints would never arise if municipal governments continued to avoid direct involvement with foreign creditors. Further, diplomatic difficulties might arise if foreign governments became important holders of taxable municipal bonds on which part of the interest was paid by the U.S. Treasury. What would have been the attitude of foreign governments to the recent New York City financial crisis if they had been holders of taxable New York City bonds? What effect would this attitude have had on the resolution of the crisis and on the future of federal-state relationships with respect to subsidized municipal borrowing?

The Financial Independence of Municipal Governments

As previously noted, one of the advantages of the taxable bond option relative to the urban development bank and other similar proposals is that the option preserves the important and guarded financial independence of municipal governments. The idea is that access to the option would be completely automatic. There would be no federal agency to decide which municipalities could and could not take advantage of the option or which projects qualified for finance by subsidized taxable bonds. Control of the option would not be used by the federal government to influence financial decisions of municipal governments or to constrain their behavior in other respects.

Proponents of the option clearly believe that preservation of the financial independence of municipal governments is an important feature of the option. Immediately following its adoption, there is little doubt that the option would function as advertised, without interference in the financial or other decisions of municipal governments. The history of other federal subsidy programs suggests, however, that a time might come when the financial independence of municipal governments would be sacrificed to "more important national needs." This happened recently with the interstate highway program when continued access to federal subsidies was made contingent on the enactment and enforcement of a speed limit of fifty-five miles an hour. Other subsidy programs have been used in a similar fashion; threats of removal of the subsidy have been used to influence the behavior of subsidy recipients in a manner not envisioned when the subsidy program was first enacted.

Further, the taxable bond option might ultimately lead to some reduction in the financial independence that municipal governments are able to exercise when they issue tax-exempt bonds. First, since the present subsidy to municipal borrowers is provided implicitly through the tax exemption, it does not seem natural and appropriate—or even practical—to attach strings and constraints on the use of this implicit subsidy. However, if strings and constraints were ultimately attached to subsidized taxable bonds, would it not seem natural and appropriate to extend those strings and constraints to tax-exempt bonds? Second, at present, the subsidy enjoyed by municipal governments is not highly visible. No annual congressional appropriation is required to finance the implicit subsidy provided by the exemption. Annual appropriations would be required, however, to finance the direct subsidy on taxable municipal bonds, and this would increase the visibility of the implicit subsidy on tax-exempt bonds. Increased visibility might lead either to increased pressure to eliminate the exemption or, at least, to attempts to charge the appropriate political price for its continued use. Third, the exemption was originally justified on the basis of the constitutional principle of reciprocal immunity. At present, there is considerable doubt as to the constitutional basis of this principle. Nevertheless, it has, over many years, proved to be a powerful argument in defeating attempts to repeal the exemption or otherwise alter the wholly tax-exempt status of municipal bonds. Under the taxable bond option, the constitutional justification for the exemption would be blurred. Tax-exempt bonds would be no more than an alternative to subsidized taxable bonds. Hence, it might be argued, why not do away with an archaic and inequitable exemption that now serves no useful purpose?

Of course, increased federal influence over the decisions of municipal governments will be exercised by responsible public officials and, presumably, will be used to serve the interests of the people. The difficulty, however, is that judgments about what serves the interests of the people will be made to an increased extent by public officials in Washington rather than by public officials in state capitals, county courthouses, and city halls. Transference of greater effective authority to the federal government, therefore, does not necessarily mean better and more responsible decision making. It means increased centralization of decision making by a group of public officials who are further removed from contact with the needs of specific communities and more subject to influence by interest groups that are organized at a national rather than a local level.

The Open-Endedness of the Taxable Bond Option

Not only has the principle of reciprocal immunity served to justify and defend the exemption, it has also limited its use to activities that fall within the legitimate purview of state and local governments. The most important exception to this general limitation has been industrial development bonds issued by municipal governments on behalf of private businesses. However, largely because such bonds did not clearly fall under the umbrella of protection provided by the principle of reciprocal immunity, it was possible in 1969 to limit them to "small issues" and to pollution control bonds. Legislation is currently pending that would eliminate the exception for pollution control bonds and limit small-issue industrial development bonds to depressed areas. This legislation, particularly the elimination of the exemption for pollution control bonds, is in accordance with the general principle that use of the exemption should be limited to those activities that clearly fall under the umbrella of reciprocal immunity.

With the taxable bond option, this basis for the limitation of the subsidy will be eroded. There is nothing special about a subsidy on interest payments that limits its applicability to municipal governments. If they are entitled to special treatment, then why not other borrowers who are also pursuing socially worthwhile projects? The list of potential candidates for subsidization is virtually endless, and the potential budgetary cost is immense. Perhaps more important than budgetary costs, decisions about what constitutes a socially worthwhile project would involve the federal government more deeply than it already is in the allocation of the economy's scarce supply of credit and capital. Previous experience does not indicate that the efficient allocation of scarce resources is a task for which the federal government possesses a comparative advantage.

Review of Major Findings

It might be argued that the six problems just discussed do not represent overriding objections to the taxable bond option. The regressivity in the distribution of benefits of the option can be offset by specific aid programs. The problem of speculation over changes in the subsidy rate will not be severe if such changes do not occur frequently. Serious abuse of the option is a potential danger, but perhaps not a likely one. The experience of Canada and Britain suggests that the international complications of municipal participation in world credit markets are manageable. The degree of control that may be exercised over municipal governments is limited, since municipal governments retain the right to issue tax-exempt bonds. Any ultimate threat to the exemption itself may be combated when and if it materializes. There is no essential reason why the applicability of the option cannot be limited to areas that have traditionally enjoyed the advantage of tax-exempt borrowing, or why the option would necessarily lead to greater federal determination of the allocation of credit and capital. Although these issues may be of problematic importance, nevertheless they must be given weight in the assessment of the taxable bond option, particularly because no substantial case can be made for the taxable bond option on the major economic issues of tax equity, fiscal efficiency, effectiveness, and stability.

To review the basis for this conclusion, it is useful to start with the complicated issues of fiscal efficiency and tax equity and proceed to effectiveness and stability. In discussing fiscal efficiency and tax equity, it is useful to focus on the extreme proposal of outright elimination of the exemption, even though this proposal is not politically viable. Outright elimination of the exemption sets an upper bound on the gain in efficiency and equity that would be achieved with the taxable bond option. The option would achieve this bound only if the direct subsidy rate on taxable municipal bonds were sufficiently high to induce municipal governments to forgo issuing any tax-exempt bonds.

The first major point concerning fiscal efficiency and tax equity was made in chapter 1: by itself, purported fiscal inefficiency of the exemption is not a very important defect. What gives force to the argument that the exemption is fiscally inefficient is the contention that this inefficiency accrues as an unjustifiable windfall to high-bracket taxpayers who escape from paying their fair share of taxes by holding municipal bonds. If this contention of tax inequity is not valid, then elimination of the exemption is nothing more than a scheme to raise more tax revenue. It has nothing to recommend it over any other such scheme, because the people who will pay the increased taxes are not necessarily those who ought to pay more taxes.

Next, we discussed the distinction between the implicit *nominal* tax rate paid by holders of municipal bonds and the implicit *real* tax rate paid by such investors. The standard criticism of the exemption relies on nominal tax rates. During periods of inflation, however, the use of nominal tax rates gives a grossly distorted picture of the tax inequity resulting from the exemption. In particular, the analysis of chapter 3 showed that during the past decade, when the implicit nominal tax rate on municipal bondholders averaged only about 30 percent, the real effective tax rate averaged over 70 percent. Since a 70 percent tax rate exceeds the maximum nominal marginal tax rate on any form of income, it is reasonable to conclude that no tax inequity resulted from municipal bondholdings during the past decade. Indeed, it could be argued that the availability of tax-exempt municipal bonds improved the equity of the U.S. tax system by ameliorating the highly distorting effects of inflation on the taxation of real interest income. For many investors, municipal bonds were the only fixed interest investment on which the real effective rate of tax did not significantly exceed 100 percent. Moreover, the theoretical analysis of chapter 3 suggests that, as long as inflation rates remain above 3 or 4 percent, the real effective rate of tax paid by holders of municipal bonds will probably average at least 50 percent. Given current projections of future inflation rates, we conclude that no significant tax inequity will result from the availability of tax-exempt municipal bonds. This conclusion is based solely on the analysis of the effects of price inflation on the real effective rate of tax paid by holders of municipal bonds and is independent of all other arguments developed in this study.

Not only is the implicit real tax rate paid by municipal bondholders much higher than the implicit nominal tax rate, but the implicit nominal tax rate is itself substantially higher than usually supposed by opponents of the exemption and proponents of the taxable bond option. The facts presented in chapter 4 establish that the proportionate yield differential between taxable bonds and tax-exempt bonds is much greater for short maturities (close to 50 percent for short-term notes) than it is for long maturities (about 30 percent for twenty-year bonds). The average proportionate yield differential in favor of municipal bonds of all maturities is at least 35 percent, a figure significantly greater than the 30 percent figure used in standard estimates of the fiscal inefficiency and tax inequity of the exemption. For this reason alone (apart from the effects of inflation or any other issue raised in this study), standard estimates of the fiscal inefficiency and tax inequity of the exemption are too high. Further, the theoretical analysis in chapter 4 established that for any investor, no matter how high his tax bracket, there is no special advantage derived from the last dollar invested in tax-exempt municipal bonds of any maturity. All things taken into account, the benefit derived from the last dollar invested in municipal bonds is no greater (and no less) than the benefit derived from the last dollar invested in any other asset. For this reason, it is incorrect to argue, as opponents of the exemption do, that high-bracket investors gain a substantial windfall from every dollar of municipal bonds that they hold. Windfall gains must be limited to inframarginal holdings of municipal bonds and, hence, are significantly smaller than suggested by opponents of the exemption.

The main point of chapter 5 was that the magnitude of the tax inequity resulting from the municipal bonds held directly by households has been seriously exaggerated. First, from the analysis of chapter 3, it is known that the inequity resulting from municipal bonds is smaller at any positive rate of inflation than at a zero rate of inflation because the real effective tax rate paid by holders of municipal bonds increases as the inflation rate increases. The standard estimate of tax inequity, however, rises as the inflation rate rises, because it is distorted by the use of nominal rather than real interest rates. Under the inflationary conditions of 1976, this distortion resulted in an exaggeration of the true upper-bound estimate of tax inequity by a factor of almost three. Second, the standard estimate of the tax inequity resulting from individual holdings of municipal bonds is exaggerated because it is based on an overestimate of the tax rate that would apply to present holders of tax-exempt municipal bonds if the exemption were eliminated. Evidence from income tax returns and inferences from data on individual portfolios indicate that the average effective marginal tax rate for present holders of municipal bonds is probably no greater than 36 percent. This contrasts with the 42 percent estimate that has been widely used by proponents of the taxable bond option. The implication of the 36 percent estimate is that the windfall gain accruing to individual holders of municipal bonds, under conditions of zero inflation, would have been no greater than $160 million in 1976. Moreover, careful theoretical analysis shows that as the inflation rate rises above zero the true measure of tax inequity must decline and ultimately become negative. In particular, at the 6 percent inflation rate that actually prevailed in 1976, the true measure of the tax inequity resulting from individual holdings of municipal bonds is minus $775 million.

The basic conclusion of chapter 6 was that no significant tax inequity results from institutional holdings of municipal bonds. This is an important conclusion, because two-thirds of the outstanding stock of municipal bonds was held by institutions (primarily commercial banks and fire and casualty insurance companies) in 1976. The standard analysis of the tax inequity associated with municipal bonds cannot validly be applied to institutions, since institutions are not the ultimate beneficiaries of any special advantage conferred by holding such bonds. The economic characteristics of commercial banking and of fire and casualty insurance indicate that the primary beneficiaries of any such advantage are the customers of these institutions. If the exemption were eliminated, equity capital invested in these industries would continue to earn its normal rate of return. The bulk of the burden of increased taxes generated by elimination of the exemption would be shifted from the owners of equity capital to the customers of banks and insurance companies. The customers that would bear the greatest share of this burden would be those with the poorest alternatives to the services of banks and insurance companies, particularly small depositors and small businesses. No gain in tax equity can reasonably be said to result from imposing this particular tax burden.

Chapter 7 focused on the fiscal efficiency that is now achieved by the exemption and on the probable fiscal cost of the taxable bond option. Contrary to the assertions of many opponents of the exemption, our analysis showed that through reduced borrowing costs state and local governments capture more than ninety-six cents of benefit for every dollar that is lost to the U.S. Treasury as a result of the exemption. This is a remarkable accomplishment for virtually any federal subsidy program, particularly one that lacks strings, constraints, and an administrative bureaucracy. Further, taking account of the fiscal effects of the increase in taxable yields that would be induced by a 40 percent taxable bond option, we estimated that the net fiscal cost of such an option to the U.S. Treasury would actually exceed the additional financial benefit to municipal governments: only about eighty-six cents of additional municipal benefit would be provided for each dollar of cost of the Treasury.

Chapter 8 developed three major points in regard to the effectiveness issue. First, contrary to what is commonly believed, the effectiveness of the exemption as a means of subsidizing the borrowing costs of municipal governments has increased substantially during the past decade. The error in the standard procedure for measuring the effectiveness of the subsidy is that it looks at nominal borrowing costs rather than real borrowing costs. During the past decade, the nominal subsidy rate, or proportionate reduction in nominal borrowing costs that can be attributed to the exemption, has averaged about 30 percent, only slightly higher than its value in the preceding decade. The real subsidy rate, or proportionate reduction in real borrowing costs, however, has averaged about 70 percent during the past decade, compared to an average of 35 percent for the late 1950s and early 1960s. Moreover, the characteristics of the U.S. tax system ensure that the real rate of subsidy enjoyed by municipal governments will continue to be at least 50 percent as long as inflation rates continue to average 4 percent per year or more. Second, past experience with the market for tax-exempt municipal bonds indicates that it should be able to absorb the increase in municipal borrowing that is likely to occur in the next decade without incurring any significant increase in real borrowing costs. Third, while it is true that a taxable bond option with a 40 percent direct interest subsidy would increase the real rate of subsidy enjoyed by municipal governments, it is questionable whether this increase is socially desirable. The greater the subsidy to municipal borrowing, the greater is the distortion of the allocation of scarce capital resources that results from encouraging municipal governments to undertake public investment projects with lower social return than the private investment projects they displace.

Chapter 9 examined the issue of stability. Theoretical analysis established that, while the taxable bond option would stabilize the nominal rate of subsidy on municipal borrowing, it would not necessarily stabilize the variable of central interest, the real borrowing costs of municipal governments. A simple empirical experiment demonstrated the practical importance of this theoretical result: If the taxable bond option, with a 40 percent direct subsidy rate, had been in operation during the past twenty-five years, the real borrowing costs of municipal governments would have been slightly more unstable than they were under the exemption. Further, it was pointed out that, while the taxable bond option might reduce the sensitivity of the municipal bonds market to certain types of economic disturbances, this reduction in sensitivity might not be desirable. The effect of the option would be not to reduce the magnitude of most disturbances but to transfer their effects out of the municipal bond market and into some other market. In particular, the taxable bond option would probably reduce the sensitivity of the municipal bond market to contractionary monetary policy, but only by decreasing the effectiveness of monetary policy and increasing the instability of the market for home mortgages.

Conclusions

Traditionally, economists have objected to the tax-exempt status of municipal bonds on three major grounds: The exemption is fiscally inefficient because it results in a greater loss of tax revenue to the U.S. Treasury than the benefit it provides to municipal governments in the form of reduced borrowing costs. The exemption is the source of tax inequity because it permits high-tax-bracket investors to escape from paying appropriate marginal tax rates by holding tax-exempt municipal bonds. The exemption results in economic inefficiency because it induces municipal governments to invest resources in public investment projects when these resources would produce a higher social return if invested in the private sector. These defects of the exemption have motivated repeated attempts to legislate its elimination. These attempts, however, have always been defeated in the Congress, largely because of the opposition of municipal governments. Whatever its defects, the exemption does confer substantial financial benefits on municipal governments and provides a highly desirable form of subsidy because the issuance of tax-exempt municipal bonds is at the discretion of municipal governments and not under the control of a federal agency.

Proponents of the taxable bond option argue that it would correct the fiscal inefficiency and tax inequity resulting from the exemption without harming the interests of municipal governments. Indeed, since under the option municipal governments could issue both tax-exempt bonds and subsidized taxable bonds, their situation could not be worsened by the option. It is argued that municipal governments would actually be better off under the option, because it would (1) increase the effective rate of subsidy enjoyed by municipal governments and (2) reduce the instability of the municipal bond market. Thus, the taxable bond option is presented as a proposal that benefits everyone except high-tax-bracket investors who presently escape from paying their fair share of tax by holding tax-exempt municipal bonds.

In this study, we have carefully examined the arguments in favor of the taxable bond option and found them to be without foundation. The increase in the inflation rate that has occurred during the past decade and seems likely to persist for some time has increased the real effective rate of tax implicitly paid by holders of long-term municipal bonds to more than 70 percent, and to significantly higher rates on short-term bonds. At these tax rates, no serious issue of tax inequity arises in connection with the tax-exempt status of municipal bonds. Further, in the case of the two-thirds of municipal bonds that are held by institutions, no issue of tax inequity arises at any inflation rate since the benefits are spread across all income classes. For the one-third of municipal bonds held directly by individuals, there is a minor question of tax inequity at a zero inflation rate. At an inflation rate of above 4 percent, however, it can be argued that there is a net gain in tax equity from the exemption that would be eliminated or reduced by the option. Without the argument of a significant increase in tax equity, the argument of improved fiscal efficiency loses its importance. At best, the option would generate a net fiscal benefit to all government units combined, at the expense of higher taxes paid by the private sector. The people who would pay higher taxes would not, however, be those who ought to pay higher taxes. Moreover, it is unlikely that the taxable bond option would generate a net fiscal benefit; the increase in the general level of government borrowing costs would probably outweigh any increase in tax revenue.

On the effectiveness issue, it is true that the taxable bond option would increase the real effective rate of subsidy enjoyed by municipal borrowers from its already high level of over 70 percent. Such an increase in the subsidy rate would not be socially desirable, however, because it would further reduce economic efficiency. On the stability issue, it is questionable whether the taxable bond option would actually improve the stability of the municipal bond market or, if it did, whether this increase in stability would be desirable. The consequence of the option might simply be to redistribute disturbances from the municipal bond market to some other market less capable of dealing with them. Finally, not only does the taxable bond option lack the advantages its proponents have claimed, it also suffers from a number of potential disadvantages: the distribution of its benefits among municipalities is regressive; the possibility of changes in the subsidy rate is a potential source of instability; the open-ended commitment to subsidize municipal borrowing costs increases the possibility of abuse; the involvement of municipal governments in international credit markets may complicate our financial and diplomatic relations with other countries; the introduction of the option increases the probability that the federal government will restrict the financial independence of municipal governments; and the option is a program that has no natural limit and that may ultimately involve the federal government more deeply in the allocation of credit and capital.

REFERENCES

Aaron, Henry, ed. 1976. *Inflation and the Income Tax.* Washington, D.C.: Brookings Institution.

Ackerman, Susan, and David Ott. 1970. "An Analysis of the Revenue Effects of Proposed Substitutes for Tax Exemption of State and Local Bonds." *National Tax Journal* 23: 397–406.

Bailey, Martin J. 1969. "Capital Gains and Income Taxation." In *The Taxation of Income from Capital*, edited by Arnold C. Harberger and Martin J. Bailey. Washington, D.C.: Brookings Institution.

Bank of Canada. *Bank of Canada Review.* Various issues.

Bedford, Margaret. 1975. "Income Taxation of Commercial Banks." *Federal Reserve Bank of Kansas City Monthly Review*, pp. 11–23.

Board of Governors of the Federal Reserve System. 1976. *Banking and Monetary Statistics, 1941–1970.* Washington, D.C.: Publications Services, Division of Administrative Services, Board of Governors of the Federal Reserve System.

Bond Buyer. *Weekly Bond Buyer.* Various issues.

Break, George, and Joseph Pechman. 1975. *Federal Tax Reform: The Impossible Dream?* Washington, D.C.: Brookings Institution.

Brinner, Roger. 1976. "Inflation and the Definition of Taxable Personal Income." In *Inflation and the Income Tax.* Henry Aaron, ed. Washington, D.C.: Brookings Institution.

Brittain, John A. 1966. *Corporate Dividend Policy.* Washington, D.C.: Brookings Institution.

Carlson, John. 1977. "Short Term Interest Rates as Predictors of Inflation: Comment." *American Economic Review* 67.

Darby, Michael. 1975. "The Financial and Tax Effects of Monetary Policy on Interest Rates." *Economic Inquiry* 13.

David, Martin. 1968. *Alternative Approaches to Capital Gains Taxation.* Washington, D.C.: Brookings Institution.

Durand, David. 1958. "A Quarterly Series of Corporate Bond Yields, 1952–1957, and Some Attendant Reservations." *Journal of Finance* 13.

Fama, Eugene. 1975. "Short Term Interest Rates as Predictors of Inflation." *American Economic Review* 65.

———. 1977. "A Pricing Model for the Municipal Bond Market." University of Chicago.

Fama, Eugene, and William Schwert. 1977. "Asset Returns and Inflation." *Journal of Financial Economics* 5.

Federal Deposit Insurance Corporation. *Bank Operating Statistics.* Various issues.

Federal Reserve Bank of Cleveland. *Economic Review.* Various issues.

Feldstein, Martin. 1976. "Personal Taxation and Portfolio Composition: An Econometric Analysis." *Econometrica* 44: 631–50.

Fisher, Irving. 1896. "Appreciation and Interest." *AEA Publications,* Series Three (II).

Fisher, Lawrence, and James Lorie. 1977. *A Half Century of Returns on Stocks and Bonds.* Chicago: University of Chicago Press.

Forbes, Ronald, and John E. Peterson. 1976. "Background Paper." In *Building a Broader Market: Report of the Twentieth Century Fund Task Force on the Municipal Bond Market.* New York: McGraw-Hill.

Fortune, Peter. 1973a. "Tax-Exemption of State and Local Interest Payments: An Economic Analysis of the Issues and an Alternative." *New England Economic Review,* pp. 3–31.

———. 1973b. "The Impact of Taxable Municipal Bonds: Policy Simulations with a Large Econometric Model." *National Tax Journal* 26: 29–42.

———. 1976. "The Municipal Bond Market: The Need for Reform." *Tax Notes* 4, no. 13: 3–8.

Galper, Harvey, and John Peterson. 1971. "An Analysis of Subsidy Plans to Support State and Local Borrowing." *National Tax Journal* 24: 205–34.

Gandolfi, Arthur. 1976. "Taxation and the Fisher Effect." *Journal of Finance* 35.

Goode, Richard. 1976. *The Individual Income Tax.* Rev. ed. Washington, D.C.: Brookings Institution.

Greenbaum, Stuart, 1967. "Competition and Efficiency in the Banking System: Empirical Research and Its Policy Implications." *Journal of Political Economy* 75.

Hufner, Robert. 1970. "Municipal Bonds: The Costs and Benefits of an Alternative." *National Tax Journal* 23: 407–16.

———. 1973. "Taxable Alternatives to Municipal Bonds: An Analysis of the Issues." Research Report #53, Federal Reserve Bank of Boston.

Ibbotson, Roger, and Rex Sinquefield. 1976. "Stocks, Bonds, Bills, and Inflation: Year by Year Historical Returns (1926–1974)." *Journal of Business* 49: 11–47.

———. 1977. *Stocks, Bonds, Bills, and Inflation: The Past (1926–1976), and the Future (1977–2000).* Charlottesville, Va.: Financial Analysts Research Foundation.

Joines, Douglas. 1977. "Short Term Interest Rates as Predictors of Inflation: Comment." *American Economic Review* 67.

Kidwell, David. 1976. "The Inclusion and Exercise of Call Provisions by State and Local Governments." *Journal of Money Credit and Banking* 8.

Kimball, Ralph. 1977. "Commercial Banks, Tax Avoidance, and the Market for State and Local Debt since 1970." *New England Economic Review*, pp. 3–21.

Klein, Benjamin. 1974. "Competitive Interest Payments on Bank Deposits and the Long-Run Demand for Money." *American Economic Review* 64, no. 6: 931–49.

Lintner, John. 1975. "Inflation and Security Returns." *Journal of Finance* 30, no. 2: 259–80.

Miller, Merton. 1977. "Debt and Taxes." *Journal of Finance* 32: 261–76.

Moody's Investors Service. *Industrial Manual*. Various years.

———. *Municipal and Government Manual*. Various years.

Morris, Frank. 1970. "The Case for Broadening the Financial Options Open to State and Local Governments." In *Financing State and Local Governments*. Boston: Federal Reserve Bank of Boston.

Mundell, Robert. 1963. "Inflation and Real Interest." *Journal of Political Economy* 71.

Mussa, Michael. 1976. *A Study in Macroeconomics*. Amsterdam: North Holland.

Nelson, Charles, and William Schwert. 1977. "On Testing the Hypothesis that the Real Rate of Interest Is Constant." *American Economic Review* 67: 478–86.

Ott, David, and Allan Meltzer. 1963. *Federal Tax Treatment of State and Local Securities*. Washington, D.C.: Brookings Institution.

Pechman, Joseph. 1977. *Federal Tax Policy*. 3rd ed. Washington, D.C.: Brookings Institution.

Peterson, John. 1971. "Responses of State and Local Governments to Varying Credit Conditions." *Federal Reserve Bulletin* 57: 209–32.

———. 1976. "Changing Conditions in the Market for State and Local Government Debt." Study prepared for the Joint Economic Committee, U.S. Congress, 94th Congress, 2nd session.

Projector, Dorothy, and Gertrude Weiss. 1966. *Survey of Financial Characteristics of Consumers*. Federal Reserve Technical Papers.

Sargent, Thomas. 1972. "Anticipated Inflation and the Nominal Rate of Interest." *Quarterly Journal of Economics* 86.

———. 1973. "Rational Expectations, the Real Rate of Interest, and the Natural Rate of Unemployment." Brookings Papers on Economic Activity. Washington, D.C.: Brookings Institution.

Skelton, Jeffrey. 1978. "A Model of Tax Effects in Coupon Bonds." University of Chicago working paper.

State of New York Insurance Department. *Annual Report of the Superintendent of Insurance*. Various years.

Surrey, Stanley. 1976. "Three Arguments for the Taxable Bond Option: Equity, Efficiency, and Marketability." *Tax Notes* 4, no. 13: 9–13.

Twentieth Century Fund Task Force on the Municipal Bond Market. 1976. *Building a Broader Market.* New York: McGraw-Hill.

U.S. Board of Governors of the Federal Reserve System. *Federal Reserve Bulletin.* Washington, D.C.: Government Printing Office, various issues.

U.S. Internal Revenue Service. *Statistics of Income: Corporate Income Tax Returns.* Washington, D.C.: Government Printing Office, various years.

――――. *Statistics of Income: Individual Income Tax Returns.* Washington, D.C.: Government Printing Office, various years.

U.S. Treasury Department. 1978. *The President's 1978 Tax Program: Detailed Descriptions and Supporting Analyses of the Proposals.* Washington, D.C.: Government Printing Office.

Van Horne, James. 1978. *Financial Market Rates and Flows.* Englewood Cliffs, N.J.: Prentice-Hall.

West, Richard. 1964. "A Study of the Relationship between Yields on New and Outstanding General Obligation Municipal Bonds." Ph.D. dissertation, University of Chicago.